Anti-Inflammatory Diet Cookbook for Beginners

1200 Days of Quick & Easy Recipes to Fight Inflammation and Balance Hormones + BONUS 30-Day No-Stress Meal Plan to Master Your Immune System

Susan Elliott

© Copyright 2022 – Susan Elliott– All rights reserved.

The content contained within this book may not be reproduced, duplicated or transmitted without direct written permission from the author or the publisher.

Under no circumstances will any blame or legal responsibility be held against the publisher, or author, for any damages, reparation, or monetary loss due to the information contained within this book, either directly or indirectly.

Legal Notice:

This book is copyright protected. It is only for personal use. You cannot amend, distribute, sell, use, quote or paraphrase any part, or the content within this book, without the consent of the author or publisher.

Disclaimer Notice:

Please note the information contained within this document is for educational and entertainment purposes only. All effort has been executed to present accurate, up to date, reliable, complete information. No warranties of any kind are declared or implied. Readers acknowledge that the author is not engaged in the rendering of legal, financial, medical or professional advice. The content within this book has been derived from various sources. Please consult a licensed professional before attempting any techniques outlined in this book.

By reading this document, the reader agrees that under no circumstances is the author responsible for any losses, direct or indirect, that are incurred as a result of the use of the information contained within this document, including, but not limited to, errors, omissions, or inaccuracies.

TABLE OF CONTENT

INTRODUCTION

   FOODS TO AVOID

   FOOD TO EAT

   BENEFIT OF ANTI-INFLAMMATORY DIET

BEANS, GRAINS AND PASTA

   Small Pasta and Beans Pot

   Wild Rice, Celery, and Cauliflower Pilaf

   Minestrone Chickpeas and Macaroni Casserole

   Slow Cooked Turkey and Brown Rice

   Papaya, Jicama, and Peas Rice Bowl

   Italian Baked Beans

   Cannellini Bean Lettuce Wraps

   Israeli Eggplant, Chickpea, and Mint Sauté

   Lentils and Rice

   Brown Rice Pilaf with Pistachios and Raisins

   Cherry, Apricot, and Pecan Brown Rice Bowl

   Curry Apple Couscous with Leeks and Pecans

   Lebanese Flavor Broken Thin Noodles

   Lemony Farro and Avocado Bowl

   Rice and Blueberry Stuffed Sweet Potatoes

   Farrotto Mix

   Feta-Grape-Bulgur Salad with Grapes and Feta

   Greek Style Meaty Bulgur

   Hearty Barley Mix

   Hearty Barley Risotto

   Hearty Freekeh Pilaf

   Herby-Lemony Farro

   Mushroom-Bulgur Pilaf

   Baked Brown Rice

   Barley Pilaf

   Basmati Rice Pilaf Mix

   Brown Rice Salad with Asparagus, Goat Cheese, and Lemon

   Carrot-Almond-Bulgur Salad

   Chickpea-Spinach-Bulgur

   Italian Seafood Risotto

   Classic Stovetop White Rice

   Classic Tabbouleh

   Farro Cucumber-Mint Salad

   Chorizo-Kidney Beans Quinoa Pilaf

   Goat Cheese 'N Red Beans Salad

   Greek Farro Salad

   White Bean and Tuna Salad

   Spicy Sweet Red Hummus

   Black Bean Chili with Mangoes

   Israeli Style Eggplant and Chickpea Salad

   Italian Sautéed Cannellini Beans

   Lentil and Vegetable Curry Stew

   Lush Moroccan Chickpea, Vegetable, and Fruit Stew

Chickpea and Rice

One-Pot Rice and Chicken

Grain Bowl with Lentil and Chickpeas

White Beans with Vegetables

Greek Wheat Berry Salad with Feta

Skillet Black-Eyed Pease and Spinach

Lentil Salad with Oranges

Chickpea Soup

Couscous Confetti Salad

Rustic Lentil-Rice Pilaf

Bulgur Pilaf with Garbanzos

Lentil Bulgur Pilaf

Simple Spanish rice

Creamy Parmesan Garlic Polenta

Mushroom Parmesan Risotto

Brown Rice Bowls with Roasted Vegetables

Spanish Chicken and Rice

Mushroom Barley Pilaf

Toasted Barley and Almond Pilaf Preparation time: 10 minutes

Mediterranean Lentils and Brown Rice

Wild Mushroom Farrotto with Parmesan

Moroccan-Style Brown Rice and Chickpea

Buckwheat Groats with Root Vegetables

Farro Risotto with Fresh Sage

Bulgur with Za'Atar, Chickpeas, and Spinach

Pearl Barley Risotto with Parmesan Cheese

Israeli Couscous with Asparagus

Freekeh Pilaf with Dates and Pistachios

Quinoa with Baby Potatoes and Broccoli

Brown Rice Pilaf with Golden Raisins

Quinoa and Chickpea Vegetable Bowls

Ritzy Veggie Chili

Spicy Italian Bean Balls with Marinara

Baked Rolled Oat with Pears and Pecans

Farro Salad Mix

Fennel-Parmesan Farro

POULTRY AND MEAT RECIPES

Duck Stew Olla Tapada

Cheesy Ranch Chicken

Turkey Crust Meatza

Simple Turkey Goulash

Chicken Frittata with Asiago Cheese and Herbs

Stuffed Chicken with Sauerkraut and Cheese

Chicken Bacon Burger

Basil Chicken Saute

Slow Cooker Jerk Chicken

Pulled Buffalo Chicken Salad with Blue Cheese

Red Pepper and Mozarella-Stuffed Chicken Caprese

Lemon-Garlic Chicken and Green Beans with Caramelized Onions

Three-Cheese Chicken Cordon Bleu

Blue Cheese Buffalo Chicken Balls

Chicken & Cheese Filled Avocados

Paprika Chicken & Pancetta in a Skillet

Cheesy Pinwheels with Chicken

Peanut-Crusted Chicken

Turnip Greens & Artichoke Chicken

Winter Chicken with Vegetables

Pancetta & Cheese Stuffed Chicken

Chili Chicken Kebab with Garlic Dressing

Chili & Lemon Marinated Chicken Wings

Cipollini & Bell Pepper Chicken Souvlaki

Tarragon Chicken with Roasted Balsamic Turnips

Tomato & Cheese Chicken Chili

Turmeric Chicken Wings with Ginger Sauce

Feta & Bacon Chicken

Chicken Pie with Bacon

Flying Jacob Casserole

BBQ Chicken Zucchini Boats

Cashew Chicken Curry

Creamy Chicken & Greens

Curry Chicken Lettuce Wraps

Nacho Chicken Casserole

Pesto & Mozzarella Chicken Casserole

Rotisserie Chicken & Cabbage Shreds

Chicken Quiche

Chicken Parmigiana

Vodka Duck Fillets

Baked Chicken Meatballs - Habanero & Green Chili

BBQ Chicken Liver and Hearts

Buffalo Balls

Turkey Chili

Beef with Carrot & Broccoli

Beef with Mushroom & Broccoli

Citrus Beef with Bok Choy

Beef with Zucchini Noodles

Beef with Asparagus & Bell Pepper

Spiced Ground Beef

Ground Beef with Cabbage

Ground Beef with Veggies

Ground Beef with Cashews & Veggies

Ground Beef with Greens & Tomatoes

Beef & Veggies Chili

Ground Beef & Veggies Curry

Spicy & Creamy Ground Beef Curry

Curried Beef Meatballs

Beef Meatballs in Tomato Gravy

Pork with Lemongrass

Pork with Olives

Pork Chops with Tomato Salsa

Mustard Pork Mix

Pork with Chili Zucchinis and Tomatoes

Pork with Thyme Sweet Potatoes

Pork with Pears and Ginger

Parsley Pork and Artichokes

Pork with Mushrooms and Cucumbers

Oregano Pork

Creamy Pork and Tomatoes

Pork with Balsamic Onion Sauce

Ground Pork Pan

Baked Pork Chops with Cashew

Cranberry Pork

Pork Tenderloin with Date Gravy and Mustard

Creamy Coconut Pork Mix

Pork Kabobs with Bell Peppers

Pork and Leeks

Almond Cinnamon Beef Meatballs

Creamy Beef Stroganoff

Spicy Beef

Beef Stuffed Cabbage

Hot Chicken Meatballs

Keto Chicken Enchaladas

Home-Style Chicken Kebab

Traditional Hungarian Gulyás

Greek Chicken Stifado

Tangy Chicken with Scallions

Double Cheese Italian Chicken

Middle Eastern Shish Kebab

Capocollo and Garlic Chicken

Cheesy Mexican-Style Chicken

Asian Saucy Chicken

VEGETABLES AND VEGAN RECIPES

Lentils with Tomatoes and Turmeric

Whole-Wheat Pasta with Tomato-Basil Sauce

Fried Rice with Kale

Nutty and Fruity Garden Salad

Roasted Root Vegetables

Stir-Fried Brussels sprouts and Carrots

Curried Veggies and Poached Eggs

Braised Kale

Braised Leeks, Cauliflower and Artichoke Hearts

Celery Root Hash Browns

Braised Carrots 'n Kale

Stir-Fried Gingery Veggies

Cauliflower Fritters

Stir-Fried Squash

Cauliflower Hash Brown

Sweet Potato Puree

Curried Okra

Vegetable Potpie

Grilled Eggplant Roll-Ups

Eggplant Gratin

Veggie Stuffed Peppers

Cheesy Gratin Zucchini

Caprese Tomatoes with Basil Dressing

Korean Barbecue Tofu

Fruit Bowl with Yogurt Topping

Collard Green Wrap

Zucchini Garlic Fries

Mashed Cauliflower

Stir-Fried Eggplant

Sautéed Garlic Mushrooms

Stir-Fried Asparagus and Bell Pepper

Wild Rice with Spicy Chickpeas

Cashew Pesto & Parsley with veggies

Spicy Chickpeas with Roasted Vegetables

Special Vegetable Kitchree

Mashed Sweet Potato Burritos

Zucchini & Pepper Lasagna

Toasted Cumin Crunch

Spicy Vegetable Burgers

Chickpea Shawarma Dip

Light Mushroom Risotto

Vegetable Pie

Turmeric Nachos

Rucola Salad

Tasty Spring Salad

Pure Delish Spinach Salad

Sexy Salsa Salad

Jalapeno Salsa

Lentil Curry

Lentils in Tomato Sauce

Black Eyed-Peas Curry

Vegan Meatballs

Tofu Fried Rice

Corn Chowder

Asian Slaw

Spinach Alfredo Soup

Artichoke Stuffed Mushroom

Asparagus with Garlic

Avocado Tomato Salad

Feta and Pesto Wrap

Cheese and Onion on Bagel

Zucchini Ravioli

Cauliflower Salad

Tofu Spinach Sauté

Zucchini Lasagna

Vegetable and Egg Casserole

Green Buddha Bowl

Spaghetti Squash

Roasted Green Beans and Mushrooms

Mexican Cauliflower Rice

Quick Collard Greens

FISH AND SEAFOOD RECIPES

Lemon-Caper Trout with Caramelized Shallots

Shrimp Scampi

Shrimp with Spicy Spinach

Shrimp with Cinnamon Sauce

Pan-Seared Scallops with Lemon-Ginger Vinaigrette

Manhattan-Style Salmon Chowder

Roasted Salmon and Asparagus

- Citrus Salmon on a Bed of Greens
- Orange and Maple-Glazed Salmon
- Salmon Ceviche
- Cod with Ginger and Black Beans
- Rosemary-Lemon Cod
- Halibut Curry
- Lemony Mussels
- Hot Tuna Steak
- Marinated Fish Steaks
- Baked Tomato Hake
- Cheesy Tuna Pasta
- Salmon and Roasted Peppers
- Shrimp and Beets
- Shrimp and Corn
- Chili Shrimp and Pineapple
- Curry Tilapia and Beans
- Balsamic Scallops
- Whitefish Curry
- Swordfish with Pineapple and Cilantro
- Sesame-Tuna Skewers
- Trout with Chard
- Sole with Vegetables
- Poached Halibut and Mushrooms
- Halibut Stir Fry
- Steamed Garlic-Dill Halibut
- Italian Halibut Chowder
- Dill Haddock
- Chili Snapper
- Lemony Mackerel
- Honey Crusted Salmon with Pecans
- Salmon and Cauliflower
- Ginger Salmon and Black Beans
- Clams with Olives Mix
- Cod Curry
- Fast Fish Pie
- Quick Chermoula Fish Parcels
- Healthy Fish Nacho Bowl
- Fish & Chickpea Stew
- Easy Crunchy Fish Tray Bake
- Ginger & Chili Sea Bass Fillets
- Nut-Crust Tilapia with Kale
- Wasabi Salmon Burgers
- Citrus & Herb Sardines
- Daring Shark Steaks
- Spicy Kingfish
- Gingered Tilapia
- Haddock with Swiss chard
- Rockfish Curry
- Coconut Rice with shrimps in Coconut curry
- Grilled fish tacos
- Curried Fish
- Herbed Rockfish
- Salmon Sushi
- Spicy herb catfish
- Stuffed Trout

Thai Chowder

Tuna-Stuffed Tomatoes

Seared Ahi Tuna

Bavette with Seafood

Quick Shrimp Moqueca

Fried ball of cod

Seafood Paella

Vietnamese Roll and Tarê

Shrimp Pie

Seafood Noodles

Potato Dumpling with Shrimp

Shrimp Rissoles

Pumpkin Shrimp

Fish Sandwich

Sardine Casserole

Mexican Salad with Mahi-Mahi

Fish Cakes

Crab Salad Cakes

Simple Founder in Brown Butter Lemon Sauce

Grilled Calamari

Souvlaki Spiced Salmon Bowls

Proscuitto-Wrapped Haddock

Grilled Salmon with Caponata

Sweet Crab Cakes

Herbed Coconut Milk Steamed Mussels

Basil Halibut Red Pepper Packets

Sherry and Butter Prawns

Clams with Garlic-Tomato Sauce

Amberjack Fillets with Cheese Sauce

Tilapia with Spicy Dijon Sauce

Garlic Butter Shrimps

Oven-Baked Sole Fillets

Keto Oodles with White Clam Sauce

Fried Codfish with Almonds

Salmon Balls

Codfish Sticks

Shrimp Risotto

Lemony Trout

Quick Fish Bowl

Tender Creamy Scallops

Salmon Cakes

Salmon with Mustard Cream

Shrimp and Black Beans Enchalada

Tuna Steaks with Shirataki Noodles

Tilapia with Parmesan Bark

Blackened Fish Tacos with Slaw:

FRUIT AND DESERT RECIPES

Almond Butter Fudge

Bounty Bars

Lean Granola

Banana Bread

Mini Lava Cakes

Crispy Apples

Ginger Cheesecake

Special Brownies

- Blueberry Scones
- Blueberries Stew
- Creamy Mint Strawberry Mix
- Vanilla Cake
- Pumpkin Cream
- Chia and Berries Smoothie Bowl
- Minty Coconut Cream
- Grapes Stew
- Blueberry Matcha Smoothie
- Pumpkin Pie Smoothie
- Fig Smoothie
- Ginger, Carrot, and Turmeric Smoothie
- Kiwi Strawberry Smoothie
- Blended Coconut Milk and Banana Breakfast Smoothie
- Kale Smoothie
- Raspberry Smoothie
- Pineapple Smoothie
- Beet Smoothie
- Blueberry Smoothie
- Strawberry Oatmeal Smoothie
- Raspberry Banana Smoothie
- Almond Blueberry Smoothie
- Green Vanilla Smoothie
- Purple Fruit Smoothie
- Vanilla Avocado Smoothie
- Triple Fruit Smoothie
- Peach Maple Smoothie
- Pink California Smoothie
- Carrot and Orange Turmeric Drink
- Voluptuous Vanilla Hot Drink
- Almond Butter Smoothies
- Baby Kale Pineapple Smoothie
- Vanilla Blueberry Smoothie
- Zesty Citrus Smoothie
- Mango and Ginger Infused Water
- White Hot Chocolate
- Peach and Raspberry Lemonade
- Hot Apple Cider
- Blueberry Lime Juice
- Sweet Cranberry Juice
- Hot Peppermint Vanilla Latte
- Berry Shrub
- Cooked Iced Tea
- Hibiscus Tea
- Apple Cinnamon Water
- Wassail
- Instant Horchata
- Jamaican Hibiscus Tea
- Ginger Ale
- Blackberry Italian Drink
- Turmeric Hot Chocolate
- Turmeric Tea
- Lemon Ginger Iced Tea
- Pineapple & Ginger Juice
- Parsley Ginger Green Juice

- Vanilla Turmeric Orange Juice
- Turmeric and Ginger Tonic
- Flu Fighting Tonic
- Golden Chai Latte
- Chocolate Latte with Reishi
- Mango Tomato Smoothie
- Spicy Tomato Smoothie
- Broccoli Smoothie
- Cherry Smoothie
- Chocolate Cherry Smoothie
- Cucumber Kiwi Green Smoothie
- Tropical Pineapple Kiwi Smoothie
- Dreamy Yummy Orange Cream Smoothie
- Peachy Keen Smoothie
- Cucumber Melon Smoothie
- Tropical Mango Coconut Smoothie
- Blueberry Pomegranate Smoothie
- Pineapple and Greens Smoothie
- Blueberry and Spinach Shake
- Wonderful Watermelon Drink
- Sweet & Savoury Smoothie
- Blackberry & Ginger Milkshake
- Fresh Cranberry and Lime Juice
- Fresh Tropical Juice
- Mixed Fruit & Nut Milkshake
- Pineapple- Ginger Smoothie
- Beet and Cherry Smoothie
- Turmeric Delight
- Hot Chocolate
- Tropical Popsicles
- Strawberry Ice Cream
- Blueberry Tarts
- Cookie Dough Bites
- Banana Cinnamon
- Banana Cinnamon Cookies
- Avocado Chia Parfait
- Choco Chia Cherry Cream
- Avocado Choco Cake
- Date Dough & Walnut Wafer
- Pineapple Pie
- Citrus Cauliflower Cake
- Creamy & Chilly Blueberry Bites
- Pistachioed Panna-Cotta Cocoa
- Pure Avocado Pudding
- Sweet Almond and Coconut Fat Bombs
- Spicy Popper Mug Cake
- The Most Elegant Parsley Soufflé Ever
- Fennel and Almond Bites
- Coconut Butter Fudge
- Raspberry Gummies
- Turmeric Milkshake
- No-Bake Carrot Cake Bites
- Chocolate Fudge Bites
- Blueberry Energy Bites
- Beet Pancakes
- Green Tea Pudding

Banana Bars

Blueberry Sour Cream Cake

Peanut Butter Balls

Black Tea Cake

Matcha and Blueberries Pudding

Spiced Tea Pudding

Lemonade Ice Pops

Café-Style Fudge

Rum Butter Cookies

Vanilla Cakes

Strawberry Shortcake

Fried Pineapple Slice

Grilled Peaches

Pumpkin Ice Cream

Lemon Sorbet

Banana & Avocado Mousse

Strawberry Soufflé

Tropical Fruit Crisp

No-Bake Cheesecake

Citrus Strawberry Granita

Glazed Banana

Refreshing Raspberry Jelly

Comforting Baked Rice Pudding

Fall-Time Custard

Creamy Frozen Yogurt

Yummy Fruity Ice-Cream

Glorious Blueberry Crumble

30 Days Meal Plan

CONCLUSION

INTRODUCTION

Inflammation has been shown to play a critical role in the manifestation of diseases such as cancer, heart disease, Alzheimer's and many others. It has also been shown that a diet high in healthy fats and low in carbohydrates allows for inflammation to be reduced. This cookbook introduces readers to this type of diet (the anti-inflammatory diet).

This book will provide you with a wide variety of recipes that are delicious and nutritious. You'll also find helpful information on the benefits of eating raw foods, probiotics, and much more. This book is an excellent resource for all types of diets including those for people with celiac disease or lactose intolerance.

Not only is this the perfect diet for people who suffer from inflammatory diseases like rheumatoid arthritis, but it also helps promote weight loss and lower the risk of diabetes. It's fair to say that this diet is one of the most powerful ways to prevent a multitude of chronic illnesses. However, it can be difficult for people with existing arthritis or other joint pain problems; it's important to keep in mind that patience and persistence are crucial when trying to adopt this lifestyle change. If you're ready to try and adopt a more healthy diet that will ultimately improve the health of your body, then we recommend getting started with this book by Marlene Snyder.

The foods in this book are identified and labeled as anti-inflammatory or pro-inflammatory for easy reference. This is a great benefit to those who need help seeing which foods have the right balance of nutrients, not to mention your body will be thanking you for eliminating processed and high-fat foods from your diet.

After reading this book, you will understand how to shop for the right foods and how to prepare them in a way that is delicious and healthy. You'll never look at food the same way again.

The anti-inflammatory diet is a diet that helps to reduce inflammation and prevent joint problems, as well as other chronic diseases such as heart disease and cancer. This cookbook provides a general overview of the diet, with over 500 recipes for common dishes. You can find easy to follow methods for preparing these dishes at whatever level of cooking ability you have by following the steps in this cookbook.

The anti-inflammatory diet has been shown to reduce inflammation. It is different than a traditional low-fat diet, as one of its main components are the high levels of healthy fats and low levels of carbohydrates. The anti-inflammatory diet is also high in omega 3 fatty acids, which have been proven to reduce inflammation.

The Anti-Inflammatory Diet Cookbook gives you over 500 delicious and nutritious recipes that are easy to follow, even for those who are out of practice. The success of this diet plan has shown people how easy it is to eat the right foods and lose weight. The majority of people have lost at least 20 pounds in the first 6 months, which is a huge improvement from the typical diet that doesn't work for most people.

The recipes in the cookbook are meant to introduce readers to the basics of this diet. This cookbook acknowledge that there are individuals out there who think that cooking and anti-inflammatory diets don't go hand-in-hand. However, they argue that good food takes as much time and attention to prepare as it does to eat fast food, but with at least one difference: eating healthy is a far tastier way to live life.

The anti-inflammatory diet can help reduce inflammation in the body. It can also help prevent chronic diseases. The authors believe that it is a healthy alternative to many various diets.

The health benefits of eating organic and local foods include cleaner water, less exposure to harmful pesticides and fertilizers and overall healthier bodies, minds and souls (and not just because they are so much tastier).

Local foods are those that are produced within a specific region, usually the same state. Organic foods are grown without using any artificial fertilizers, pesticides or genetically engineered seeds.

The health benefits of eating and supporting organic foods go beyond just what we put in our mouths. In fact, supporting organic and local food producers can help local economies thrive and keep farmers on the land and not in urban areas where pollution is at its highest.

It is well-known that inflammatory responses are important to protect us from infection. However, it turns out that not all inflammation is necessary and good for us. There are actually two different types of inflammation: acute inflammation, which is short-lived and resolves after the invader has been eliminated; and chronic or slow-burning inflammation, which creates long-lasting harm as an aftermath to immunity.

The dietary factors that cause chronic inflammation are called "inflammatory foods". These include sugar and refined carbs, Tran's fats (partially hydrogenated oils), saturated fats, vegetable oils (corn oil, soybean oil, safflower oil etc.) or omega-6 polyunsaturated fats in excess of omega-3 polyunsaturated fatty acids.

The chronic inflammation we frequently experience today is a root cause of many diseases and health problems. Therefore, reduction to chronic inflammation is the key to achieving overall good health. What do you think of when you hear the word "inflammation"? If you are like most people, the first answer that comes to mind is pain and swelling. However, it is not only these two symptoms that are associated with inflammation. It also brings about other symptoms, such as fatigue, joint stiffness and tingling, brain fog and anxiety.

FOODS TO AVOID

Artificial sweeteners – As I've previously mentioned before, artificial sweeteners are very different from natural sugars that come from fruits and other plants. Artificial sweeteners are known to contribute to obesity and digestive problems and some studies have even linked them to cancer and premature death in lab animals. The liver goes into overdrive when you consume artificial sweeteners, spiking insulin levels which can lead to chronic inflammation in the body.

Tran's fats – A lot of people don't realize that the "trans" in trans-fat actually stands for "transported." Tran's fats are all about the oil companies creating cheaper oils that are dirtier and less healthy for you than oils made from wholesome plant sources. Because they're cheaper to produce, these oils are also more commonly used in processed foods.

Animal products – Meat, poultry, fish and dairy are all good at contributing to inflammation in your body. The reason is two-fold: First, these foods contain saturated fats that are known triggers for inflammation in your system. Second, they're also loaded with sodium, which raises blood pressure and contributes to an unhealthy heart rate.

Refined grains –They're linked to some serious health problems like inflammation, type 2 diabetes and bowel disorders such as leaky gut syndrome (which can lead to autoimmune diseases). It's best to limit the amount of these types of foods you're eating to a small serving (ideally less than one cup per day) so you can enjoy optimal health while eating some carboy goodness.

Processed foods – Though there are a few exceptions (like canned tomatoes, or packaged plain dried beans), most processed foods contain ingredients that are nowhere near their natural state. For example, if you buy a package of "peanut butter," it won't actually be ground up peanuts – instead, it'll probably be heavily processed peanut oil, sugar and salt. Additionally many processed foods contain high fructose corn syrup and other artificial ingredients that your body doesn't recognize as real food. If you're eating too much of this type of food you're very likely contributing to inflammation in your body (and setting yourself up for some serious health issues down the road).

FOOD TO EAT

Strawberries are great for improving brain health and preventing cognitive decline. They contain a significant amount of Vitamin C, Bromelain, Potassium, Vitamin A and Vitamin K which all contribute to better brain function and protecting your nervous system. They are a member of the "Brain Berry" family with blueberries and acerola cherries.

Spinach is a great source of Vitamin K which helps to prevent excessive blood clotting. It also helps to lower blood pressure levels and it protects against cardiovascular disease too! It's a great source of Lutein and Zeaxanthin which is important for vision health. Studies have shown that spinach helps to improve memory retention in the brain and it lowers oxidative stress too!

Blueberries are full of antioxidants and anti-inflammatory properties. They lower the level of "bad" LDL cholesterol, they improve blood sugar control and they reduce oxidative stress in your body. They help to protect against colon cancer, breast cancer, prostate cancer and lung cancer.

BENEFIT OF ANTI-INFLAMMATORY DIET

Anti-inflammatory diet is a healthy diet that can help reduce inflammation and its effects. Inflammation increases the risk of heart disease, arthritis, and Alzheimer's disease. Diet is a proven way to manage the symptoms of inflammatory diseases. It can also help those who are not diagnosed with chronic illness but want to prevent it.

A diet with all of the nutrients needed to maintain good health can reduce inflammation, which increases the risk of chronic diseases and leads to weight gain.

A diet that is good for the body and the mind, a diet that helps you battle stress from different sources. The anti-inflammatory diet is one that can make you feel better physically and mentally. Check out the benefits of this amazing diet. You will find yourself feeling energetic, happy, and most of all satisfied now with a new taste for food!

All it takes to improve your mood is eating an anti-inflammatory diet which can also help improve your weight loss odds when following this recipe. By incorporating this anti-inflammatory diet in your regular meal, you are now taking control of your own health. It can be hard at first, especially if you do not eat well. But soon enough and with time, it will come naturally as you develop a taste for this special way to eat.

Anti-inflammatory diet is important because it can also help improve your overall health and mood.

The anti-inflammatory diet works by inhibiting the production of inflammatory proteins that are produced when your body is under stress. These proteins cause inflammation, which is the root cause of a lot of diseases from heart diseases to arthritis and cancer. To reduce inflammation and its damaging effects, you have to reduce the production of inflammatory proteins in your body.

However, this can be achieved with a healthy diet that contains foods that are rich in antioxidants. Antioxidants can also help increase the number of white blood cells in the body.

The most beneficial antioxidants are: vitamin C, vitamin E, beta-carotene, selenium, zinc and copper.

Antioxidants work by fighting free radicals in your body. Free radicals are a type of molecule that is created when different parts of your body break down. They are destructive to other molecules and can cause changes in health and mood as well. Antioxidants neutralize free radicals and prevent them from causing damage in the body.

The anti-inflammatory diet starves these free radicals from the food it needs to survive. Foods that contain inflammatory fats help in producing inflammatory proteins. Therefore, avoiding these foods will reduce inflammation in the body and fight various health problems as well. The foods that you have to avoid are: red meat, sugary products, processed and refined foods, fried foods, high fat dairy products and alcohol which all contain pro-inflammatory fats.

The anti-inflammatory diet is made up of food that is rich in vitamins, minerals and antioxidants. These are: leafy green vegetables, nuts, seeds and dried fruits.

These foods are not only rich in the nutrients needed to maintain a healthy body but also help eliminate toxins from the body as well through urine or bowel movements. Other foods that are part of this diet are: olive oil, avocados, salmon and sardines which contain omega-3 fatty acids. These fats are good for the body, especially heart health.

The anti-inflammatory diet is important because it will improve your health and mood. It can also be an effective weight loss tool.

This diet is hard at first to follow especially if you are used to eating unhealthy foods. But as time passes, with some effort and a little commitment, it will only become easier to follow as you adopt it into your lifestyle and eventually your taste buds.

When following this anti-inflammatory diet, you will feel better physically and mentally. With a better sense of self-control and discipline, you can also increase your personal achievements in life. You will have more energy, feel better mentally, and have more clarity of mind so that you can focus on what's important to you.

This is a diet that helps fight stress from different sources, but the two major sources are eating unhealthy foods and giving up on healthy food choices. This diet can help you overcome this and thus feel better about yourself. With a renewed sense of self-esteem, you will find yourself more productive and happier with your results.

This anti-inflammatory diet is rich in vitamins, minerals and antioxidants. The majority of these nutrients are able to reduce inflammation in the body, which is the root cause of a lot of diseases such as heart disease, cancer and arthritis. With less stress in your life, you can live a healthier lifestyle as well as increase your longevity.

The anti-inflammatory diet is important because doing it can help improve your health and mood. It can also be an effective weight loss tool. Reducing inflammation in the body will also reduce the damage done to other parts of the body by free radicals. It will even help improve your skin tone, which is another huge benefit of this diet.

This diet is hard at first to follow especially if you are used to eating unhealthy foods. But as time passes, with some effort and a little commitment, it will only become easier to follow as you adopt it into your lifestyle and eventually your taste buds.

When following this diet, you will feel better physically and mentally. With a better sense of self-control and discipline, you can also increase your personal achievements in life. You will have more energy, feel better mentally and have more clarity of mind so that you can focus on what's important to you.

BEANS, GRAINS AND PASTA

Small Pasta and Beans Pot

Preparation time: 15 minutes

Cooking time: 15 minutes

Servings: 2-4

Ingredients:

- 1 pound (454 g) small whole wheat pasta
- 1 (14.5-ounce / 411-g) can diced tomatoes, juice reserved
- 1 (15-ounce / 425-g) can cannellini beans, drained and rinsed
- 2 tablespoons no-salt-added tomato paste
- 1 red or yellow bell pepper, chopped
- 1 yellow onion, chopped
- 1 tablespoon Italian seasoning mix
- 3 garlic cloves, minced
- ¼ teaspoon crushed red pepper flakes, optional
- 1 tablespoon extra-virgin olive oil
- 5 cups water
- 1 bunch kale, stemmed and chopped
- ½ cup pitted Klamath olives, chopped
- 1 cup sliced basil

Directions:

1. Except for the kale, olives, and basil, combine all the ingredients in a pot. Stir to mix well. Bring to a boil over high heat. Stir constantly.
2. Reduce the heat to medium high and add the kale. Cook for 10 minutes or until the pasta is al dente. Stir constantly. Transfer all of them on a large plate and serve with olives and basil on top.

Nutrition:

Calories: 357

Fat: 7.6g

Protein: 18.2g

Carbs: 64.5g

Wild Rice, Celery, and Cauliflower Pilaf

Preparation time: 15 minutes

Cooking time: 45 minutes

Servings: 4

Ingredients:

- 1 tablespoon olive oil, plus more for greasing the baking dish
- 1 cup wild rice
- 2 cups low-sodium chicken broth
- 1 sweet onion, chopped
- 2 stalks celery, chopped
- 1 teaspoon minced garlic
- 2 carrots, peeled, halved lengthwise, and sliced
- ½ cauliflower head, cut into small florets
- 1 teaspoon chopped fresh thyme
- Sea salt, to taste

Directions:

1. Preheat the oven to 350°f (180°c). Line a baking sheet with parchment paper and grease with olive oil.
2. Put the wild rice in a saucepan, then pour in the chicken broth. Bring to a boil. Reduce the heat to low and simmer for 30 minutes or until the rice is plump.
3. Meanwhile, heat the remaining olive oil in an oven-proof skillet over medium-high heat until shimmering.
4. Add the onion, celery, and garlic to the skillet and sauté for 3 minutes or until the onion is translucent.
5. Add the carrots and cauliflower to the skillet and sauté for 5 minutes. Turn off the heat and set aside.
6. Pour the cooked rice in the skillet with the vegetables. Sprinkle with thyme and salt. Set the skillet in the preheated oven and bake for 15 minutes or until the vegetables are soft. Serve immediately.

Nutrition:

Calories: 214

Fat: 3.9g

Protein: 7.2g

Carbs: 37.9g

Minestrone Chickpeas and Macaroni Casserole

Preparation time: 15 minutes

Cooking time: 7 hours & 25 minutes

Servings: 5

Ingredients:

- 1 (15-ounce / 425-g) can chickpeas, drained and rinsed
- 1 (28-ounce / 794-g) can diced tomatoes, with the juice
- 1 (6-ounce / 170-g) can no-salt-added tomato paste
- 3 medium carrots, sliced
- 3 cloves garlic, minced
- 1 medium yellow onion, chopped
- 1 cup low-sodium vegetable soup
- ½ teaspoon dried rosemary
- 1 teaspoon dried oregano
- 2 teaspoons maple syrup
- ½ teaspoon sea salt
- ¼ teaspoon ground black pepper
- ½ pound (227-g) fresh green beans, trimmed and cut into bite-size pieces
- 1 cup macaroni pasta
- 2 ounces (57 g) Parmesan cheese, grated

Directions:

1. Except for the green beans, pasta, and Parmesan cheese, combine all the ingredients in the slow cooker and stir to mix well. Put the slow cooker lid on and cook on low for 7 hours.
2. Fold in the pasta and green beans. Put the lid on and cook on high for 20 minutes or until the vegetable are soft and the pasta is al dente.
3. Pour them in a large serving bowl and spread with Parmesan cheese before serving.

Nutrition:

Calories: 349

Fat: 6.7g

Protein: 16.5g

Carbs: 59.9g

Slow Cooked Turkey and Brown Rice

Preparation time: 15 minutes

Cooking time: 3 hours & 10 minutes

Servings: 6

Ingredients:

- 1 tablespoon extra-virgin olive oil
- 1½ pounds (680 g) ground turkey
- 2 tablespoons chopped fresh sage, divided
- 2 tablespoons chopped fresh thyme, divided
- 1 teaspoon sea salt
- ½ teaspoon ground black pepper
- 2 cups brown rice
- 1 (14-ounce / 397-g) can stewed tomatoes, with the juice
- ¼ cup pitted and sliced Klamath olives
- 3 medium zucchinis, sliced thinly
- ¼ cup chopped fresh flat-leaf parsley
- 1 medium yellow onion, chopped
- 1 tablespoon plus 1 teaspoon balsamic vinegar
- 2 cups low-sodium chicken stock
- 2 garlic cloves, minced
- ½ cup grated Parmesan cheese, for serving

Directions:

1. Heat the olive oil in a nonstick skillet over medium-high heat until shimmering. Add the ground turkey and sprinkle with 1 tablespoon of sage, 1 tablespoon of thyme, salt and ground black pepper.
2. Sauté for 10 minutes or until the ground turkey is lightly browned. Pour them in the slow cooker, then pour in the remaining ingredients, except for the Parmesan. Stir to mix well.
3. Put the lid on and cook on high for 3 hours or until the rice and vegetables are tender. Pour them in a large serving bowl, then

spread with Parmesan cheese before serving.

Nutrition:

Calories: 499

Fat: 16.4g

Protein: 32.4g

Carbs: 56.5g

Papaya, Jicama, and Peas Rice Bowl

Preparation time: 15 minutes

Cooking time: 45 minutes

Servings: 4

Ingredients:

Sauce:

- Juice of ¼ lemon
- 2 teaspoons chopped fresh basil
- 1 tablespoon raw honey
- 1 tablespoon extra-virgin olive oil
- Sea salt, to taste

Rice:

- 1½ cups wild rice
- 2 papayas, peeled, seeded, and diced
- 1 jicama, peeled and shredded
- 1 cup snow peas, julienned
- 2 cups shredded cabbage
- 1 scallion, white and green parts, chopped

Directions:

1. Combine the ingredients for the sauce in a bowl. Stir to mix well. Set aside until ready to use. Pour the wild rice in a saucepan, then pour in enough water to cover. Bring to a boil.
2. Reduce the heat to low, then simmer for 45 minutes or until the wild rice is soft and plump. Drain and transfer to a large serving bowl.
3. Top the rice with papayas, jicama, peas, cabbage, and scallion. Pour the sauce over and stir to mix well before serving.

Nutrition:

Calories: 446

- Fat: 7.9g
- Protein: 13.1g
- Carbs: 85.8g

Italian Baked Beans

Preparation time: 5 minutes

Cooking time: 15 minutes

Servings: 6

Ingredients:

- 2 teaspoons extra-virgin olive oil
- ½ cup minced onion (about ¼ onion)
- 1 (12-ounce) can low-sodium tomato paste
- ¼ cup red wine vinegar
- 2 tablespoons honey
- ¼ teaspoon ground cinnamon
- ½ cup water
- 2 (15-ounce) cans cannellini or great northern beans, undrained

Directions:

1. In a medium saucepan over medium heat, heat the oil. Add the onion and cook for 5 minutes, stirring frequently.
2. Add the tomato paste, vinegar, honey, cinnamon, and water, and mix well. Turn the heat to low. Drain and rinse one can of the beans in a colander and add to the saucepan.
3. Pour the entire second can of beans (including the liquid) into the saucepan. Let it cook for 10 minutes, stirring occasionally, and serve.
4. Ingredient tip: Switch up this recipe by making new variations of the homemade ketchup. Instead of the cinnamon, try ¼ teaspoon of smoked paprika and 1 tablespoon of hot sauce. Serve.

Nutrition:

Calories: 236

Fat: 3g

Carbohydrates: 42g

Protein: 10g

Cannellini Bean Lettuce Wraps

Preparation time: 15 minutes

Cooking time: 10 minutes

Servings: 4

Ingredients:

- 1 tablespoon extra-virgin olive oil
- ½ cup diced red onion (about ¼ onion)
- ¾ cup chopped fresh tomatoes (about 1 medium tomato)
- ¼ teaspoon freshly ground black pepper
- 1 (15-ounce) can cannellini or great northern beans, drained and rinsed
- ¼ cup finely chopped fresh curly parsley
- ½ cup Lemony Garlic Hummus or ½ cup prepared hummus
- 8 romaine lettuce leaves

Directions:

- In a large skillet over medium heat, heat the oil. Add the onion and cook for 3 minutes, stirring occasionally.
- Add the tomatoes and pepper and cook for 3 more minutes, stirring occasionally. Add the beans and cook for 3 more minutes, stirring occasionally. Remove from the heat, and mix in the parsley.
- Spread 1 tablespoon of hummus over each lettuce leaf. Evenly spread the warm bean mixture down the center of each leaf.
- Fold one side of the lettuce leaf over the filling lengthwise, then fold over the other side to make a wrap and serve.

Nutrition:

Calories: 211

Fat: 8g

Carbohydrates: 28g

Protein: 10g

Israeli Eggplant, Chickpea, and Mint Sauté

Preparation time: 5 minutes

Cooking time: 20 minutes

Servings: 6

Ingredients:

- Nonstick cooking spray
- 1 medium globe eggplant (about 1 pound), stem removed
- 1 tablespoon extra-virgin olive oil
- 2 tablespoons freshly squeezed lemon juice (from about 1 small lemon)
- 2 tablespoons balsamic vinegar
- 1 teaspoon ground cumin
- ¼ teaspoon kosher or sea salt
- 1 (15-ounce) can chickpeas, drained and rinsed
- 1 cup sliced sweet onion (about ½ medium Walla Walla or Vidalia onion)
- ¼ cup loosely packed chopped or torn mint leaves
- 1 tablespoon sesame seeds, toasted if desired
- 1 garlic clove, finely minced (about ½ teaspoon)

Directions:

1. Place one oven rack about 4 inches below the broiler element. Turn the broiler to the highest setting to preheat. Spray a large, rimmed baking sheet with nonstick cooking spray.
2. On a cutting board, cut the eggplant lengthwise into four slabs (each piece should be about ½- to 1/8-inch thick). Place the eggplant slabs on the prepared baking sheet. Set aside.
3. In a small bowl, whisk together the oil, lemon juice, vinegar, cumin, and salt. Brush or drizzle 2 tablespoons of the lemon dressing over both sides of the eggplant slabs. Reserve the remaining dressing.
4. Broil the eggplant directly under the heating element for 4 minutes, flip them, and then broil for another 4 minutes, until golden brown.
5. While the eggplant is broiling, in a serving bowl, combine the chickpeas, onion, mint, sesame seeds, and garlic. Add the reserved

dressing, and gently mix to incorporate all the ingredients.
6. When the eggplant is done, using tongs, transfer the slabs from the baking sheet to a cooling rack and cool for 3 minutes.
7. When slightly cooled, place the eggplant on a cutting board and slice each slab crosswise into ½-inch strips.
8. Add the eggplant to the serving bowl with the onion mixture. Gently toss everything together and serve warm or at room temperature.

Nutrition:

Calories: 159

Fat: 4g

Carbohydrates: 26g

Protein: 6g

Lentils and Rice

Preparation time: 5 minutes

Cooking time: 25 minutes

Servings: 4

Ingredients:

- 2¼ cups low-sodium or no-salt-added vegetable broth
- ½ cup uncooked brown or green lentils
- ½ cup uncooked instant brown rice
- ½ cup diced carrots (about 1 carrot)
- ½ cup diced celery (about 1 stalk)
- 1 (2.25-ounce) can sliced olives, drained (about ½ cup)
- ¼ cup diced red onion (about 1/8 onion)
- ¼ cup chopped fresh curly-leaf parsley
- 1½ tablespoons extra-virgin olive oil
- 1 tablespoon freshly squeezed lemon juice (from about ½ small lemon)
- 1 garlic clove, minced (about ½ teaspoon)
- ¼ teaspoon kosher or sea salt
- ¼ teaspoon freshly ground black pepper

Directions:

1. In a medium saucepan over high heat, bring the broth and lentils to a boil, cover, and lower the heat to medium-low. Cook for 8 minutes.
2. Raise the heat to medium and stir in the rice. Cover the pot and cook the mixture for 15 minutes, or until the liquid is absorbed. Remove the pot from the heat and let it sit, covered, for 1 minute, then stir.
3. While the lentils and rice are cooking, mix together the carrots, celery, olives, onion, and parsley in a large serving bowl.
4. In a small bowl, whisk together the oil, lemon juice, garlic, salt, and pepper. Set aside. When the lentils and rice are cooked, add them to the serving bowl.
5. Pour the dressing on top and mix everything together. Serve warm or cold, or store in a sealed container in the refrigerator for up to 7 days.

Nutrition:

Calories: 230

Fat: 8g

Carbohydrates: 34g

Protein: 8g

Brown Rice Pilaf with Pistachios and Raisins

Preparation time: 15 minutes

Cooking time: 15 minutes

Servings: 6

Ingredients:

- 1 tablespoon extra-virgin olive oil
- 1 cup chopped onion
- ½ cup shredded carrot
- ½ teaspoon ground cinnamon
- 1 teaspoon ground cumin
- 2 cups brown rice
- 1¾ cups pure orange juice
- ¼ cup water
- ½ cup shelled pistachios
- 1 cup golden raisins
- ½ cup chopped fresh chives

Directions:

1. Heat the olive oil in a saucepan over medium-high heat until shimmering. Add the onion and sauté for 5 minutes or until translucent.
2. Add the carrots, cinnamon, and cumin, then sauté for 1 minutes or until aromatic.
3. Pour into the brown rice, orange juice, and water. Bring to a boil. Reduce the heat to medium-low and simmer for 7 minutes or until the liquid is almost absorbed.
4. Transfer the rice mixture in a large serving bowl, then spread with pistachios, raisins, and chives. Serve immediately.

Nutrition:

Calories: 264

Fat: 7.1g

Protein: 5.2g

Carbs: 48.9g

Cherry, Apricot, and Pecan Brown Rice Bowl

Preparation time: 15 minutes

Cooking time: 1 hour & 1 minute

Servings: 2

Ingredients:

- 2 tablespoons olive oil
- 2 green onions, sliced
- ½ cup brown rice
- 1 cup low-sodium chicken stock
- 2 tablespoons dried cherries
- 4 dried apricots, chopped
- 2 tablespoons pecans, toasted and chopped
- Sea salt and freshly ground pepper, to taste

Directions:

1. Heat the olive oil in a medium saucepan over medium-high heat until shimmering. Add the green onions and sauté for 1 minutes or until fragrant.
2. Add the rice. Stir to mix well, then pour in the chicken stock. Bring to a boil. Reduce the heat to low. Cover and simmer for 50 minutes or until the brown rice is soft.
3. Add the cherries, apricots, and pecans, and simmer for 10 more minutes or until the fruits are tender.
4. Pour them in a large serving bowl. Fluff with a fork. Sprinkle with sea salt and freshly ground pepper. Serve immediately.

Nutrition:

Calories: 451

Fat: 25.9g

Protein: 8.2g

Carbs: 50.4g

Curry Apple Couscous with Leeks and Pecans

Preparation time: 15 minutes

Cooking time: 8 minutes

Servings: 4

Ingredients:

- 2 teaspoons extra-virgin olive oil
- 2 leeks, white parts only, sliced
- 1 apple, diced
- 2 cups cooked couscous
- 2 tablespoons curry powder
- ½ cup chopped pecans

Directions:

1. Heat the olive oil in a skillet over medium heat until shimmering. Add the leeks and sauté for 5 minutes or until soft.
2. Add the diced apple and cook for 3 more minutes until tender. Add the couscous and curry powder. Stir to combine. Transfer them in a large serving bowl, then mix in the pecans and serve.

Nutrition:

Calories: 254

Fat: 11.9g

Protein: 5.4g

Carbs: 34.3g

Lebanese Flavor Broken Thin Noodles

Preparation time: 15 minutes

Cooking time: 25 minutes

Servings: 6

Ingredients:

- 1 tablespoon extra-virgin olive oil
- 1 (3-ounce / 85-g) cup vermicelli, broken into 1- to 1½-inch pieces
- 3 cups shredded cabbage
- 1 cup brown rice
- 3 cups low-sodium vegetable soup
- ½ cup water
- 2 garlic cloves, mashed
- ¼ teaspoon sea salt
- 1/8 teaspoon crushed red pepper flakes
- ½ cup coarsely chopped cilantro
- Fresh lemon slices, for serving

Directions:

1. Heat the olive oil in a saucepan over medium-high heat until shimmering. Add the vermicelli and sauté for 3 minutes or until toasted. Add the cabbage and sauté for 4 minutes or until tender.
2. Pour in the brown rice, vegetable soup, and water. Add the garlic and sprinkle with salt and red pepper flakes.
3. Bring to a boil over high heat. Reduce the heat to medium low. Put the lid on and simmer for another 10 minutes. Turn off the heat, then let sit for 5 minutes without opening the lid.
4. Pour them on a large serving platter and spread with cilantro. Squeeze the lemon slices over and serve warm.

Nutrition:

Calories: 127

Fat: 3.1g

Protein: 4.2g

Carbs: 22.9g

Lemony Farro and Avocado Bowl

Preparation time: 15 minutes

Cooking time: 25 minutes

Servings: 4

Ingredients:

- 1 tablespoon plus 2 teaspoons extra-virgin olive oil, divided
- ½ medium onion, chopped
- 1 carrot, shredded
- 2 garlic cloves, minced
- 1 (6-ounce / 170-g) cup pearled farro
- 2 cups low-sodium vegetable soup
- 2 avocados, peeled, pitted, and sliced
- Zest and juice of 1 small lemon
- ¼ teaspoon sea salt

Directions:

1. Heat 1 tablespoon of olive oil in a saucepan over medium-high heat until shimmering. Add the onion and sauté for 5 minutes or until translucent. Add the carrot and garlic and sauté for 1 minute or until fragrant.
2. Add the farro and pour in the vegetable soup. Bring to a boil over high heat. Reduce the heat to low. Put the lid on and simmer for 20 minutes or until the farro is al dente.
3. Transfer the farro in a large serving bowl, then fold in the avocado slices. Sprinkle with lemon zest and salt, then drizzle with lemon juice and 2 teaspoons of olive oil. Stir to mix well and serve immediately.

Nutrition:

Calories: 210

Fat: 11.1g

Protein: 4.2g

Carbs: 27.9g

Rice and Blueberry Stuffed Sweet Potatoes

Preparation time: 15 minutes

Cooking time: 20 minutes

Servings: 4

Ingredients:

- 2 cups cooked wild rice
- ½ cup dried blueberries
- ½ cup chopped hazelnuts
- ½ cup shredded Swiss chard
- 1 teaspoon chopped fresh thyme
- 1 scallion, white and green parts, peeled and thinly sliced
- Sea salt and freshly ground black pepper, to taste
- 4 sweet potatoes, baked in the skin until tender

Directions:

1. Preheat the oven to 400°f (205°c). Combine all the ingredients, except for the sweet potatoes, in a large bowl. Stir to mix well.
2. Cut the top third of the sweet potato off length wire, then scoop most of the sweet potato flesh out. Fill the potato with the wild rice mixture, then set the sweet potato on a greased baking sheet.
3. Bake in the preheated oven for 20 minutes or until the sweet potato skin is lightly charred. Serve immediately.

Nutrition:

Calories: 393

Fat: 7.1g

Protein: 10.2g

Carbs: 76.9g

Farrotto Mix

Preparation time: 15 minutes

Cooking time: 40 minutes

Servings: 6

Ingredients:

- ½ onion, chopped fine
- 1 cup frozen peas, thawed
- 1 garlic clove, minced
- 1 tablespoon minced fresh chives
- 1 teaspoon grated lemon zest plus 1 teaspoon juice
- 1½ cups whole farro
- 1½ ounces Parmesan cheese, grated (¾ cup)
- 2 tablespoons extra-virgin olive oil
- 2 teaspoons minced fresh tarragon
- 3 cups chicken broth
- 3 cups water
- 4 ounces asparagus, trimmed and cut on bias into 1-inch lengths
- 4 ounces pancetta, cut into ¼-inch pieces
- Salt and pepper

Directions:

1. Pulse farro using a blender until about half of grains are broken into smaller pieces, about 6 pulses.
2. Bring broth and water to boil in moderate-sized saucepan on high heat. Put in asparagus and cook until crisp-tender, 2 to 3 minutes.
3. Use a slotted spoon to move asparagus to a container and set aside. Decrease heat to low, cover broth mixture, and keep warm.
4. Cook pancetta in a Dutch oven on moderate heat until lightly browned and fat has rendered, approximately 5 minutes.
5. Put in 1 tablespoon oil and onion and cook till they become tender, approximately 5 minutes. Mix in garlic and cook until aromatic, approximately half a minute.
6. Put in farro and cook, stirring often, until grains are lightly toasted, approximately three minutes.
7. Stir 5 cups warm broth mixture into farro mixture, decrease the heat to low, cover, and cook until almost all liquid has been absorbed and farro is just al dente, about 25 minutes, stirring twice during cooking.
8. Put in peas, tarragon, ¾ teaspoon salt, and ½ teaspoon pepper and cook, stirring continuously, until farro becomes creamy, approximately 5 minutes.
9. Remove from the heat, mix in Parmesan, chives, lemon zest and juice, remaining 1 tablespoon oil, and reserved asparagus.
10. Adjust consistency with remaining warm broth mixture as required (you may have

broth left over). Sprinkle with salt and pepper to taste. Serve.

Nutrition:

Calories: 218

Carbs: 41g

Fat: 2g

Protein: 7g

Feta-Grape-Bulgur Salad with Grapes and Feta

Preparation time: 15 minutes

Cooking time: 1 hour & 30 minutes

Servings: 4-6

Ingredients:

- ¼ cup chopped fresh mint
- ¼ cup extra-virgin olive oil
- ¼ teaspoon ground cumin
- ½ cup slivered almonds, toasted
- 1 cup water
- 1½ cups medium-grind bulgur, rinsed
- 2 ounces feta cheese, crumbled (½ cup)
- 2 scallions, sliced thin
- 5 tablespoons lemon juice (2 lemons)
- 6 ounces seedless red grapes, quartered (1 cup)
- Pinch cayenne pepper
- Salt and pepper

Directions:

1. Mix bulgur, water, ¼ cup lemon juice, and ¼ teaspoon salt in a container. Cover and allow to sit at room temperature until grains are softened and liquid is fully absorbed, about 1½ hours.
2. Beat remaining 1 tablespoon lemon juice, oil, cumin, cayenne, and ¼ teaspoon salt together in a big container.
3. Put in bulgur, grapes, 1/3 cup almonds, 1/3 cup feta, scallions, and mint and gently toss to combine. Sprinkle with salt and pepper to taste. Sprinkle with remaining almonds and remaining feta before you serve.

Nutrition:

Calories: 500

Carbs: 45g

Fat: 14g

Protein: 50g

Greek Style Meaty Bulgur

Preparation time: 15 minutes

Cooking time: 30 minutes

Servings: 4-6

Ingredients:

- ½ cup jarred roasted red peppers, rinsed, patted dry, and chopped
- 1 bay leaf
- 1 cup medium-grind bulgur, rinsed
- 1 onion, chopped fine
- 1 tablespoon chopped fresh dill
- 1 teaspoon extra-virgin olive oil
- 1 1/3 cups vegetable broth
- 2 teaspoons minced fresh marjoram or ½ teaspoon dried
- 3 garlic cloves, minced
- 8 ounces ground lamb
- Lemon wedges
- Salt and pepper

Directions:

1. Heat oil in a big saucepan on moderate to high heat until just smoking. Put in lamb, ½ teaspoon salt, and ¼ teaspoon pepper and cook, breaking up meat with wooden spoon, until browned, 3 to 5 minutes.
2. Mix in onion and red peppers and cook until onion is softened, 5 to 7 minutes. Mix in garlic and marjoram and cook until aromatic, approximately half a minute.
3. Mix in bulgur, broth, and bay leaf and bring to simmer. Decrease heat to low, cover, and simmer gently until bulgur is tender, 16 to 18 minutes.
4. Remove from the heat, lay clean dish towel underneath lid and let bulgur sit for about 10 minutes.

5. Put in dill and fluff gently with fork to combine. Sprinkle with salt and pepper to taste. Serve with lemon wedges.

Nutrition:

Calories: 137

Carbs: 16g

Fat: 5g

Protein: 7g

Hearty Barley Mix

Preparation time: 15 minutes

Cooking time: 50 minutes

Servings: 4

Ingredients:

- 1/8 teaspoon ground cardamom
- ½ cup plain yogurt
- ½ teaspoon ground cumin
- 2/3 cup raw sunflower seeds
- ¾ teaspoon ground coriander
- 1 cup pearl barley
- 1½ tablespoons minced fresh mint
- 1½ teaspoons grated lemon zest plus 1½ tablespoons juice
- 3 tablespoons extra-virgin olive oil
- 5 carrots, peeled
- 8 ounces snow peas, strings removed, halved along the length
- Salt and pepper

Directions:

1. Beat yogurt, ½ teaspoon lemon zest and 1½ teaspoons juice, 1½ teaspoons mint, ¼ teaspoon salt, and 1/8 teaspoon pepper together in a small-sized container; cover put inside your fridge until ready to serve.
2. Bring 4 quarts water to boil in a Dutch oven. Put in barley and 1 tablespoon salt, return to boil, and cook until tender, 20 to 40 minutes. Drain barley, return to now-empty pot, and cover to keep warm.
3. In the meantime, halve carrots crosswise, then halve or quarter along the length to create uniformly sized pieces.
4. Heat 1 tablespoon oil in 12-inch frying pan on moderate to high heat until just smoking. Put in carrots and ½ teaspoon coriander and cook, stirring intermittently, until mildly charred and just tender, 5 to 7 minutes.
5. Put in snow peas and cook, stirring intermittently, until spotty brown, 3 to 5 minutes; move to plate.
6. Heat 1½ teaspoons oil in now-empty frying pan on moderate heat until it starts to shimmer. Put in sunflower seeds, cumin, cardamom, remaining ¼ teaspoon coriander, and ¼ teaspoon salt.
7. Cook, stirring continuously, until seeds are toasted, approximately 2 minutes; move to small-sized container.
8. Beat remaining 1 teaspoon lemon zest and 1 tablespoon juice, remaining 1 tablespoon mint, and remaining 1½ tablespoons oil together in a big container.
9. Put in barley and carrot–snow pea mixture and gently toss to combine. Sprinkle with salt and pepper to taste. Serve, topping individual portions with spiced sunflower seeds and drizzling with yogurt sauce.

Nutrition:

Calories: 193

Carbs: 44g

Fat: 1g

Protein: 4g

Hearty Barley Risotto

Preparation time: 15 minutes

Cooking time: 60 minutes

Servings: 4-6

Ingredients:

- 1 carrot, peeled and chopped fine
- 1 cup dry white wine
- 1 onion, chopped fine
- 1 teaspoon minced fresh thyme or ¼ teaspoon dried
- 1½ cups pearl barley
- 2 ounces Parmesan cheese, grated (1 cup)
- 2 tablespoons extra-virgin olive oil

- 4 cups chicken or vegetable broth
- 4 cups water
- Salt and pepper

Directions:

1. Bring broth and water to simmer in moderate-sized saucepan. Decrease heat to low and cover to keep warm.
2. Heat 1 tablespoon oil in a Dutch oven on moderate heat until it starts to shimmer. Put in onion and carrot and cook till they become tender, 5 to 7 minutes.
3. Put in barley and cook, stirring frequently, until lightly toasted and aromatic, about 4 minutes. Put in wine and cook, stirring often, until fully absorbed, approximately two minutes.
4. Mix in 3 cups warm broth and thyme, bring to simmer, and cook, stirring intermittently, until liquid is absorbed and bottom of pot is dry, 22 to 25 minutes.
5. Mix in 2 cups warm broth, bring to simmer, and cook, stirring intermittently, until liquid is absorbed and bottom of pot is dry, fifteen to twenty minutes.
6. Carry on cooking risotto, stirring frequently and adding warm broth as required to stop pot bottom from becoming dry, until barley is cooked through, 15 to 20 minutes.
7. Remove from the heat, adjust consistency with remaining warm broth as required. Mix in Parmesan and residual 1 tablespoon oil and sprinkle with salt and pepper to taste. Serve.

Nutrition:

Calories: 222

Carbs: 33g

Fat: 5g

Protein: 6g

Hearty Freekeh Pilaf

Preparation time: 15 minutes

Cooking time: 60 minutes

Servings: 4-6

Ingredients:

- ¼ cup chopped fresh mint
- ¼ cup extra-virgin olive oil, plus extra for serving
- ¼ cup shelled pistachios, toasted and coarsely chopped
- ¼ teaspoon ground coriander
- ¼ teaspoon ground cumin
- 1 head cauliflower (2 pounds), cored and cut into ½-inch florets
- 1 shallot, minced
- 1½ cups whole freekeh
- 1½ tablespoons lemon juice
- 1½ teaspoons grated fresh ginger
- 3 ounces pitted dates, chopped (½ cup)
- Salt and pepper

Directions:

1. Bring 4 quarts water to boil in a Dutch oven. Put in freekeh and 1 tablespoon salt, return to boil, and cook until grains are tender, 30 to 45 minutes. Drain freekeh, return to now-empty pot, and cover to keep warm.
2. Heat 2 tablespoons oil in 12-inch non-stick frying pan on moderate to high heat until it starts to shimmer.
3. Put in cauliflower, ½ teaspoon salt, and ¼ teaspoon pepper, cover, and cook until florets are softened and start to brown, approximately five minutes.
4. Remove lid and continue to cook, stirring intermittently, until florets turn spotty brown, about 10 minutes.
5. Put in remaining 2 tablespoons oil, dates, shallot, ginger, coriander, and cumin and cook, stirring often, until dates and shallot are softened and aromatic, approximately 3 minutes.
6. Decrease heat to low, put in freekeh, and cook, stirring often, until heated through, about 1 minute. Remove from the heat, mix in pistachios, mint, and lemon juice.
7. Sprinkle with salt and pepper to taste and drizzle with extra oil. Serve.

Nutrition:

Calories: 520

Carbs: 54g

Fat: 14g

Protein: 36g

Herby-Lemony Farro

Preparation time: 15 minutes

Cooking time: 40 minutes

Servings: 4-6

Ingredients:

- ¼ cup chopped fresh mint
- ¼ cup chopped fresh parsley
- 1 garlic clove, minced
- 1 onion, chopped fine
- 1 tablespoon lemon juice
- 1½ cups whole farro
- 3 tablespoons extra-virgin olive oil
- Salt and pepper

Directions:

1. Bring 4 quarts water to boil in a Dutch oven. Put in farro and 1 tablespoon salt, return to boil, and cook until grains are soft with slight chew, 15 to 30 minutes. Drain farro, return to now-empty pot, and cover to keep warm.
2. Heat 2 tablespoons oil in 12-inch frying pan on moderate heat until it starts to shimmer. Put in onion and ¼ teaspoon salt and cook till they become tender, approximately five minutes.
3. Mix in garlic and cook until aromatic, approximately half a minute. Put in residual 1 tablespoon oil and farro and cook, stirring often, until heated through, approximately two minutes.
4. Remove from the heat, mix in parsley, mint, and lemon juice. Sprinkle with salt and pepper to taste. Serve.

Nutrition:

Calories: 243

Carbs: 22g

Fat: 14g

Protein: 10g

Mushroom-Bulgur Pilaf

Preparation time: 15 minutes

Cooking time: 30 minutes

Servings: 4

Ingredients:

- ¼ cup minced fresh parsley
- ¼ ounce dried porcini mushrooms, rinsed and minced
- ¾ cup chicken or vegetable broth
- ¾ cup water
- 1 cup medium-grind bulgur, rinsed
- 1 onion, chopped fine
- 2 garlic cloves, minced
- 2 tablespoons extra-virgin olive oil
- 8 ounces cremini mushrooms, trimmed, halved if small or quartered if large
- Salt and pepper

Directions:

1. Heat oil in a big saucepan on moderate heat until it starts to shimmer. Put in onion, porcini mushrooms, and ½ teaspoon salt and cook until onion is softened, approximately 5 minutes.
2. Mix in cremini mushrooms, increase heat to medium-high, cover, and cook until cremini release their liquid and begin to brown, about 4 minutes.
3. Mix in garlic and cook until aromatic, approximately half a minute. Mix in bulgur, broth, and water and bring to simmer.
4. Decrease heat to low, cover, and simmer gently until bulgur is tender, 16 to 18 minutes. Remove from the heat, lay clean dish towel underneath lid and let pilaf sit for about ten minutes.
5. Put in parsley to pilaf and fluff gently with fork to combine. Sprinkle with salt and pepper to taste. Serve.

Nutrition:

Calories: 259

Carbs: 50g

Fat: 3g

Protein: 11g

Baked Brown Rice

Preparation time: 15 minutes

Cooking time: 1 hour & 25 minutes

Servings: 4-6

Ingredients:

- ½ cup minced fresh parsley
- ¾ cup jarred roasted red peppers, rinsed, patted dry, and chopped
- 1 cup chicken or vegetable broth
- 1½ cups long-grain brown rice, rinsed
- 2 onions, chopped fine
- 2¼ cups water
- 4 teaspoons extra-virgin olive oil
- Grated Parmesan cheese
- Lemon wedges
- Salt and pepper

Directions:

1. Place the oven rack in the center of the oven and pre-heat your oven to 375 degrees. Heat oil in a Dutch oven on moderate heat until it starts to shimmer.
2. Put in onions and 1 teaspoon salt and cook, stirring intermittently, till they become tender and well browned, 12 to 14 minutes.
3. Mix in water and broth and bring to boil. Mix in rice, cover, and move pot to oven. Bake until rice becomes soft and liquid is absorbed, 65 to 70 minutes.
4. Remove pot from oven. Sprinkle red peppers over rice, cover, and allow to sit for about five minutes.
5. Put in parsley to rice and fluff gently with fork to combine. Sprinkle with salt and pepper to taste. Serve with grated Parmesan and lemon wedges.

Nutrition:

Calories: 100

Carbs: 27g

Fat: 21g

Protein: 2g

Barley Pilaf

Preparation time: 15 minutes

Cooking time: 45 minutes

Servings: 4-6

Ingredients:

- ¼ cup minced fresh parsley
- 1 small onion, chopped fine
- 1½ cups pearl barley, rinsed
- 1½ teaspoons lemon juice
- 1½ teaspoons minced fresh thyme or ½ teaspoon dried
- 2 garlic cloves, minced
- 2 tablespoons minced fresh chives
- 2½ cups water
- 3 tablespoons extra-virgin olive oil
- Salt and pepper

Directions:

1. Heat oil in a big saucepan on moderate heat until it starts to shimmer. Put in onion and ½ teaspoon salt and cook till they become tender, approximately 5 minutes.
2. Mix in barley, garlic, and thyme and cook, stirring often, until barley is lightly toasted and aromatic, approximately three minutes.
3. Mix in water and bring to simmer. Decrease heat to low, cover, and simmer until barley becomes soft and water is absorbed, 20 to 40 minutes.
4. Remove from the heat, lay clean dish towel underneath lid and let pilaf sit for about ten minutes. Put in parsley, chives, and lemon juice to pilaf and fluff gently with fork to combine. Sprinkle with salt and pepper to taste. Serve.

Nutrition:

Calories: 39

Carbs: 8g

Fat: 1g

Protein: 1g

Basmati Rice Pilaf Mix

Preparation time: 15 minutes

Cooking time: 25 minutes

Servings: 4-6

Ingredients:

- ¼ cup currants
- ¼ cup sliced almonds, toasted
- ¼ teaspoon ground cinnamon
- ½ teaspoon ground turmeric
- 1 small onion, chopped fine
- 1 tablespoon extra-virgin olive oil
- 1½ cups basmati rice, rinsed
- 2 garlic cloves, minced
- 2¼ cups water
- Salt and pepper

Directions:

1. Heat oil in a big saucepan on moderate heat until it starts to shimmer. Put in onion and ¼ teaspoon salt and cook till they become tender, approximately 5 minutes.
2. Put in rice, garlic, turmeric, and cinnamon and cook, stirring often, until grain edges begin to turn translucent, approximately three minutes.
3. Mix in water and bring to simmer. Decrease heat to low, cover, and simmer gently until rice becomes soft and water is absorbed, 16 to 18 minutes.
4. Remove from the heat, drizzle currants over pilaf. Cover, laying clean dish towel underneath lid, and let pilaf sit for about ten minutes.
5. Put in almonds to pilaf and fluff gently with fork to combine. Sprinkle with salt and pepper to taste. Serve.

Nutrition:

Calories: 180

Carbs: 36g

Fat: 2g

Protein: 4g

Brown Rice Salad with Asparagus, Goat Cheese, and Lemon

Preparation time: 15 minutes

Cooking time: 35 minutes

Servings: 4-6

Ingredients:

- ¼ cup minced fresh parsley
- ¼ cup slivered almonds, toasted
- 1 pound asparagus, trimmed and cut into 1-inch lengths
- 1 shallot, minced
- 1 teaspoon grated lemon zest plus 3 tablespoons juice
- 1½ cups long-grain brown rice
- 2 ounces goat cheese, crumbled (½ cup)
- 3½ tablespoons extra-virgin olive oil
- Salt and pepper

Directions:

1. Bring 4 quarts water to boil in a Dutch oven. Put in rice and 1½ teaspoons salt and cook, stirring intermittently, until rice is tender, about half an hour.
2. Drain rice, spread onto rimmed baking sheet, and drizzle with 1 tablespoon lemon juice. Allow it to cool completely, about 15 minutes.
3. Heat 1 tablespoon oil in 12-inch frying pan on high heat until just smoking. Put in asparagus, ¼ teaspoon salt, and ¼ teaspoon pepper and cook, stirring intermittently, until asparagus is browned and crisp-tender, about 4 minutes; move to plate and allow to cool slightly.
4. Beat remaining 2½ tablespoons oil, lemon zest and remaining 2 tablespoons juice, shallot, ½ teaspoon salt, and ½ teaspoon pepper together in a big container.
5. Put in rice, asparagus, 2 tablespoons goat cheese, 3 tablespoons almonds, and 3 tablespoons parsley. Gently toss to combine and allow to sit for about 10 minutes.
6. Sprinkle with salt and pepper to taste. Move to serving platter and drizzle with remaining 2 tablespoons goat cheese,

remaining 1 tablespoon almonds, and remaining 1 tablespoon parsley. Serve.

Nutrition:

Calories: 197

Carbs: 6g

Fat: 16g

Protein: 7g

Carrot-Almond-Bulgur Salad

Preparation time: 1 hour & 45 minutes

Cooking time: 0 minutes

Servings: 4-6

Ingredients:

- 1/8 teaspoon cayenne pepper
- 1/3 cup chopped fresh cilantro
- 1/3 cup chopped fresh mint
- 1/3 cup extra-virgin olive oil
- ½ cup sliced almonds, toasted
- ½ teaspoon ground cumin
- 1 cup water
- 1½ cups medium-grind bulgur, rinsed
- 3 scallions, sliced thin
- 4 carrots, peeled and shredded
- 6 tablespoons lemon juice (2 lemons)
- Salt and pepper

Directions:

1. Mix bulgur, water, ¼ cup lemon juice, and ¼ teaspoon salt in a container. Cover and allow to sit at room temperature until grains are softened and liquid is fully absorbed, about 1½ hours.
2. Beat remaining 2 tablespoons lemon juice, oil, cumin, cayenne, and ½ teaspoon salt together in a big container.
3. Put in bulgur, carrots, scallions, almonds, mint, and cilantro and gently toss to combine. Sprinkle with salt and pepper to taste. Serve.

Nutrition:

Calories: 240

Carbs: 54g

Fat: 2g

Protein: 7g

Chickpea-Spinach-Bulgur

Preparation time: 15 minutes

Cooking time: 23 minutes

Servings: 4-6

Ingredients:

- ¾ cup chicken or vegetable broth
- ¾ cup water
- 1 (15-ounce) can chickpeas, rinsed
- 1 cup medium-grind bulgur, rinsed
- 1 onion, chopped fine
- 1 tablespoon lemon juice
- 2 tablespoons za'atar
- 3 garlic cloves, minced
- 3 ounces (3 cups) baby spinach, chopped
- 3 tablespoons extra-virgin olive oil
- Salt and pepper

Directions:

1. Heat 2 tablespoons oil in a big saucepan on moderate heat until it starts to shimmer. Put in onion and ½ teaspoon salt and cook till they become tender, approximately 5 minutes.
2. Mix in garlic and 1 tablespoon za'atar and cook until aromatic, approximately half a minute. Mix in bulgur, chickpeas, broth, and water and bring to simmer. Decrease heat to low, cover, and simmer gently until bulgur is tender, 16 to 18 minutes.
3. Remove from the heat, lay clean dish towel underneath lid and let bulgur sit for about ten minutes.
4. Put in spinach, lemon juice, remaining 1 tablespoon za'atar, and residual 1 tablespoon oil and fluff gently with fork to combine. Sprinkle with salt and pepper to taste. Serve.

Nutrition:

Calories: 319

Carbs: 43g

Fat: 12g

Protein: 10g

Italian Seafood Risotto

Preparation time: 15 minutes

Cooking time: 60 minutes

Servings: 4-6

Ingredients:

- 1/8 teaspoon saffron threads, crumbled
- 1 (14.5-ounce) can diced tomatoes, drained
- 1 cup dry white wine
- 1 onion, chopped fine
- 1 tablespoon lemon juice
- 1 teaspoon minced fresh thyme or ¼ teaspoon dried
- 12 ounces large shrimp (26 to 30 per pound), peeled and deveined, shells reserved
- 12 ounces small bay scallops
- 2 bay leaves
- 2 cups Arborio rice
- 2 cups chicken broth
- 2 tablespoons minced fresh parsley
- 2½ cups water
- 4 (8-ounce) bottles clam juice
- 5 garlic cloves, minced
- 5 tablespoons extra-virgin olive oil
- Salt and pepper

Directions:

1. Bring shrimp shells, broth, water, clam juice, tomatoes, and bay leaves to boil in a big saucepan on moderate to high heat. Decrease the heat to a simmer and cook for 20 minutes.
2. Strain mixture through fine-mesh strainer into big container, pressing on solids to extract as much liquid as possible; discard solids. Return broth to now-empty saucepan, cover, and keep warm on low heat.
3. Heat 2 tablespoons oil in a Dutch oven on moderate heat until it starts to shimmer. Put in onion and cook till they become tender, approximately 5 minutes.
4. Put in rice, garlic, thyme, and saffron and cook, stirring often, until grain edges begin to turn translucent, approximately 3 minutes.
5. Put in wine and cook, stirring often, until fully absorbed, approximately three minutes. Mix in 3½ cups warm broth, bring to simmer, and cook, stirring intermittently, until almost fully absorbed, about 15 minutes.
6. Carry on cooking rice, stirring often and adding warm broth, 1 cup at a time, every few minutes as liquid is absorbed, until rice is creamy and cooked through but still somewhat firm in center, about 15 minutes.
7. Mix in shrimp and scallops and cook, stirring often, until opaque throughout, approximately three minutes. Remove pot from heat, cover, and allow to sit for about 5 minutes.
8. Adjust consistency with remaining warm broth as required. Mix in remaining 3 tablespoons oil, parsley, and lemon juice and sprinkle with salt and pepper to taste. Serve.

Nutrition:

Calories: 450

Carbs: 12g

Fat: 40g

Protein: 31g

Classic Stovetop White Rice

Preparation time: 15 minutes

Cooking time: 22 minutes

Servings: 4-6

Ingredients:

- 1 tablespoon extra-virgin olive oil
- 2 cups long-grain white rice, rinsed
- 3 cups water
- Basmati, jasmine, or Texmati rice can be substituted for the long-grain rice.
- Salt and pepper

Directions:

1. Heat oil in a big saucepan on moderate heat until it starts to shimmer. Put in rice

and cook, stirring frequently, until grain edges begin to turn translucent, approximately 2 minutes.
2. Put in water and 1 teaspoon salt and bring to simmer. Cover, decrease the heat to low, and simmer gently until rice becomes soft and water is absorbed, approximately 20 minutes.
3. Remove from the heat, lay clean dish towel underneath lid and let rice sit for about ten minutes. Gently fluff rice with fork. Sprinkle with salt and pepper to taste. Serve.

Nutrition:

Calories: 160

Carbs: 36g

Fat: 0g

Protein: 3g

Classic Tabbouleh

Preparation time: 2 hours

Cooking time: 0 minutes

Servings: 4-6

Ingredients:

- 1/8 teaspoon cayenne pepper
- ¼ cup lemon juice (2 lemons)
- ½ cup medium-grind bulgur, rinsed
- ½ cup minced fresh mint
- 1½ cups minced fresh parsley
- 2 scallions, sliced thin
- 3 tomatoes, cored and cut into ½-inch pieces
- 6 tablespoons extra-virgin olive oil
- Salt and pepper

Directions:

1. Toss tomatoes with ¼ teaspoon salt using a fine-mesh strainer set over bowl and let drain, tossing occasionally, for 30 minutes; reserve 2 tablespoons drained tomato juice.
2. Toss bulgur with 2 tablespoons lemon juice and reserved tomato juice in a container and allow to sit until grains start to become tender, 30 to 40 minutes.
3. Beat remaining 2 tablespoons lemon juice, oil, cayenne, and ¼ teaspoon salt together in a big container. Put in tomatoes, bulgur, parsley, mint, and scallions and toss gently to combine.
4. Cover and allow to sit at room temperature until flavors have blended and bulgur is tender, about 1 hour. Before serving, toss salad to recombine and sprinkle with salt and pepper to taste.

Nutrition:

Calories: 150

Carbs: 8g

Fat: 12g

Protein: 4g

Farro Cucumber-Mint Salad

Preparation time: 15 minutes

Cooking time: 30 minutes

Servings: 4-6

Ingredients:

- 1 cup baby arugula
- 1 English cucumber, halved along the length, seeded, and cut into ¼-inch pieces
- 1½ cups whole farro
- 2 tablespoons lemon juice
- 2 tablespoons minced shallot
- 2 tablespoons plain Greek yogurt
- 3 tablespoons chopped fresh mint
- 3 tablespoons extra-virgin olive oil
- 6 ounces cherry tomatoes, halved
- Salt and pepper

Directions:

1. Bring 4 quarts water to boil in a Dutch oven. Put in farro and 1 tablespoon salt, return to boil, and cook until grains are soft with slight chew, 15 to 30 minutes.
2. Drain farro, spread in rimmed baking sheet, and allow to cool completely, about fifteen minutes.

3. Beat oil, lemon juice, shallot, yogurt, ¼ teaspoon salt, and ¼ teaspoon pepper together in a big container.
4. Put in farro, cucumber, tomatoes, arugula, and mint and toss gently to combine. Sprinkle with salt and pepper to taste. Serve.

Nutrition:

Calories: 97

Carbs: 15g

Fat: 4g

Protein: 2g

Chorizo-Kidney Beans Quinoa Pilaf

Preparation time: 15 minutes

Cooking time: 37 minutes

Servings: 4

Ingredients:

- ¼ pound dried Spanish chorizo diced (about 2/3 cup)
- ¼ teaspoon red pepper flakes
- ¼ teaspoon smoked paprika
- ½ teaspoon cumin
- ½ teaspoon sea salt
- 1 3/4 cups water
- 1 cup quinoa
- 1 large clove garlic minced
- 1 small red bell pepper finely diced
- 1 small red onion finely diced
- 1 tablespoon tomato paste
- 1 15-ounce can kidney beans rinsed and drained

Directions:

1. Place a nonstick pot on medium high fire and heat for 2 minutes. Add chorizo and sauté for 5 minutes until lightly browned. Stir in peppers and onion. Sauté for 5 minutes.
2. Add tomato paste, red pepper flakes, salt, paprika, cumin, and garlic. Sauté for 2 minutes. Stir in quinoa and mix well. Sauté for 2 minutes.
3. Add water and beans. Mix well. Cover and simmer for 20 minutes or until liquid is fully absorbed. Turn off fire and fluff quinoa. Let it sit for 5 minutes more while uncovered. Serve and enjoy.

Nutrition:

Calories: 260

Protein: 9.6g

Carbs: 40.9g

Fat: 6.8g

Goat Cheese 'N Red Beans Salad

Preparation time: 15 minutes

Cooking time: 0 minutes

Servings: 6

Ingredients:

- 2 cans of Red Kidney Beans, drained and rinsed well
- Water or vegetable broth to cover beans
- 1 bunch parsley, chopped
- 1 1/2 cups red grape tomatoes, halved
- 3 cloves garlic, minced
- 3 tablespoons olive oil
- 3 tablespoons lemon juice
- 1/2 teaspoon salt
- 1/2 teaspoon white pepper
- 6 ounces goat cheese, crumbled

Directions:

1. In a large bowl, combine beans, parsley, tomatoes and garlic. Add olive oil, lemon juice, salt and pepper.
2. Mix well and refrigerate until ready to serve. Spoon into individual dishes topped with crumbled goat cheese.

Nutrition:

Calories: 385

Protein: 22.5g

Carbs: 44.0g

Fat: 15.0g

Greek Farro Salad

Preparation time: 15 minutes

Cooking time: 20 minutes

Servings: 4

INGREDIENTS:

Farro:

- ½ teaspoon fine-grain sea salt
- 1 cup farro, rinsed
- 1 tablespoon olive oil
- 2 garlic cloves, pressed or minced
- Salad:
- ½ small red onion, chopped and then rinsed under water to mellow the flavor
- 1 avocado, sliced into strips
- 1 cucumber, sliced into thin rounds
- 15 pitted Klamath olives, sliced into rounds
- 1-pint cherry tomatoes, sliced into rounds
- 2 cups cooked chickpeas (or one 14-ounce can, rinsed and drained)
- 5 ounces mixed greens
- Lemon wedges

Herbed Yogurt Ingredients:

- 1/8 teaspoon salt
- 1 ¼ cups plain Greek yogurt
- 1 ½ tablespoon lightly packed fresh dill, roughly chopped
- 1 ½ tablespoon lightly packed fresh mint, torn into pieces
- 1 tablespoon lemon juice (about ½ lemon)
- 1 tablespoon olive oil

Directions:

1. In a blender, blend and puree all herbed yogurt ingredients and set aside. Then cook the farro by placing in a pot filled halfway with water.
2. Bring to a boil, reduce fire to a simmer and cook for 15 minutes or until farro is tender. Drain well. Mix in salt, garlic, and olive oil and fluff to coat.
3. Evenly divide the cooled farro into 4 bowls. Evenly divide the salad ingredients on the 4 farro bowl. Top with ¼ of the yogurt dressing. Serve and enjoy.

Nutrition:

Calories: 428

Protein: 17.7g

Carbs: 47.6g

Fat: 24.5g

White Bean and Tuna Salad

Preparation time: 15 minutes

Cooking time: 8 minutes

Servings: 4

Ingredients:

- 1 (12 ounce) can solid white albacore tuna, drained
- 1 (16 ounce) can Great Northern beans, drained and rinsed
- 1 (2.25 ounce) can sliced black olives, drained
- 1 teaspoon dried oregano
- 1/2 teaspoon finely grated lemon zest
- 1/4 medium red onion, thinly sliced
- 3 tablespoons lemon juice
- 3/4-pound green beans, trimmed and snapped in half
- 4 large hard-cooked eggs, peeled and quartered
- 6 tablespoons extra-virgin olive oil
- Salt and ground black pepper, to taste

Directions:

1. Place a saucepan on medium high fire. Add a cup of water and the green beans. Cover and cook for 8 minutes. Drain immediately once tender.
2. In a salad bowl, whisk well oregano, olive oil, lemon juice, and lemon zest. Season generously with pepper and salt and mix until salt is dissolved.
3. Stir in drained green beans, tuna, beans, olives, and red onion. Mix thoroughly to coat. Adjust seasoning to taste. Spread eggs on top. Serve and enjoy.

Nutrition:

Calories: 551

Protein: 36.3g

Carbs: 33.4g

Fat: 30.3g

Spicy Sweet Red Hummus

Preparation time: 15 minutes

Cooking time: 0 minutes

Servings: 8

Ingredients:

- 1 (15 ounce) can garbanzo beans, drained
- 1 (4 ounce) jar roasted red peppers
- 1 1/2 tablespoons tahini
- 1 clove garlic, minced
- 1 tablespoon chopped fresh parsley
- 1/2 teaspoon cayenne pepper
- 1/2 teaspoon ground cumin
- 1/4 teaspoon salt
- 3 tablespoons lemon juice

Directions:

1. In a blender, add all ingredients and process until smooth and creamy. Adjust seasoning to taste if needed. Can be stored in an airtight container for up to 5 days.

Nutrition:

Calories: 64

Protein: 2.5g

Carbs: 9.6g

Fat: 2.2g

Black Bean Chili with Mangoes

Preparation time: 15 minutes

Cooking time: 10 minutes

Servings: 4

Ingredients:

- 2 tablespoons coconut oil
- 1 onion, chopped
- 2 (15-ounce / 425-g) cans black beans, drained and rinsed
- 1 tablespoon chili powder
- 1 teaspoon sea salt
- ¼ teaspoon freshly ground black pepper
- 1 cup water
- 2 ripe mangoes, sliced thinly
- ¼ cup chopped fresh cilantro, divided
- ¼ cup sliced scallions, divided

Directions:

1. Heat the coconut oil in a pot over high heat until melted. Put the onion in the pot and sauté for 5 minutes or until translucent.
2. Add the black beans to the pot. Sprinkle with chili powder, salt, and ground black pepper. Pour in the water. Stir to mix well.
3. Bring to a boil. Reduce the heat to low, then simmering for 5 minutes or until the beans are tender. Turn off the heat and mix in the mangoes, then garnish with scallions and cilantro before serving.

Nutrition:

Calories: 430

Fat: 9.1g

Protein: 20.2g

Carbs: 71.9g

Israeli Style Eggplant and Chickpea Salad

Preparation time: 5 minutes

Cooking time: 20 minutes

Servings: 6

Ingredients:

- 2 tablespoons balsamic vinegar
- 2 tablespoons freshly squeezed lemon juice
- 1 teaspoon ground cumin
- ¼ teaspoon sea salt
- 2 tablespoons olive oil, divided

- 1 (1-pound / 454-g) medium globe eggplant, stem removed, cut into flat cubes (about ½ inch thick)
- 1 (15-ounce / 425-g) can chickpeas, drained and rinsed
- ¼ cup chopped mint leaves
- 1 cup sliced sweet onion
- 1 garlic clove, finely minced
- 1 tablespoon sesame seeds, toasted

Directions:

1. Preheat the oven to 550°f (288°c) or the highest level of your oven or broiler. Grease a baking sheet with 1 tablespoon of olive oil.
2. Combine the balsamic vinegar, lemon juice, cumin, salt, and 1 tablespoon of olive oil in a small bowl. Stir to mix well.
3. Arrange the eggplant cubes on the baking sheet, then brush with 2 tablespoons of the balsamic vinegar mixture on both sides.
4. Broil in the preheated oven for 8 minutes or until lightly browned. Flip the cubes halfway through the cooking time.
5. Meanwhile, combine the chickpeas, mint, onion, garlic, and sesame seeds in a large serving bowl. Drizzle with remaining balsamic vinegar mixture. Stir to mix well.
6. Remove the eggplant from the oven. Allow to cool for 5 minutes, then slice them into ½-inch strips on a clean work surface.
7. Add the eggplant strips in the serving bowl, then toss to combine well before serving.

Nutrition:

Calories: 125

Fat: 2.9g

Protein: 5.2g

Carbs: 20.9g

Italian Sautéed Cannellini Beans

Preparation time: 15 minutes

Cooking time: 15 minutes

Servings: 6

Ingredients:

- 2 teaspoons extra-virgin olive oil
- ½ cup minced onion
- ¼ cup red wine vinegar
- 1 (12-ounce / 340-g) can no-salt-added tomato paste
- 2 tablespoons raw honey
- ½ cup water
- ¼ teaspoon ground cinnamon
- 2 (15-ounce / 425-g) cans cannellini beans

Directions:

1. Heat the olive oil in a saucepan over medium heat until shimmering. Add the onion and sauté for 5 minutes or until translucent.
2. Pour in the red wine vinegar, tomato paste, honey, and water. Sprinkle with cinnamon. Stir to mix well.
3. Reduce the heat to low, then pour all the beans into the saucepan. Cook for 10 more minutes. Stir constantly. Serve immediately.

Nutrition:

Calories: 435

Fat: 2.1g

Protein: 26.2g

Carbs: 80.3g

Lentil and Vegetable Curry Stew

Preparation time: 15 minutes

Cooking time: 4 hours & 7 minutes

Servings: 8

Ingredients:

- 1 tablespoon coconut oil
- 1 yellow onion, diced
- ¼ cup yellow Thai curry paste
- 2 cups unsweetened coconut milk
- 2 cups dry red lentils, rinsed well and drained
- 3 cups bite-sized cauliflower florets
- 2 golden potatoes, cut into chunks
- 2 carrots, peeled and diced

- 8 cups low-sodium vegetable soup, divided
- 1 bunch kale, stems removed and roughly chopped
- Sea salt, to taste
- ½ cup fresh cilantro, chopped
- Pinch crushed red pepper flakes

Directions:

1. Heat the coconut oil in a nonstick skillet over medium-high heat until melted. Add the onion and sauté for 5 minutes or until translucent.
2. Pour in the curry paste and sauté for another 2 minutes, then fold in the coconut milk and stir to combine well. Bring to a simmer and turn off the heat.
3. Put the lentils, cauliflower, potatoes, and carrot in the slow cooker. Pour in 6 cups of vegetable soup and the curry mixture. Stir to combine well.
4. Cover and cook on high for 4 hours or until the lentils and vegetables are soft. Stir periodically.
5. During the last 30 minutes, fold the kale in the slow cooker and pour in the remaining vegetable soup. Sprinkle with salt.
6. Pour the stew in a large serving bowl and spread the cilantro and red pepper flakes on top before serving hot.

Nutrition:

Calories: 530

Fat: 19.2g

Protein: 20.3g

Carbs: 75.2g

Lush Moroccan Chickpea, Vegetable, and Fruit Stew

Preparation time: 15 minutes

Cooking time: 6 hours & 4 minutes

Servings: 6

Ingredients:

- 1 large bell pepper, any color, chopped
- 6 ounces (170 g) green beans, trimmed and cut into bite-size pieces
- 3 cups canned chickpeas, rinsed and drained
- 1 (15-ounce / 425-g) can diced tomatoes, with the juice
- 1 large carrot, cut into ¼-inch rounds
- 2 large potatoes, peeled and cubed
- 1 large yellow onion, chopped
- 1 teaspoon grated fresh ginger
- 2 garlic cloves, minced
- 1¾ cups low-sodium vegetable soup
- 1 teaspoon ground cumin
- 1 tablespoon ground coriander
- ¼ teaspoon ground red pepper flakes
- Sea salt and ground black pepper, to taste
- 8 ounces (227 g) fresh baby spinach
- ¼ cup diced dried figs
- ¼ cup diced dried apricots
- 1 cup plain Greek yogurt

Directions:

1. Place the bell peppers, green beans, chicken peas, tomatoes and juice, carrot, potatoes, onion, ginger, and garlic in the slow cooker.
2. Pour in the vegetable soup and sprinkle with cumin, coriander, red pepper flakes, salt, and ground black pepper. Stir to mix well.
3. Put the slow cooker lid on and cook on high for 6 hours or until the vegetables are soft. Stir periodically. Open the lid and fold in the spinach, figs, apricots, and yogurt. Stir to mix well.
4. Cook for 4 minutes or until the spinach is wilted. Pour them in a large serving bowl. Allow to cool for at least 20 minutes, then serve warm.

Nutrition:

Calories: 611

Fat: 9.0g

Protein: 30.7g

Carbs: 107.4g

Chickpea and Rice

Preparation Time: 30 min.

Cooking Time: 45 min.

Servings: 4

Ingredients:

- 0.3 lb. long - grain rice, soaked in water for 20 minutes
- 0.3 lb. chickpeas, cooked
- Salt and pepper, to taste
- 1 bay leaf
- 2 tablespoons chopped parsley
- 1 garlic clove minced
- 0.4 quarts of chicken broth
- 3 tablespoons olive oil
- 1 medium onion, sliced
- 1 teaspoon lime juice

Directions:

1. Drain the rice and set aside.
2. Heat oil in saucepan and cook onion with garlic until onion is softened.
3. Add chickpeas, bay leaf, salt, and pepper. Stir fry for 1-2 minutes.
4. Add chicken broth and let it simmer on medium heat until bubbles appear at the surface.
5. Add rice and lime juice and stir well. Let it simmer for 4-5 minutes or until bubbles appear at the surface or the rice. Now cover the saucepans with a lid and let rice cook on low flame for 20 minutes.
6. Add to serving dish and top with parsley.
7. Serve and enjoy!

Nutrition:

Calories 321

Fat 17 g

Carbs 35 g

Protein 21 g

One-Pot Rice and Chicken

Preparation Time: 30 min.

Cooking Time: 45 min.

Servings: 4

Ingredients:

- 4-5 chicken thighs
- 0.3 lb. long - grain rice, soaked in water for 20 minutes
- ¼ teaspoons cumin seeds
- 1 teaspoon dried oregano
- Salt and pepper, to taste
- 1 garlic clove, minced
- 0.4 quarts of water
- 3 tablespoons olive oil
- 1 medium onion, sliced
- 1 teaspoon lime juice
- 1 tablespoon vinegar

Directions:

1. In a bowl add chicken, some salt, some black pepper, oregano, cumin, and vinegar. Mix well. Let it marinate for about 20 minutes.
2. Heat some oil in a pan and place chicken in the pan. Let the chicken cook for about 5-6 minutes per side or until nicely golden from both sides. Keep turning the chicken over after a few minutes.
3. Drain the rice and set aside.
4. Preheat oven to 355° F.
5. In a skillet heat some olive oil and cook onion with garlic until onion is softened.
6. Add salt and pepper. Stir fry for 1-2 minutes.
7. Add water and let it simmer on medium heat until bubbles appear at the surface.
8. Add rice and lime juice and stir well. Let it simmer for 6-10 minutes or until bubbles appear at the surface or the rice and liquid are dried a little. Place chicken on top of rice.
9. Cover the skillet with a lid and place it in the oven. Bake for 20 minutes.
10. Serve and enjoy!

Nutrition:

Calories 240

Fat 15 g

Carbs 3 g

Protein ½ g

Grain Bowl with Lentil and Chickpeas

Preparation Time: 10 min.

Cooking Time: 5-8 min.

Servings: 3-4

Ingredients:

- 6 tablespoons virgin olive oil
- Salt, to taste
- 1 zucchini squash, sliced into rounds
- 0.6 lb. farro, cooked
- 0.5 lb. cooked brown lentils, cooked
- ½ lb. chickpeas, cooked
- 0.3 lb. cherry tomatoes, halved
- 2 shallots, sliced
- 2 avocados, peeled, pitted and sliced
- 0.3 lb. fresh parsley, chopped
- 5-6 Kalamata olives
- 2 tablespoons lemon juice
- Some crumbled feta cheese, optional
- 2 tablespoons Dijon mustard
- 1-2 garlic cloves, minced
- 1 teaspoon sumac, ground
- Mixed spices, of choice

Directions:

1. Heat 1-2 tablespoons oil in a pan and sauté zucchini until tender. Removed from heat and set aside.
2. In a bowl add Dijon mustard, some salt, sumac powder, mix spices, remaining olive oil, garlic, and lemon juice; mix well and set aside.
3. Add zucchini, avocado, shallots, farro, lentils, tomatoes, chickpeas, olives, feta, and parsley into serving bowls. Season with Dijon mustard dressing.
4. Serve and enjoy.

Nutrition:

Calories 625

Fat 45 g

Carbs 0 g

Protein 15 g

White Beans with Vegetables

Preparation Time: 10 min.

Cooking Time: 0 min.

Servings: 4

Ingredients:

- ½ lb. white beans, cooked
- 1 onion, chopped
- 1 tablespoon lemon juice
- 7-8 cherry tomatoes, chopped
- 1 tablespoon oregano
- Ground pepper, to taste
- 2-3 tablespoons cilantro, chopped
- Salt, to taste

Directions:

1. In a large bowl combine white beans, onion, tomatoes, cilantro, oregano, salt, pepper, and lemon juice.
2. Add mixture to a serving dish.

Enjoy.

Nutrition:

Calories 345

Fat 27 g

Carbs 67 g

Protein 21 g

Greek Wheat Berry Salad with Feta

Preparation Time: 10 min.

Cooking Time: 0 min.

Servings: 1

Ingredients:

- 0.6 lb. wheat berries, cooked
- 0.2 lb. spring onion, chopped
- A handful of black olives, chopped
- 2-3 roasted red bell peppers, chopped
- 3-4 tomatoes, chopped
- 1-2 onions, sliced
- 0.3 lb. feta cheese, crumbled
- 2 chilies, sliced

- 2 tablespoons honey
- 1 teaspoon lemon juice
- Salt, to taste
- ¼ tablespoons black pepper
- 2 tablespoons olive oil
- 2 tablespoons thyme
- 4-5 tablespoons balsamic vinegar
- 1 tablespoon Dijon mustard
- 4 tablespoons olive oil
  - lb. parsley, chopped

Directions:

1. In a bowl combine honey, mustard, bell peppers, salt, pepper, vinegar, olive oil. Mix well and set aside.
2. In a mixing bowl add wheat berries, thyme, onion, tomato, spring onion, parsley, chilies, and olive. Mix well.
3. Drizzle dressing on salad, add feta cheese, and mix everything.
4. Serve and enjoy.

Nutrition:

Calories 354

Fat 29 g

Carbs 10 g

Protein 7.2 g

Skillet Black-Eyed Pease and Spinach

Preparation Time: 10min.

Cooking Time: 35 min.

Serving: 3-4

Ingredients:

- ½ lb. dry black-eyed peas, cooked
- 4 tablespoons extra virgin olive oil
- 1 onion, chopped
- 1 carrot, sliced
- 1 red bell pepper, chopped
- 1 lb. fresh spinach, washed
- 0.2 lb. tomatoes, crushed
- ½ tablespoons fine salt
- Lemon for serving
- Ground black pepper, to taste
- 1 tablespoon fresh parsley chopped
- 0.3 quarts chicken broth

Directions:

1. Heat oil in a skillet and cook onion with carrots for about 3-4 minutes.
2. Add spinach leaves, salt, and pepper; stir fry for 1-2 minutes.
3. Add peas, crushed tomatoes, and chicken broth; simmer for 10-15 minutes on low flame.
4. Add to serving platter and top with parsley and lemon.
5. Serve and enjoy!

Nutrition:

Calories 241

Fat 15 g

Carbs 19 g

Protein 9 g

Lentil Salad with Oranges

Preparation Time: 15 min.

Cooking Time: 0 min.

Serving: 2

Ingredients:

- 0.4 lb. dry lentils, cooked
- 1 garlic clove, minced
- 0.3 lb. cherry tomatoes, diced
- 1 orange, peeled and cut into chunks
- ½ onion, diced
- 5-6 tablespoons fresh parsley, chopped
- 3 tablespoons extra virgin olive oil
- 2 tablespoons red wine vinegar
- Salt and pepper, as needed

Directions:

1. In a large mixing bowl add lentils, onion, tomatoes, parsley, and orange; mix thoroughly.
2. In a bowl add salt, pepper, garlic, olive oil, and red wine; stir to combine.
3. Drizzle dressing on salad. Toss well.
4. Serve and enjoy!

Nutrition:

Calories 398

Fat 15 g

Carbs 47 g

Protein 17 g

Chickpea Soup

Preparation Time: 2-3 min.

Cooking Time: 55 min.

Serving: 3

Ingredients:

- ½ lb. chickpeas, cooked
- 1 large onion, diced
- 1 garlic clove, cut in half
- 4 tablespoons olive oil
- Salt and pepper, to taste
- Lemon for serving
- Parsley or oregano, for serving, optional
- 0.4 quarts of water

Directions:

1. Heat oil in a saucepan and cook onion with garlic until fragrant.
2. Add water, chickpeas, salt, pepper, and oregano; mix well. Let simmer for 50 minutes on low heat.
3. Garnish with parsley and lemon.
4. Serve and enjoy!

Nutrition:

Calories 675

Fat 34 g

Carbs 76 g

Protein 22 g

Couscous Confetti Salad

Preparation time: 5 minutes

Cooking time: 20 minutes

Servings 4 to 6

Ingredients:

- 3 tablespoons extra-virgin olive oil
- 1 large onion, chopped
- 2 carrots, chopped
- 1 cup fresh peas
- ½ cup golden raisins
- 1 teaspoon salt
- 2 cups vegetable broth
- 2 cups couscous

Directions:

1. In a medium pot over medium heat, gently toss the olive oil, onions, carrots, peas, and raisins together and let cook for 5 minutes.
2. Add the salt and broth and stir to combine. Bring to a boil, and let ingredients boil for 5 minutes.
3. Add the couscous. Stir, turn the heat to low, cover, and let cook for 10 minutes. Fluff with a fork and serve.

Nutrition:

Calories: 511

Fat: 12g

Protein: 14g

Carbs: 92g

Fiber: 7g

Sodium: 504mg

Rustic Lentil-Rice Pilaf

Preparation time: 5 minutes

Cooking time: 50 minutes

Servings 6

Ingredients:

- ¼ cup extra-virgin olive oil
- 1 large onion, chopped
- 6 cups water
- 1 teaspoon ground cumin
- 1 teaspoon salt
- 2 cups brown lentils, picked over and rinsed

- 1 cup basmati rice

Directions:

1. In a medium pot over medium heat, cook the olive oil and onions for 7 to 10 minutes until the edges are browned.
2. Turn the heat to high, add the water, cumin, and salt, and bring this mixture to a boil, boiling for about 3 minutes.
3. Add the lentils and turn the heat to medium-low. Cover the pot and cook for 20 minutes, stirring occasionally.
4. Stir in the rice and cover; cook for an additional 20 minutes.
5. Fluff the rice with a fork and serve warm.

Nutrition:

Calories: 397

Fat: 11g

Protein: 18g

Carbs: 60g

Fiber: 18g

Sodium: 396mg

Bulgur Pilaf with Garbanzos

Preparation time: 5 minutes

Cooking time: 20 minutes

Servings 4 to 6

Ingredients:

- 3 tablespoons extra-virgin olive oil
- 1 large onion, chopped
- 1 (16-ounce / 454-g) can garbanzo beans, rinsed and drained
- 2 cups bulgur wheat, rinsed and drained
- 1½ teaspoons salt
- ½ teaspoon cinnamon
- 4 cups water

Directions:

1. In a large pot over medium heat, cook the olive oil and onion for 5 minutes.
2. Add the garbanzo beans and cook for another 5 minutes.
3. Add the bulgur, salt, cinnamon, and water and stir to combine. Cover the pot, turn the heat to low, and cook for 10 minutes.
4. When the cooking is done, fluff the pilaf with a fork. Cover and let sit for another 5 minutes.

Nutrition:

Calories: 462

Fat: 13g

Protein: 15g

Carbs: 76g

Fiber: 19g

Sodium: 890mg

Lentil Bulgur Pilaf

Preparation time: 10 minutes

Cooking time: 50 minutes

Servings: 6

Ingredients:

- ½ cup extra-virgin olive oil
- 4 large onions, chopped
- 2 teaspoons salt, divided
- 6 cups water
- 2 cups brown lentils, picked over and rinsed
- 1 teaspoon freshly ground black pepper
- 1 cup bulgur wheat

Directions:

1. In a large pot over medium heat, cook and stir the olive oil, onions, and 1 teaspoon of salt for 12 to 15 minutes, until the onions are a medium brown/golden color.
2. Put half of the cooked onions in a bowl.
3. Add the water, remaining 1 teaspoon of salt, and lentils to the remaining onions. Stir. Cover and cook for 30 minutes.
4. Stir in the black pepper and bulgur, cover, and cook for 5 minutes. Fluff with a fork, cover, and let stand for another 5 minutes.

5. Spoon the lentils and bulgur onto a serving plate and top with the reserved onions. Serve warm.

Nutrition:

Calories: 479

Fat: 20g

Protein: 20g

Carbs: 60g

Fiber: 24g

Sodium: 789mg

Simple Spanish rice

Preparation time: 10 minutes

Cooking time: 20 minutes

Servings 4

Ingredients:

- 2 tablespoons extra-virgin olive oil
- 1 medium onion, finely chopped
- 1 large tomato, finely diced
- 2 tablespoons tomato paste
- 1 teaspoon smoked paprika
- 1 teaspoon salt
- 1½ cups basmati rice
- 3 cups water

Directions:

1. In a medium pot over medium heat, cook the olive oil, onion, and tomato for 3 minutes.
2. Stir in the tomato paste, paprika, salt, and rice. Cook for 1 minute.
3. Add the water, cover the pot, and turn the heat to low. Cook for 12 minutes.
4. Gently toss the rice, cover, and cook for another 3 minutes.

Nutrition:

Calories: 328

Fat: 7g

Protein: 6g

Carbs: 60g

Fiber: 2g

Sodium: 651mg

Creamy Parmesan Garlic Polenta

Preparation time: 5 minutes

Cooking time: 30 minutes

Servings 4

Ingredients:

- 4 tablespoons (½ stick) unsalted butter, divided (optional)
- 1 tablespoon garlic, finely chopped
- 4 cups water
- 1 teaspoon salt
- 1 cup polenta
- ¾ cup Parmesan cheese, divided

Directions:

1. In a large pot over medium heat, cook 3 tablespoons of butter (if desired) and the garlic for 2 minutes.
2. Add the water and salt, and bring to a boil. Add the polenta and immediately whisk until it starts to thicken, about 3 minutes. Turn the heat to low, cover, and cook for 25 minutes, whisking every 5 minutes.
3. Using a wooden spoon, stir in ½ cup of the Parmesan cheese.
4. To serve, pour the polenta into a large serving bowl. Sprinkle the top with the remaining 1 tablespoon butter (if desired) and ¼ cup of remaining Parmesan cheese. Serve warm.

Nutrition:

Calories: 297

Fat: 16g

Protein: 9g

Carbs: 28g

Fiber: 2g

Sodium: 838mg

Mushroom Parmesan Risotto

Preparation time: 10 minutes

Cooking time: 30 minutes

Servings 4

Ingredients:

- 6 cups vegetable broth
- 3 tablespoons extra-virgin olive oil, divided
- 1 pound (454 g) cremini mushrooms, cleaned and sliced
- 1 medium onion, finely chopped
- 2 cloves garlic, minced
- 1½ cups Arborio rice
- 1 teaspoon salt
- ½ cup freshly grated Parmesan cheese
- ½ teaspoon freshly ground black pepper

Directions:

1. In a saucepan over medium heat, bring the broth to a low simmer.
2. In a large skillet over medium heat, cook 1 tablespoon olive oil and the sliced mushrooms for 5 to 7 minutes. Set cooked mushrooms aside.
3. In the same skillet over medium heat, add the 2 remaining tablespoons of olive oil, onion, and garlic. Cook for 3 minutes.
4. Add the rice, salt, and 1 cup of broth to the skillet. Stir the ingredients together and cook over low heat until most of the liquid is absorbed. Continue adding ½ cup of broth at a time, stirring until it is absorbed. Repeat until all of the broth is used up.
5. With the final addition of broth, add the cooked mushrooms, Parmesan cheese, and black pepper. Cook for 2 more minutes. Serve immediately.

Nutrition:

Calories: 410

Fat: 12g

Protein: 11g

Carbs: 65g

Fiber: 3g

Sodium: 2086mg

Brown Rice Bowls with Roasted Vegetables

Preparation time: 15 minutes

Cooking time: 20 minutes

Servings 4

Ingredients:

- Nonstick cooking spray
- 2 cups broccoli florets
- 2 cups cauliflower florets
- 1 (15-ounce / 425-g) can chickpeas, drained and rinsed
- 1 cup carrots sliced 1 inch thick
- 2 to 3 tablespoons extra-virgin olive oil, divided
- Salt and freshly ground black pepper, to taste
- 2 to 3 tablespoons sesame seeds, for garnish
- 2 cups cooked brown rice

Dressing:

- 3 to 4 tablespoons tahini
- 2 tablespoons honey
- 1 lemon, juiced
- 1 garlic clove, minced
- Salt and freshly ground black pepper, to taste

Directions:

1. Preheat the oven to 400°F (205°C). Spray two baking sheets with cooking spray.
2. Cover the first baking sheet with the broccoli and cauliflower and the second with the chickpeas and carrots. Toss each sheet with half of the oil and season with salt and pepper before placing in oven.
3. Cook the carrots and chickpeas for 10 minutes, leaving the carrots still just crisp, and the broccoli and cauliflower for 20 minutes, until tender. Stir each halfway through cooking.

4. To make the dressing, in a small bowl, mix the tahini, honey, lemon juice, and garlic. Season with salt and pepper and set aside.
5. Divide the rice into individual bowls, then layer with vegetables and drizzle dressing over the dish.

Nutrition:

Calories: 454

Fat: 18g

Protein: 12g

Carbs: 62g

Fiber: 11g

sodium: 61mg

Spanish Chicken and Rice

Preparation time: 15 minutes

Cooking time: 30 minutes

Servings 2

Ingredients:

- 2 teaspoons smoked paprika
- 2 teaspoons ground cumin
- 1½ teaspoons garlic salt
- ¾ teaspoon chili powder
- ¼ teaspoon dried oregano
- 1 lemon
- 2 boneless, skinless chicken breasts
- 3 tablespoons extra-virgin olive oil, divided
- 2 large shallots, diced
- 1 cup uncooked white rice
- 2 cups vegetable stock
- 1 cup broccoli florets
- 1/3 cup chopped parsley

Directions:

1. In a small bowl, whisk together the paprika, cumin, garlic salt, chili powder, and oregano. Divide in half and set aside. Into another small bowl, juice the lemon and set aside.
2. Put the chicken in a medium bowl. Coat the chicken with 2 tablespoons of olive oil and rub with half of the seasoning mix.
3. In a large pan, heat the remaining 1 tablespoon of olive oil and cook the chicken for 2 to 3 minutes on each side, until just browned but not cooked through.
4. Add shallots to the same pan and cook until translucent, then add the rice and cook for 1 more minute to toast. Add the vegetable stock, lemon juice, and the remaining seasoning mix and stir to combine. Return the chicken to the pan on top of the rice. Cover and cook for 15 minutes.
5. Uncover and add the broccoli florets. Cover and cook an additional 5 minutes, until the liquid is absorbed, rice is tender, and chicken is cooked through.
6. Top with freshly chopped parsley and serve immediately.

Nutrition:

Calories: 750

Fat: 25g

Protein: 36g

Carbs: 101g

Fiber: 7g

Sodium: 1823mg

Mushroom Barley Pilaf

Preparation time: 5 minutes

Cooking time: 37 minutes

Servings 4

Ingredients:

- Olive oil cooking spray
- 2 tablespoons olive oil
- 8 ounces (227 g) button mushrooms, diced
- ½ yellow onion, diced
- 2 garlic cloves, minced
- 1 cup pearl barley
- 2 cups vegetable broth

- 1 tablespoon fresh thyme, chopped
- ½ teaspoon salt
- ¼ teaspoon smoked paprika
- Fresh parsley, for garnish

Directions:

1. Preheat the air fryer to 380°F (193°C). Lightly coat the inside of a 5-cup capacity casserole dish with olive oil cooking spray. (The shape of the casserole dish will depend upon the size of the air fryer, but it needs to be able to hold at least 5 cups.)
2. In a large skillet, heat the olive oil over medium heat. Add the mushrooms and onion and cook, stirring occasionally, for 5 minutes, or until the mushrooms begin to brown.
3. Add the garlic and cook for an additional 2 minutes. Transfer the vegetables to a large bowl.
4. Add the barley, broth, thyme, salt, and paprika.
5. Pour the barley-and-vegetable mixture into the prepared casserole dish, and place the dish into the air fryer. Bake for 15 minutes.
6. Stir the barley mixture. Reduce the heat to 360°F (182°C), then return the barley to the air fryer and bake for 15 minutes more.
7. Remove from the air fryer and let sit for 5 minutes before fluffing with a fork and topping with fresh parsley.

Nutrition:

Calories: 263

Fat: 8g

Protein: 7g

Carbs: 44g

Fiber: 9g

Sodium: 576mg

Toasted Barley and Almond Pilaf
Preparation time: 10 minutes

Cooking time: 5 minutes

Servings 2

Ingredients:

- 1 tablespoon olive oil
- 1 garlic clove, minced
- 3 scallions, minced
- 2 ounces (57 g) mushrooms, sliced
- ¼ cup sliced almonds
- ½ cup uncooked pearled barley
- 1½ cups low-sodium chicken stock
- ½ teaspoon dried thyme
- 1 tablespoon fresh minced parsley
- Salt, to taste

Directions:

1. Heat the oil in a saucepan over medium-high heat. Add the garlic, scallions, mushrooms, and almonds, and sauté for 3 minutes.
2. Add the barley and cook, stirring, for 1 minute to toast it.
3. Add the chicken stock and thyme and bring the mixture to a boil.
4. Cover and reduce the heat to low. Simmer the barley for 30 minutes, or until the liquid is absorbed and the barley is tender.
5. Sprinkle with fresh parsley and season with salt before serving.

Nutrition:

Calories: 333

Fat: 13g

Protein: 10g

Carbs: 46g

Fiber: 9g

Sodium: 141mg

Mediterranean Lentils and Brown Rice

Preparation time: 15 minutes

Cooking time: 23 minutes

Servings 4

Ingredients:

- 2¼ cups low-sodium or no-salt-added vegetable broth
- ½ cup uncooked brown or green lentils
- ½ cup uncooked instant brown rice
- ½ cup diced carrots
- ½ cup diced celery
- 1 (2¼-ounce / 64-g) can sliced olives, drained
- ¼ cup diced red onion
- ¼ cup chopped fresh curly-leaf parsley
- 1½ tablespoons extra-virgin olive oil
- 1 tablespoon freshly squeezed lemon juice
- 1 garlic clove, minced
- ¼ teaspoon kosher or sea salt
- ¼ teaspoon freshly ground black pepper

Directions:

1. In a medium saucepan over high heat, bring the broth and lentils to a boil, cover, and lower the heat to medium-low. Cook for 8 minutes.
2. Raise the heat to medium, and stir in the rice. Cover the pot and cook the mixture for 15 minutes, or until the liquid is absorbed. Remove the pot from the heat and let it sit, covered, for 1 minute, then stir.
3. While the lentils and rice are cooking, mix together the carrots, celery, olives, onion, and parsley in a large serving bowl.
4. In a small bowl, whisk together the oil, lemon juice, garlic, salt, and pepper. Set aside.
5. When the lentils and rice are cooked, add them to the serving bowl. Pour the dressing on top, and mix everything together. Serve warm or cold, or store in a sealed container in the refrigerator for up to 7 days.

Nutrition:

Calories: 170

Fat: 5g

Protein: 5g

Carbs: 25g

Fiber: 2g

Sodium: 566mg

Wild Mushroom Farrotto with Parmesan

Preparation time: 15 minutes

Cooking time: 7 minutes

Servings 4

Ingredients:

- 1½ cups whole farro
- 3 tablespoons extra-virgin olive oil, divided, plus extra for drizzling
- 12 ounces (340 g) cremini or white mushrooms, trimmed and sliced thin
- ½ onion, chopped fine
- ½ teaspoon table salt
- ¼ teaspoon pepper
- 1 garlic clove, minced
- ¼ ounce (7 g) dried porcini mushrooms, rinsed and chopped fine
- 2 teaspoons minced fresh thyme or ½ teaspoon dried
- ¼ cup dry white wine
- 2½ cups chicken or vegetable broth, plus extra as needed
- 2 ounces (57 g) Parmesan cheese, grated, plus extra for serving
- 2 teaspoons lemon juice
- ½ cup chopped fresh parsley

Directions:

1. Pulse farro in blender until about half of grains are broken into smaller pieces, about 6 pulses.
2. Using highest sauté function, heat 2 tablespoons oil in Instant Pot until shimmering. Add cremini mushrooms, onion, salt, and pepper, partially cover, and cook until mushrooms are softened and have released their liquid, about 5 minutes. Stir in farro, garlic, porcini mushrooms, and thyme and cook until fragrant, about 1 minute. Stir in wine and cook until nearly evaporated, about 30 seconds. Stir in broth.

3. Lock lid in place and close pressure release valve. Select high pressure cook function and cook for 12 minutes. Turn off Instant Pot and quick-release pressure. Carefully remove lid, allowing steam to escape away from you.
4. If necessary adjust consistency with extra hot broth, or continue to cook ferrite, using highest sauté function, stirring frequently, until proper consistency is achieved. (Farrotto should be slightly thickened, and spoon dragged along bottom of multicore should leave trail that quickly fills in.) Add Parmesan and remaining 1 tablespoon oil and stir vigorously until ferrite becomes creamy. Stir in lemon juice and season with salt and pepper to taste. Sprinkle individual portions with parsley and extra Parmesan, and drizzle with extra oil before serving.

Nutrition:

Calories: 280

Fat: 9g

Protein: 13g

Carbs: 35g

Fiber: 3g

Sodium: 630mg

Moroccan-Style Brown Rice and Chickpea

Preparation time: 15 minutes

Cooking time: 45 minutes

Servings 6

Ingredients:

- Olive oil cooking spray
- 1 cup long-grain brown rice
- 2¼ cups chicken stock
- 1 (15½-ounce / 439-g) can chickpeas, drained and rinsed
- ½ cup diced carrot
- ½ cup green peas
- 1 teaspoon ground cumin
- ½ teaspoon ground turmeric
- ½ teaspoon ground ginger
- ½ teaspoon onion powder
- ½ teaspoon salt
- ¼ teaspoon ground cinnamon
- ¼ teaspoon garlic powder
- ¼ teaspoon black pepper
- Fresh parsley, for garnish

Direction:

1. Preheat the air fryer to 380°F (193°C). Lightly coat the inside of a 5-cup capacity casserole dish with olive oil cooking spray. (The shape of the casserole dish will depend upon the size of the air fryer, but it needs to be able to hold at least 5 cups.)
2. In the casserole dish, combine the rice, stock, chickpeas, carrot, peas, cumin, turmeric, ginger, onion powder, salt, cinnamon, garlic powder, and black pepper. Stir well to combine.
3. Cover loosely with aluminum foil.
4. Place the covered casserole dish into the air fryer and bake for 20 minutes. Remove from the air fryer and stir well.
5. Place the casserole back into the air fryer, uncovered, and bake for 25 minutes more.
6. Fluff with a spoon and sprinkle with fresh chopped parsley before serving.

Nutrition:

Calories: 204

Fat: 1g

Protein: 7g

Carbs: 40g

Fiber: 4g

Sodium: 623mg

Buckwheat Groats with Root Vegetables

Preparation time: 15 minutes

Cooking time: 40 minutes

Servings 6

Ingredients:

- Olive oil cooking spray
- 2 large potatoes, cubed
- 2 carrots, sliced
- 1 small rutabaga, cubed
- 2 celery stalks, chopped
- ½ teaspoon smoked paprika
- ¼ cup plus 1 tablespoon olive oil, divided
- 2 rosemary sprigs
- 1 cup buckwheat groats
- 2 cups vegetable broth
- 2 garlic cloves, minced
- ½ yellow onion, chopped
- 1 teaspoon salt

Directions:

1. Preheat the air fryer to 380°F (193°C). Lightly coat the inside of a 5-cup capacity casserole dish with olive oil cooking spray. (The shape of the casserole dish will depend upon the size of the air fryer, but it needs to be able to hold at least 5 cups.)
2. In a large bowl, toss the potatoes, carrots, rutabaga, and celery with the paprika and ¼ cup olive oil.
3. Pour the vegetable mixture into the prepared casserole dish and top with the rosemary sprigs. Place the casserole dish into the air fryer and bake for 15 minutes.
4. While the vegetables are cooking, rinse and drain the buckwheat groats.
5. In a medium saucepan over medium-high heat, combine the groats, vegetable broth, garlic, onion, and salt with the remaining 1 tablespoon olive oil. Bring the mixture to a boil, then reduce the heat to low, cover, and cook for 10 to 12 minutes.
6. Remove the casserole dish from the air fryer. Remove the rosemary sprigs and discard. Pour the cooked buckwheat into the dish with the vegetables and stir to combine. Cover with aluminum foil and bake for an additional 15 minutes.
7. Stir before serving.

Nutrition:

Calories: 344

Fat: 12g

Protein: 8g

Carbs: 50g

Fiber: 7g

Sodium: 876mg

Farro Risotto with Fresh Sage

Preparation time: 10 minutes

Cooking time: 35 minutes

Servings 6

Ingredients:

- Olive oil cooking spray
- 1½ cups uncooked farro
- 2 ½ cups chicken broth
- 1 cup tomato sauce
- 1 yellow onion, diced
- 3 garlic cloves, minced
- 1 tablespoon fresh sage, chopped
- ½ teaspoon salt
- 2 tablespoons olive oil
- 1 cup Parmesan cheese, grated, divided

Directions:

1. Preheat the air fryer to 380°F (193°C). Lightly coat the inside of a 5-cup capacity casserole dish with olive oil cooking spray. (The shape of the casserole dish will depend upon the size of the air fryer, but it needs to be able to hold at least 5 cups.)
2. In a large bowl, combine the farro, broth, tomato sauce, onion, garlic, sage, salt, olive oil, and ½ cup of the Parmesan.
3. Pour the farro mixture into the prepared casserole dish and cover with aluminum foil.
4. Bake for 20 minutes, then uncover and stir. Sprinkle the remaining ½ cup Parmesan over the top and bake for 15 minutes more.
5. Stir well before serving.

Nutrition:

Calories: 284

Fat: 9g

Protein: 12g

Carbs: 40g

Fiber: 3g

Sodium: 564mg

Bulgur with Za'Atar, Chickpeas, and Spinach

Preparation time: 10 minutes

Cooking time: 7 minutes

Servings 4 to 6

Ingredients:

- 3 tablespoons extra-virgin olive oil, divided
- 1 onion, chopped fine
- ½ teaspoon table salt
- 3 garlic cloves, minced
- 2 tablespoons za'atar, divided
- 1 cup medium-grind bulgur, rinsed
- 1 (15-ounce / 425-g) can chickpeas, rinsed
- 1½ cups water
- 5 ounces (142 g) baby spinach, chopped
- 1 tablespoon lemon juice, plus lemon wedges for serving

Directions:

1. Using highest sauté function, heat 2 tablespoons oil in Instant Pot until shimmering. Add onion and salt and cook until onion is softened, about 5 minutes. Stir in garlic and 1 tablespoon za'atar and cook until fragrant, about 30 seconds. Stir in bulgur, chickpeas, and water.
2. Lock lid in place and close pressure release valve. Select high pressure cook function and cook for 1 minute. Turn off Instant Pot and quick-release pressure. Carefully remove lid, allowing steam to escape away from you.
3. Gently fluff bulgur with fork. Lay clean dish towel over pot, replace lid, and let sit for 5 minutes. Add spinach, lemon juice, remaining 1 tablespoon za'atar, and remaining 1 tablespoon oil and gently toss to combine. Season with salt and pepper to taste. Serve with lemon wedges.

Nutrition:

Calories: 200

Fat: 8g

Protein: 6g

Carbs: 28g

Fiber: 6g

Sodium: 320mg

Pearl Barley Risotto with Parmesan Cheese

Preparation time: 5 minutes

Cooking time: 20 minutes

Servings 6

Ingredients:

- 4 cups low-sodium or no-salt-added vegetable broth
- 1 tablespoon extra-virgin olive oil
- 1 cup chopped yellow onion
- 2 cups uncooked pearl barley
- ½ cup dry white wine
- 1 cup freshly grated Parmesan cheese, divided
- ¼ teaspoon kosher or sea salt
- ¼ teaspoon freshly ground black pepper
- Fresh chopped chives and lemon wedges, for serving (optional)

Directions:

1. Pour the broth into a medium saucepan and bring to a simmer.
2. Heat the olive oil in a large stockpot over medium-high heat. Add the onion and cook for about 4 minutes, stirring occasionally.
3. Add the barley and cook for 2 minutes, stirring, or until the barley is toasted. Pour in the wine and cook for about 1 minute, or until most of the liquid evaporates. Add 1 cup of the warm broth into the pot and cook, stirring, for about 2 minutes, or until most of the liquid is absorbed.
4. Add the remaining broth, 1 cup at a time, cooking until each cup is absorbed (about 2 minutes each time) before adding the

next. The last addition of broth will take a bit longer to absorb, about 4 minutes.
5. Remove the pot from the heat, and stir in ½ cup of the cheese, and the salt and pepper.
6. Serve with the remaining ½ cup of the cheese on the side, along with the chives and lemon wedges (if desired).

Nutrition:

Calories: 421

Fat: 11g

Protein: 15g

Carbs: 67g

Fiber: 11g

Sodium: 641mg

Israeli Couscous with Asparagus

Preparation time: 5 minutes

Cooking time: 25 minutes

Servings 6

Ingredients:

- 1½ pounds (680 g) asparagus spears, ends trimmed and stalks chopped into 1-inch pieces
- 1 garlic clove, minced
- 1 tablespoon extra-virgin olive oil
- ¼ teaspoon freshly ground black pepper
- 1¾ cups water
- 1 (8-ounce / 227-g) box uncooked whole-wheat or regular Israeli couscous (about 1 1/3 cups)
- ¼ teaspoon kosher salt
- 1 cup garlic-and-herb goat cheese, at room temperature

Directions:

1. Preheat the oven to 425°F (220°C).
2. In a large bowl, stir together the asparagus, garlic, oil, and pepper. Spread the asparagus on a large, rimmed baking sheet and roast for 10 minutes, stirring a few times. Remove the pan from the oven and spoon the asparagus into a large serving bowl. Set aside.
3. While the asparagus is roasting, bring the water to a boil in a medium saucepan. Add the couscous and season with salt, stirring well.
4. Reduce the heat to medium-low. Cover and cook for 12 minutes, or until the water is absorbed.
5. Pour the hot couscous into the bowl with the asparagus. Add the goat cheese and mix thoroughly until completely melted.
6. Serve immediately.

Nutrition:

Calories: 103

Fat: 2g

Protein: 6g

Carbs: 18g

Fiber: 5g

Sodium: 343mg

Freekeh Pilaf with Dates and Pistachios

Preparation time: 10 minutes

Cooking time: 10 minutes

Servings 4 to 6

Ingredients:

- 2 tablespoons extra-virgin olive oil, plus extra for drizzling
- 1 shallot, minced
- 1½ teaspoons grated fresh ginger
- ¼ teaspoon ground coriander
- ¼ teaspoon ground cumin
- Salt and pepper, to taste
- 1¾ cups water
- 1½ cups cracked freekeh, rinsed
- 3 ounces (85 g) pitted dates, chopped
- ¼ cup shelled pistachios, toasted and coarsely chopped
- 1½ tablespoons lemon juice
- ¼ cup chopped fresh mint

Directions:

1. Set the Instant Pot to Sauté mode and heat the olive oil until shimmering.

2. Add the shallot, ginger, coriander, cumin, salt, and pepper to the pot and cook for about 2 minutes, or until the shallot is softened. Stir in the water and freekeh.
3. Secure the lid. Select the Manual mode and set the cooking time for 4 minutes at High Pressure. Once cooking is complete, do a quick pressure release. Carefully open the lid.
4. Add the dates, pistachios and lemon juice and gently fluff the freekeh with a fork to combine. Season to taste with salt and pepper.
5. Transfer to a serving dish and sprinkle with the mint. Serve drizzled with extra olive oil.

Nutrition:

Calories: 280

Fat: 8g

Protein: 8g

Carbs: 46g

Fiber: 9g

Sodium: 200mg

Quinoa with Baby Potatoes and Broccoli

Preparation time: 5 minutes

Cooking time: 10 minutes

Servings 4

Ingredients:

- 2 tablespoons olive oil
- 1 cup baby potatoes, cut in half
- 1 cup broccoli florets
- 2 cups cooked quinoa
- Zest of 1 lemon
- Sea salt and freshly ground pepper, to taste

Directions:

1. Heat the olive oil in a large skillet over medium heat until shimmering.
2. Add the potatoes and cook for about 6 to 7 minutes, or until softened and golden brown. Add the broccoli and cook for about 3 minutes, or until tender.
3. Remove from the heat and add the quinoa and lemon zest. Season with salt and pepper to taste, then serve.

Nutrition:

Calories: 205

Fat: 8g

Protein: 5g

Carbs: 27g

Fiber: 3g

Sodium: 158mg

Brown Rice Pilaf with Golden Raisins

Preparation time: 5 minutes

Cooking time: 15 minutes

Servings: 6

Ingredients:

- 1 tablespoon extra-virgin olive oil
- 1 cup chopped onion (about ½ medium onion)
- ½ cup shredded carrot (about 1 medium carrot)
- 1 teaspoon ground cumin
- ½ teaspoon ground cinnamon
- 2 cups instant brown rice
- 1¾ cups 100% orange juice
- ¼ cup water
- 1 cup golden raisins
- ½ cup shelled pistachios
- Chopped fresh chives (optional)

Directions:

1. In a medium saucepan over medium-high heat, heat the oil. Add the onion and cook for 5 minutes, stirring frequently.
2. Add the carrot, cumin, and cinnamon, and cook for 1 minute, stirring frequently. Stir in the rice, orange juice, and water.
3. Bring to a boil, cover, then lower the heat to medium-low. Simmer for 7 minutes, or until the rice is cooked through and the

liquid is absorbed. Stir in the raisins, pistachios, and chives (if using) and serve.

Nutrition:

Calories: 320

Fat: 7g

Carbohydrates: 61g

Protein: 6g

Quinoa and Chickpea Vegetable Bowls

Preparation time: 15 minutes

Cooking time: 15 minutes

Servings: 4

Ingredients:

- 1 cup red dry quinoa, rinsed and drained
- 2 cups low-sodium vegetable soup
- 2 cups fresh spinach
- 2 cups finely shredded red cabbage
- 1 (15-ounce / 425-g) can chickpeas, drained and rinsed
- 1 ripe avocado, thinly sliced
- 1 cup shredded carrots
- 1 red bell pepper, thinly sliced
- 4 tablespoons Mango Sauce
- ½ cup fresh cilantro, chopped

Mango Sauce:

- 1 mango, diced
- ¼ cup fresh lime juice
- ½ teaspoon ground turmeric
- 1 teaspoon finely minced fresh ginger
- ¼ teaspoon sea salt
- Pinch of ground red pepper
- 1 teaspoon pure maple syrup
- 2 tablespoons extra-virgin olive oil

Directions:

1. Pour the quinoa and vegetable soup in a saucepan. Bring to a boil. Reduce the heat to low. Cover and cook for 15 minutes or until tender. Fluffy with a fork.
2. Meanwhile, combine the ingredients for the mango sauce in a food processor. Pulse until smooth.
3. Divide the quinoa, spinach, and cabbage into 4 serving bowls, then top with chickpeas, avocado, carrots, and bell pepper.
4. Dress them with the mango sauce and spread with cilantro. Serve immediately.

Nutrition:

Calories: 366

Fat: 11.1g

Protein: 15.5g

Carbs: 55.6g

Ritzy Veggie Chili

Preparation time: 15 minutes

Cooking time: 5 hours

Servings: 4

Ingredients:

- 1 (28-ounce / 794-g) can chopped tomatoes, with the juice
- 1 (15-ounce / 425-g) can black beans, drained and rinsed
- 1 (15-ounce / 425-g) can redly beans, drained and rinsed
- 1 medium green bell pepper, chopped
- 1 yellow onion, chopped
- 1 tablespoon onion powder
- 1 teaspoon paprika
- 1 teaspoon cayenne pepper
- 1 teaspoon garlic powder
- ½ teaspoon sea salt
- ½ teaspoon ground black pepper
- 1 tablespoon olive oil
- 1 large has avocado, pitted, peeled, and chopped, for garnish

Directions:

1. Combine all the ingredients, except for the avocado, in the slow cooker. Stir to mix well.

2. Put the slow cooker lid on and cook on high for 5 hours or until the vegetables are tender and the mixture has a thick consistency.
3. Pour the chili in a large serving bowl. Allow to cool for 30 minutes, then spread with chopped avocado and serve.

Nutrition:

Calories: 633

Fat: 16.3g

Protein: 31.7g

Carbs: 97.0g

Spicy Italian Bean Balls with Marinara

Preparation time: 15 minutes

Cooking time: 30 minutes

Servings: 2-4

Ingredients:

- Bean Balls:
- 1 tablespoon extra-virgin olive oil
- ½ yellow onion, minced
- 1 teaspoon fennel seeds
- 2 teaspoons dried oregano
- ½ teaspoon crushed red pepper flakes
- 1 teaspoon garlic powder
- 1 (15-ounce / 425-g) can white beans (cannellini or navy), drained and rinsed
- ½ cup whole-grain bread crumbs
- Sea salt and ground black pepper, to taste

Marinara:

- 1 tablespoon extra-virgin olive oil
- 3 garlic cloves, minced
- Handful basil leaves
- 1 (28-ounce / 794-g) can chopped tomatoes with juice reserved
- Sea salt, to taste

Directions:

1. Preheat the oven to 350°F (180°C). Line a baking sheet with parchment paper. Heat the olive oil in a nonstick skillet over medium heat until shimmering.
2. Add the onion and sauté for 5 minutes or until translucent. Sprinkle with fennel seeds, oregano, red pepper flakes, and garlic powder, then cook for 1 minute or until aromatic.
3. Pour the sautéed mixture in a food processor and add the beans and bread crumbs. Sprinkle with salt and ground black pepper, then pulse to combine well and the mixture holds together.
4. Shape the mixture into balls with a 2-ounce (57-g) cookie scoop, then arrange the balls on the baking sheet.
5. Bake in the preheated oven for 30 minutes or until lightly browned. Flip the balls halfway through the cooking time.
6. While baking the bean balls, heat the olive oil in a saucepan over medium-high heat until shimmering. Add the garlic and basil and sauté for 2 minutes or until fragrant.
7. Fold in the tomatoes and juice. Bring to a boil. Reduce the heat to low. Put the lid on and simmer for 15 minutes. Sprinkle with salt.
8. Transfer the bean balls on a large plate and baste with marinara before serving.

Nutrition:

Calories: 351

Fat: 16.4g

Protein: 11.5g

Carbs: 42.9g

Baked Rolled Oat with Pears and Pecans

Preparation time: 15 minutes

Cooking time: 30 minutes

Servings: 6

Ingredients:

- 2 tablespoons coconut oil, melted, plus more for greasing the pan
- 3 ripe pears, cored and diced
- 2 cups unsweetened almond milk

- 1 tablespoon pure vanilla extract
- ¼ cup pure maple syrup
- 2 cups gluten-free rolled oats
- ½ cup raisins
- ¾ cup chopped pecans
- ¼ teaspoon ground nutmeg
- 1 teaspoon ground cinnamon
- ½ teaspoon ground ginger
- ¼ teaspoon sea salt

Directions:

1. Preheat the oven to 350°F (180°C). Grease a baking dish with melted coconut oil, then spread the pears in a single layer on the baking dish evenly.
2. Combine the almond milk, vanilla extract, maple syrup, and coconut oil in a bowl. Stir to mix well.
3. Combine the remaining ingredients in a separate large bowl. Stir to mix well. Fold the almond milk mixture in the bowl, then pour the mixture over the pears.
4. Place the baking dish in the preheated oven and bake for 30 minutes or until lightly browned and set. Serve immediately.

Nutrition:

Calories: 479

Fat: 34.9g

Protein: 8.8g

Carbs: 50.1g

Farro Salad Mix

Preparation time: 15 minutes

Cooking time: 33 minutes

Servings: 4-6

Ingredients:

- 1 teaspoon Dijon mustard
- 1½ cups whole farro
- 2 ounces feta cheese, crumbled (½ cup)
- 2 tablespoons lemon juice
- 2 tablespoons minced shallot
- 3 tablespoons chopped fresh dill
- 3 tablespoons extra-virgin olive oil
- 6 ounces asparagus, trimmed and cut into 1-inch lengths
- 6 ounces cherry tomatoes, halved
- 6 ounces sugar snap peas, strings removed, cut into 1-inch lengths
- Salt and pepper

Directions:

1. Bring 4 quarts water to boil in a Dutch oven. Put in asparagus, snap peas, and 1 tablespoon salt and cook until crisp-tender, approximately 3 minutes.
2. Use a slotted spoon to move vegetables to large plate and allow to cool completely, about 15 minutes. Put in farro to water, return to boil, and cook until grains are soft with slight chew, 15 to 30 minutes.
3. Drain farro, spread in rimmed baking sheet, and allow to cool completely, about 15 minutes.
4. Beat oil, lemon juice, shallot, mustard, ¼ teaspoon salt, and ¼ teaspoon pepper together in a big container.
5. Put in vegetables, farro, tomatoes, dill, and ¼ cup feta and toss gently to combine. Sprinkle with salt and pepper to taste. Move to serving platter and drizzle with remaining ¼ cup feta. Serve.

Nutrition:

Calories: 240

Carbs: 26g

Fat: 12g

Protein: 9g

Fennel-Parmesan Farro

Preparation time: 15 minutes

Cooking time: 50 minutes

Servings: 4-6

Ingredients:

- ¼ cup minced fresh parsley
- 1 onion, chopped fine
- 1 ounce Parmesan cheese, grated (½ cup)
- 1 small fennel bulb, stalks discarded, bulb halved, cored, and chopped fine

- 1 teaspoon minced fresh thyme or ¼ teaspoon dried
- 1½ cups whole farro
- 2 teaspoons sherry vinegar
- 3 garlic cloves, minced
- 3 tablespoons extra-virgin olive oil
- Salt and pepper

Directions:

1. Bring 4 quarts water to boil in a Dutch oven. Put in farro and 1 tablespoon salt, return to boil, and cook until grains are soft with slight chew, 15 to 30 minutes.
2. Drain farro, return to now-empty pot, and cover to keep warm. Heat 2 tablespoons oil in 12-inch frying pan on moderate heat until it starts to shimmer.
3. Put in onion, fennel, and ¼ teaspoon salt and cook, stirring intermittently, till they become tender, 8 to 10 minutes. Put in garlic and thyme and cook until aromatic, approximately half a minute.
4. Put in residual 1 tablespoon oil and farro and cook, stirring often, until heated through, approximately 2 minutes.
5. Remove from the heat, mix in Parmesan, parsley, and vinegar. Sprinkle with salt and pepper to taste. Serve.

Nutrition:

Calories: 338

Carbs: 56g

Fat: 10g

Protein: 11g

POULTRY AND MEAT RECIPES

Duck Stew Olla Tapada

Preparation Time: 15 minutes

Cooking Time: 30 minutes

Servings: 3

Ingredients:

- 1 red bell pepper, deveined and chopped
- 1 pound duck breasts, boneless, skinless, and chopped into small chunks
- 1/2 cup chayote, peeled and cubed
- 1 shallot, chopped
- 1 teaspoon Mexican spice mix

Directions:

1. In a clay pot, heat 2 teaspoons of canola oil over a medium-high flame. Sauté the peppers and shallot until softened about 4 minutes.
2. Add in the remaining ingredients; pour in 1 ½ cups of water or chicken bone broth. Once your mixture starts boiling, reduce the heat to medium-low.
3. Let it simmer, partially covered, for 18 to 22 minutes, until cooked through. Enjoy!

Nutrition:

228 Calorie

9.5g Fat

3.3g Carbs

30.6g Protein

1g Fiber

Cheesy Ranch Chicken

Preparation Time: 10 minutes

Cooking Time: 20 minutes

Servings: 4

Ingredients:

- 2 chicken breasts
- 1/2 tablespoon ranch seasoning mix
- 4 slices bacon, chopped
- 1/2 cup Monterey-Jack cheese, grated
- 4 ounces Ricotta cheese, room temperature

Directions:

1. Preheat your oven to 360 degrees F.
2. Rub the chicken with ranch seasoning mix.
3. Heat a saucepan over medium-high flame. Now, sear the chicken for about 8 minutes. Lower the chicken into a lightly greased casserole dish.
4. Top with cheese and bacon and bake in the preheated oven for about 10 minutes until hot and bubbly. Serve with freshly snipped scallions, if desired.

Nutrition:

295 Calories

19.5g Fat

2.9g Carbs

25.5g Protein

0.4g Fiber

Turkey Crust Meatza

Preparation Time: 15 minutes

Cooking Time: 35 minutes

Servings: 4

Ingredients:

- 1/2 pound ground turkey
- 2 slices Canadian bacon
- 1 tomato, chopped
- 1 tablespoon pizza spice mix
- 1 cup Mozzarella cheese, grated

Directions:

1. Mix the ground turkey and cheese; season with salt and black pepper and mix until everything is well combined.
2. Press the mixture into a foil-lined baking pan. Bake in the preheated oven at 380 degrees F for 25 minutes.

3. Top the crust with Canadian bacon, tomato, and pizza spice mix. Continue to bake for a further 8 minutes.
4. Let it rest for a few minutes before slicing and serving. Bon appétit!

Nutrition:

360 Calories

22.7g Fat

5.9g Carbs

32.6g Protein

0.7g Fiber

Simple Turkey Goulash

Preparation Time: 15 minutes

Cooking Time: 45 minutes

Servings: 4

Ingredients:

- 2 tablespoons olive oil
- 1 large-sized leek, chopped
- 2 cloves garlic, minced
- 2 pounds turkey thighs, skinless, boneless and chopped
- 2 celery stalks, chopped

Directions:

1. In a clay pot, heat 2 olive oil over a medium-high flame. Then, cook the leeks until tender and translucent.
2. Then, continue to sauté the garlic for 30 seconds to 1 minute.
3. Stir in the turkey, celery, and 4 cups of water. Once your mixture starts boiling, let it simmer, partially covered, for about 40 minutes.
4. Bon appétit!

Nutrition:

220 Calories

7.4g Fat

2.7g Carbs

35.5g Protein

1g Fiber

Chicken Frittata with Asiago Cheese and Herbs

Preparation Time: 10 minutes

Cooking Time: 30 minutes

Servings: 4

Ingredients:

- 1 pound chicken breasts, chopped into small strips
- 4 slices of bacon
- 1 cup Asiago cheese, shredded
- 6 eggs
- 1/2 cup yogurt

Directions:

1. Preheat an oven-proof skillet. Then, fry the bacon until crisp and reserve. Then, in the pan drippings, cook the chicken for about 8 minutes or until no longer pink.
2. Add the reserved bacon back to the skillet.
3. In a mixing dish, thoroughly combine the eggs and yogurt; season with Italian spice mix.
4. Pour the egg mixture over the chicken and bacon. Top with cheese and bake in the preheated oven at 380 degrees F for 22 minutes until hot and bubbly.
5. Let it sit for 1-2 minutes before slicing and serving. Bon appétit!

Nutrition:

484 Calories

31.8g Fat

5.8g Carbs

41.9g Protein

0.7g Fiber

Stuffed Chicken with Sauerkraut and Cheese

Preparation Time: 10 minutes

Cooking Time: 35 minutes

Servings: 4

Ingredients:

- 5 chicken cutlets
- 1 cup Romano cheese, shredded
- 2 garlic cloves, minced
- 5 Italian peppers, deveined and chopped
- 5 tablespoons sauerkraut, for serving

Directions:

1. Spritz a baking pan with 1 tablespoon of the olive oil. Brush the chicken with another tablespoon of olive oil.
2. Season the chicken with Italian spice mix. You can spread Dijon mustard on one side of each chicken cutlet if desired.
3. Divide the garlic, peppers and Romano cheese between chicken cutlets; roll them up.
4. Bake at 360°F for 25 to 33 minutes until nicely brown on all sides. Serve with the sauerkraut and serve. Bon appétit!

Nutrition:

376 Calories

16.7g Fat

5.8g Carbs

47g Protein

1g Fiber

Chicken Bacon Burger

Preparation Time: 10 minutes

Cooking Time: 15 minutes

Servings: 8

Ingredients:

- 4 chicken breasts
- 4 slices of bacon
- 1/4 medium onion
- 2 cloves of garlic
- 1/4 cup (60 ml) avocado oil, to cook with

Directions:

1. Food process the chicken, bacon, onion, and garlic and form 8 patties. You need to do this in batches.
2. Fry patties in the avocado oil in batches. Make sure burgers are fully cooked.
3. Serve with guacamole (see page 131 for recipe).

Nutrition:

Calories: 319

Fat: 24 g

Net Carbohydrates: 1 g

Protein: 25 g

Basil Chicken Saute

Preparation Time: 10 minutes

Cooking Time: 15 minutes

Servings: 2

Ingredients:

- 1 chicken breast, minced or chopped very small
- 2 cloves of garlic, minced
- 1 chili pepper, diced (optional)
- 1 cup) basil leaves, finely chopped
- 1 Tablespoon tamari sauce
- 2 Tablespoons avocado or coconut oil to cook in
- Salt, to taste

Directions:

1. Add oil to a frying pan and saute the garlic and pepper.
2. Then add in the minced chicken and saute until the chicken is cooked.
3. Add the tamari sauce and salt to taste. Add in the basil leaves and mix it in.

Nutrition:

Calories: 320

Fat: 24 g

Net Carbohydrates: 2 g

Protein: 24 g

Slow Cooker Jerk Chicken

Preparation Time: 10 minutes

Cooking Time: 5 hours

Servings: 4

Ingredients:

- chicken drumsticks and 8 chicken wings
- 4 teaspoons (20 g) salt
- 4 teaspoons (9 g) paprika
- 1 teaspoon (2 g) cayenne pepper
- 2 teaspoons (5 g) onion powder
- 2 teaspoons (3 g) dried thyme
- 2 teaspoons (4 g) white pepper
- 2 teaspoons (6 g) garlic powder
- 1 teaspoon (2 g) black pepper

Directions:

1. Put all the spices in a bowl, then mix to make a rub for the chicken.
2. Wash the chicken meat in cold water briefly. Place the washed chicken meat into the bowl with the rub, and rub the spices onto the meat thoroughly, including under the skin.
3. Place each piece of chicken covered with the spices into the slow cooker (no liquid required).
4. Set the slow cooker on medium heat, and cook for 5 hours or until the chicken meat falls off the bone.

Nutrition:

Calories: 480

Fat: 30 g

Net Carbohydrates: 4 g

Protein: 45 g

Pulled Buffalo Chicken Salad with Blue Cheese

Preparation Time: 10 minutes

Cooking Time: 30 minutes

Servings: 2

Ingredients:

- 2 boneless, skinless free-range chicken breasts
- 4 uncured center-cut bacon strips
- ¼ cup Buffalo Sauce
- 4 cups chopped romaine lettuce, divided
- ½ cup blue cheese dressing, divided
- ½ cup crumbled organic blue cheese, divided
- ¼ cup chopped red onion, divided

Directions:

1. Place a large pot of water to a boil over high heat.
2. Put the chicken breasts to the water, lower the heat then simmer the breasts until their internal temperature reaches 180°F, about 30 minutes.
3. Take the chicken to a bowl and let it cool for about 10 minutes.
4. On the other hand, crisp the bacon strips in a skillet over medium heat, about 3 minutes per side. Drain the bacon on a paper towel.
5. Shred the chicken using a fork and toss it with the buffalo sauce.
6. Divide the lettuce into 2 bowls. Top each with half of the pulled chicken, half of the blue cheese dressing, blue cheese crumbles, and chopped red onion. Crumble the bacon over the salads and serve.

Nutrition:

Calories: 843

Total Fat: 65g

Saturated Fat: 14g

Protein: 59g

Cholesterol: 156mg

Carbohydrates: 6g

Fiber: 1g

Net Carbs: 5g

Red Pepper and Mozzarella-Stuffed Chicken Caprese

Preparation Time: 10 minutes

Cooking Time: 40 minutes

Servings: 2

Ingredients:

- 2 tablespoons extra-virgin olive oil
- 2 chicken breasts, butterflied
- 10 fresh basil leaves
- 1 (8-ounce) ball mozzarella cheese, cut into 4 pieces
- 1 cup Roasted Red Peppers
- 2 tablespoons Italian seasoning
- Sea salt
- Freshly ground black pepper

Directions:

1. Preheat the oven to 400°F.
2. Line a rimmed baking sheet using a parchment paper.
3. Place 5 basil leaves inside each chicken breast.
4. Place 2 mozzarella slices inside each breast.
5. Divide the roasted red peppers into 2 breasts. Sprinkle the Italian seasoning generously over each breast and season them with salt and pepper. Close each breast to envelop the filling.
6. Put the breasts on the baking sheet and bake until cooked through about 40 minutes. Serve hot.

Nutrition:

Calories: 539

Total Fat: 30g

Saturated Fat: 5g

Protein: 63g

Cholesterol 152mg

Carbohydrates: 4g

Fiber: 1g

Net Carbs: 3g

Lemon-Garlic Chicken and Green Beans with Caramelized Onions

Preparation Time: 10 minutes

Cooking Time: 65 minutes

Servings: 2

Ingredients:

- 3 tbsp. extra-virgin olive oil
- 3 tbsp. freshly squeezed lemon juice
- 2 tbsp. minced garlic
- 1 tsp. sea salt, plus additional for seasoning
- ¼ tsp. freshly ground black pepper
- ¼ tsp. paprika
- ⅛ tsp. red pepper flakes
- 2 large boneless, skinless free-range chicken breasts
- 1 yellow onion, quartered
- 2 cups trimmed green beans
- ¼ cup Golden Ghee, melted

Directions:

1. In .a medium bowl or a zipper-top plastic bag, combine the olive oil, lemon juice, garlic, salt, black pepper, paprika, and red pepper flakes.
2. Put the chicken then coat it in the marinade.
3. Cover the bowl or seal the bag then marinate the chicken in the fridge for at least 1 hour, or overnight if possible.
4. Preheat the oven to 350°F.
5. Dice 1 of the onion quarters, and cut the remaining 3 quarters into large chunks.
6. Put the larger chunks of onion across the bottom of a cast iron or ovenproof skillet.
7. Put the green beans, then scatter the diced onion above. Place on the top the green beans and onion with the ghee. Put the marinated chicken breasts on the green beans then spoon the remaining marinade at the chicken. Season the dish with a sprinkle of sea salt.
8. Bake the chicken until its internal temperature reaches at least 165°F, about 65 minutes. Serve hot.

Nutrition:

Calories: 803

Total Fat: 61g

Saturated Fat: 23g

Protein: 53g

Cholesterol: 217mg

Carbohydrates: 14g

Fiber: 5g

Net Carbs: 9g

Three-Cheese Chicken Cordon Bleu

Preparation Time: 10 minutes

Cooking Time: 50 minutes

Servings: 2

Ingredients:

- ½ cup shredded organic Gruyère cheese
- ½ cup shredded organic Emmentaler (Swiss) cheese
- ¼ cup shredded organic Appenzeller cheese
- ⅛ teaspoon ground nutmeg
- 2 large boneless, skinless, free-range chicken breasts, butterflied and pounded thin
- 4 slices nitrate-free ham
- 2 teaspoons Dijon mustard (optional)
- 1 tablespoon extra-virgin olive oil
- ½ cup grated organic Parmesan cheese
- ½ teaspoon Seasoned Salt (here)

Directions:

1. Preheat the oven to 375°F.
2. Line a rimmed baking sheet using parchment paper.
3. In a small bowl, combine the Gruyère, Emmentaler, and Appenzeller cheeses with the nutmeg.
4. Lay the butterflied chicken breasts flat on a work surface and divide the cheese mixture between the two breasts.
5. Then place 2 slices of ham on top of the cheese on each breast, followed by 1 teaspoon of Dijon mustard in the middle (if using). Fold the chicken breast over to enclose the filling.
6. Brush the olive oil into a chicken, and sprinkle it with the Parmesan cheese and seasoned salt.
7. Place the stuffed chicken breasts on the baking sheet and bake until the internal temperature reaches at least 165°F, about 50 minutes. Serve hot.

Nutrition:

Calories: 848

Total Fat: 52g

Saturated Fat: 23g

Protein: 88g

Cholesterol: 278mg

Carbohydrates: 4g

Fiber: 1g

Net Carbs: 3g

Blue Cheese Buffalo Chicken Balls

Preparation Time: 10 minutes

Cooking Time: 18 minutes

Servings: 4-6

Ingredients:

- 1 pound free-range ground chicken
- 1 large free-range egg, lightly beaten
- 1 cup shredded organic mozzarella cheese
- ½ cup crumbled organic blue cheese
- ¼ cup chopped celery
- 2 tablespoons water
- 1 teaspoon onion powder
- ½ teaspoon sea salt
- ½ teaspoon freshly ground black pepper
- 1 recipe Buffalo Sauce

Directions:

1. Preheat the oven to 450°F.
2. Line a baking pan with parchment paper.
3. In a large bowl, put and combine the chicken, egg, mozzarella, blue cheeses, celery, water, onion powder, salt, and pepper. Use your hands to mix the ingredients well.
4. Make 20 meatballs into a mixture then place them in the baking pan as you do.
5. Bake until the internal temperature reaches 165°F, about 18 minutes.
6. On the other hand, warm the buffalo sauce in a medium saucepan over low heat.
7. When the meatballs are done, toss them in the warm sauce and serve.

Nutrition:

Calories: 340

Total Fat: 17g

Saturated Fat: 6g

Protein: 44g

Cholesterol: 157mg

Carbohydrates: 2g

Fiber: 0g

Net Carbs: 2g

Chicken & Cheese Filled Avocados

Preparation Time: 10 minutes

Cooking Time: 0 minutes

Servings: 2

Ingredients:

- 2 avocados
- ¼ cup mayonnaise
- 1 tsp dried thyme
- 2 tbsp. cream cheese
- 1 ½ cups chicken, cooked and shredded
- Salt and black pepper, to taste
- ¼ tsp cayenne pepper
- ½ tsp onion powder
- ½ tsp garlic powder
- 1 tsp paprika
- Salt and black pepper, to taste
- 2 tbsp. lemon juice

Directions:

1. Halve the avocados and scoop the insides.
2. Put the flesh in a bowl, then add in the chicken; stir in the remaining ingredients.
3. Fill the avocado cups with chicken mixture and serve.

Nutrition:

Calories 518

Fat 41.6

Net Carbs 5.3g

Protein 23.2g

Paprika Chicken & Pancetta in a Skillet

Preparation Time: 20 minutes

Cooking Time: 10 minutes

Servings: 2

Ingredients:

- 1 tbsp. olive oil
- 5 pancetta strips, chopped
- 1/3 cup Dijon mustard
- Salt and black pepper, to taste
- 1 onion, chopped
- 1 cup chicken stock
- 2 chicken breasts, skinless and boneless
- ¼ tsp sweet paprika
- 2 tbsp. oregano, chopped

Directions:

1. In a bowl, combine the paprika, black pepper, salt, and mustard. Sprinkle this mixture the chicken breasts and massage.
2. Heat a skillet over medium heat, stir in the pancetta, cook until it browns, for about 3-4 minutes, and remove to a plate.
3. To the pancetta fat, add olive oil and cook the chicken breasts for 2 minutes per side. Place in the stock, black pepper, pancetta, salt, and onion. Sprinkle with oregano and serve.

Nutrition:

Calories 323

Fat 21g

Net Carbs 4.8g

Protein 24.5g

Cheesy Pinwheels with Chicken

Preparation Time: 10 minutes

Cooking Time: 30 minutes

Servings: 2

Ingredients:

- 2 tbsp. ghee

- 1 garlic, minced
- 1/3 pound chicken breasts, cubed
- 1 tsp creole seasoning
- 1/3 red onion, chopped
- 1 tomato, chopped
- ½ cup chicken stock
- ¼ cup whipping cream
- ½ cup mozzarella cheese, grated
- ¼ cup fresh cilantro, chopped
- Salt and black pepper, to taste
- 4 ounces cream cheese
- 5 eggs
- A pinch of garlic powder

Directions:

1. Season the chicken with creole seasoning. Heat a pan at medium heat and warm 1 tbsp. ghee. Put chicken and cook per side for 2 minutes; remove to a plate.
2. Melt the rest of the ghee and stir in garlic and tomato; cook for 4 minutes. Return the chicken to the pan and pour in stock; cook for 15 minutes. Place in whipping cream, red onion, salt, mozzarella cheese, and black pepper; cook for 2 minutes.
3. In a blender, mix the cream cheese with garlic powder, salt, eggs, and black pepper, and pulse well. Place the mixture into a lined baking sheet, and then bake for 10 minutes in the oven at 320 F. Allow the cheese sheet to cool down, place on a cutting board, roll, and slice into medium slices.
4. Organize the slices on a serving plate and top with chicken mixture. Sprinkle with cilantro to serve.

Nutrition:

Calories 463

Fat 36.4g

Net Carbs 6.3g

Protein 35.2g

Peanut-Crusted Chicken

Preparation Time: 15 minutes

Cooking Time: 15 minutes

Servings: 2

Ingredients:

- 1 egg
- Salt and black pepper, to taste
- 3 tbsp. canola oil
- 1 ½ cups peanuts, ground
- 2 chicken breast halves, boneless and skinless
- Lemon slices for garnish

Directions:

1. Whisk egg in one bowl and pour the peanuts in another one. Season the chicken, dip in the egg, and then in peanuts. Warm oil in a pan over medium heat and brown the chicken for 2 minutes per side.
2. Remove the chicken pieces to a baking sheet, set in the oven, and bake for 10 minutes at 360 F. Serve topped with lemon slices.

Nutrition:

Calories 634

Fat 51g

Net Carbs 4.7g

Protein 43.6g

Turnip Greens & Artichoke Chicken

Preparation Time: 5 minutes

Cooking Time: 30 minutes

Servings: 2

Ingredients:

- 4 ounces cream cheese
- 2 chicken breasts
- 4 oz. canned artichoke hearts, chopped
- 1 cup turnip greens
- ¼ cup Pecorino cheese, grated
- ½ tbsp. onion powder
- ½ tbsp. garlic powder
- Salt and black pepper, to taste
- 2 ounces Monterrey Jack cheese, shredded

Directions:

1. Line a baking dish using parchment paper and place it in the chicken breasts. Season with black pepper and salt. Set in the oven at 350 F and bake for 35 minutes.
2. In a bowl, combine the artichokes with onion powder, Pecorino cheese, salt, turnip greens, cream cheese, garlic powder, and black pepper. Take off the chicken from the oven, cut each piece in half, divide artichokes mixture on top, spread with Monterrey cheese, and bake for 5 more minutes.

Nutrition:

Calories 443

Fat 24.5g

Net Carbs 4.2g

Protein 35.4g

Winter Chicken with Vegetables

Preparation Time: 5 minutes

Cooking Time: 30 minutes

Servings: 2

Ingredients:

- 2 tbsp. olive oil
- 2 cups whipping cream
- 1 pound chicken breasts, chopped
- 1 onion, chopped
- 1 carrot, chopped
- 2 cups chicken stock
- Salt and black pepper, to taste
- 1 bay leaf
- 1 turnip, chopped
- 1 parsnip, chopped
- 1 cup green beans, chopped
- 2 tsp fresh thyme, chopped

Directions:

1. Heat a pan at medium heat and warm the olive oil. Sauté the onion for 3 minutes, pour in the stock, carrot, turnip, parsnip, chicken, and bay leaf. Place to a boil, and simmer for 20 minutes.
2. Add in the asparagus and cook for 7 minutes. Discard the bay leaf, stir in the whipping cream, adjust the seasoning, and scatter it with fresh thyme to serve.

Nutrition:

Calories 483

Fat 32.5g

Net Carbs 6.9g

Protein 33g

Pancetta & Cheese Stuffed Chicken

Preparation Time: 15 minutes

Cooking Time: 25 minutes

Servings: 2

Ingredients:

- 4 slices pancetta
- 2 tbsp. olive oil
- 2 chicken breasts
- 1 garlic clove, minced
- 1 shallot, finely chopped
- 2 tbsp. dried oregano
- 4 oz. mascarpone cheese
- 1 lemon, zested
- Salt and black pepper to taste

Directions:

1. Warm the oil in a small skillet, then sauté the garlic and shallots for 3 minutes. Stir in salt, black pepper, and lemon zest. Transfer to a bowl and let it cool. Stir in the mascarpone cheese and oregano.
2. Score a pocket in each chicken's breast, fill the holes with the cheese mixture and cover it with the cut-out chicken. Wrap each breast with two pancetta slices and secure the ends with a toothpick.
3. Set the chicken on a greased baking sheet and cook in the oven for 20 minutes at 380 F.

Nutrition:

Calories 643

Fat 44.5g

Net Carbs 6.2g

Protein 52.8g

Chili Chicken Kebab with Garlic Dressing

Preparation Time: 7 minutes

Cooking Time: 10 minutes

Servings: 2-4

Ingredients:

- Skewers
- 2 tbsp. olive oil
- 3 tbsp. soy sauce, sugar-free
- 1 tbsp. ginger paste
- 2 tbsp. swerve brown sugar
- Chili pepper to taste
- 2 chicken breasts, cut into cubes
- Dressing
- ½ cup tahini
- 1 tbsp. parsley, chopped
- 1 garlic clove, minced
- Salt and black pepper to taste
- ¼ cup warm water

Directions:

1. To make the marinade:
2. In a small bowl, place and mix the soy sauce, ginger paste, brown sugar, chili pepper, and olive oil. Put the chicken in a zipper bag, pour the marinade over, seal, and shake for an even coat. Marinate in the fridge for 2 hours.
3. Preheat a grill to high heat. Thread the chicken on skewers and cook for 10 minutes, with three to four turnings to be golden brown. Transfer to a plate.
4. Mix the tahini, garlic, salt, parsley, and warm water in a bowl. Serve the chicken skewers topped with the tahini dressing.

Nutrition:

Calories 410

Fat 32g

Net Carbs 4.8g

Protein 23.5g

Chili & Lemon Marinated Chicken Wings

Preparation Time: 5 minutes

Cooking Time: 12 minutes

Servings: 2-4

Ingredients:

- 3 tbsp. olive oil
- 1 tsp coriander seeds
- 1 tsp xylitol
- 1 pound wings
- Juice from 1 lemon
- ½ cup fresh parsley, chopped
- 2 garlic cloves, minced
- 1 red chili pepper, chopped
- Salt and black pepper, to taste
- Lemon wedges, for serving
- ½ tsp cilantro

Directions:

1. Using a bowl, stir together lemon juice, xylitol, garlic, salt, red chili pepper, cilantro, olive oil, and black pepper. Place in the chicken wings and toss well to coat. Refrigerate for 2 hours.
2. Preheat grill over high heat. Add the chicken wings, and grill each side for 6 minutes. Serve the chicken wings with lemon wedges.

Nutrition:

Calories 223

Fat 12g

Net Carbs 5.1g

Protein 16.8g

Cipollini & Bell Pepper Chicken Souvlaki

Preparation Time: 5 minutes

Cooking Time: 12 minutes

Servings: 2-4

Ingredients:

- 2 chicken breasts, cubed
- 2 tbsp. olive oil
- 2 cloves garlic, minced
- 1 red bell pepper, cut into chunks
- 8 oz. small cipollini
- ½ cup lemon juice
- Salt and black pepper to taste
- 1 tsp rosemary leaves to garnish
- 2 to 4 lemon wedges to garnish

Directions:

1. Thread the chicken, bell pepper, and cipollini onto skewers and set aside. In a bowl, mix half of the oil, garlic, salt, black pepper, and lemon juice, and add the chicken skewers. Cover the bowl and let the chicken marinate for at least 2 hours in the refrigerator.
2. Preheat a grill to high heat and grill the skewers for 6 minutes on each side. Remove and serve garnished with rosemary leaves and lemons wedges.

Nutrition:

Calories 363

Fat 14.2g

Net Carbs 4.2g

Protein 32.5g

Tarragon Chicken with Roasted Balsamic Turnips

Preparation Time: 10 minutes

Cooking Time: 50 minutes

Servings: 2-4

Ingredients:

- 1 pound chicken thighs
- 2 lb. turnips, cut into wedges
- 2 tbsp. olive oil
- 1 tbsp. balsamic vinegar
- 1 tbsp. tarragon
- Salt and black pepper, to taste

Directions:

1. Set the oven to 400°F then grease a baking dish with olive oil. Cook turnips in boiling water for 10 minutes, drain and set aside. Add the chicken and turnips to the baking dish.
2. Sprinkle with tarragon, black pepper, and salt. Roast for 35 minutes. Remove the baking dish, drizzle the turnip wedges with balsamic vinegar and return to the oven for another 5 minutes.

Nutrition:

Calories: 383

Fat: 26g

Net Carbs: 9.5g

Protein: 21.3g

Tomato & Cheese Chicken Chili

Preparation Time: 5 minutes

Cooking Time: 25 minutes

Servings: 2-4

Ingredients:

- 1 tbsp. butter
- 1 tbsp. olive oil
- 1 pound chicken breasts, skinless, boneless, cubed
- ½ onion, chopped
- 2 cups chicken broth
- 2 cups tomatoes, chopped
- 2 oz. tomato puree
- 1 tbsp. chili powder
- 1 tbsp. cumin
- 1 garlic clove, minced
- 1 habanero pepper, minced
- ½ cup mozzarella cheese, shredded
- Salt and black pepper to taste

Directions:

1. Season the chicken using salt and pepper. Set a large pan at medium heat and add the chicken; cover it with water, and bring it to a boil. Cook until no longer pink, for 10 minutes.

2. Transfer the chicken to a flat surface to shred with forks. In a pot, pour in the butter and olive oil and set over medium heat. Sauté onion and garlic until transparent for 5 minutes.
3. Stir in the chicken, tomatoes, cumin, habanero pepper, tomato puree, broth, and chili powder. Adjust the seasoning and let the mixture boil.
4. Reduce heat to simmer for about 10 minutes. Top with shredded cheese to serve.

Nutrition:

Calories: 322

Fat: 16.6g

Net Carbs: 6.2g

Protein: 29g

Turmeric Chicken Wings with Ginger Sauce

Preparation Time: 5 minutes

Cooking Time: 20 minutes

Servings: 2-4

Ingredients:

- 2 tbsp. olive oil
- 1 pound chicken wings, cut in half
- 1 tbsp. turmeric
- 1 tbsp. cumin
- 3 tbsp. fresh ginger, grated
- Salt and black pepper, to taste
- Juice of ½ lime
- 1 cup thyme leaves
- ¾ cup cilantro, chopped
- 1 tbsp. water
- 1 jalapeño pepper

Directions:

1. In a bowl, stir together 1 tbsp. ginger, cumin, and salt, half of the olive oil, black pepper, turmeric, and cilantro. Place in the chicken wings pieces, toss to coat, and refrigerate for 20 minutes.
2. Heat the grill to high heat. Remove the wings from the marinade, drain, and grill for 20 minutes, turning from time to time, then set aside.
3. Using a blender, combine thyme, remaining ginger, salt, jalapeno pepper, black pepper, lime juice, the remaining olive oil, and water, and blend well. Serve the chicken wings topped with the sauce.

Nutrition:

Calories 253

Fat 16.1g

Net Carbs 4.1g

Protein 21.7g

Feta & Bacon Chicken

Preparation Time: 20 minutes

Cooking Time: 10minutes

Servings: 2-4

Ingredients:

- 4 oz. bacon, chopped
- 1 pound chicken breasts
- 3 green onions, chopped
- 2 tbsp. coconut oil
- 4 oz. feta cheese, crumbled
- 1 tbsp. parsley

Directions:

1. Place a pan over medium heat and coat with cooking spray. Add in the bacon and cook until crispy. Remove to paper towels, drain the grease and crumble.
2. To the same pan, add in the oil and cook the chicken breasts for 4-5 minutes, then flip to the other side; cook for an additional 4-5 minutes. Place the chicken breasts to a baking dish. Place the green onions, set in the oven, turn on the broiler, and cook for 5 minutes at high temperature. Remove to serving plates and serve topped with bacon, feta cheese, and parsley.

Nutrition:

Calories 459

Fat 35g

Net Carbs 3.1g

Protein 31.5g

Chicken Pie with Bacon

Preparation Time: 20 minutes

Cooking Time: 35 minutes

Servings: 24

Ingredients:

- 3 tbsp. butter
- 1 onion, chopped
- 4 oz. bacon, sliced
- 1 carrot, chopped
- 3 garlic cloves, minced
- Salt and black pepper, to taste
- ¾ cup crème fraîche
- ½ cup chicken stock
- 1 pound chicken breasts, cubed
- 2 tbsp. yellow mustard
- ¾ cup cheddar cheese, shredded
- Dough
- 1 egg
- ¾ cup almond flour
- 3 tbsp. cream cheese
- 1 ½ cups mozzarella cheese, shredded
- 1 tsp onion powder
- 1 tsp garlic powder
- Salt and black pepper, to taste

Directions:

1. Sauté the onion, garlic, black pepper, bacon, and carrot in melted butter for 5 minutes. Add in the chicken and cook for 3 minutes. Stir in the crème fraîche, salt, mustard, black pepper, and stock, and cook for 7 minutes. Add in the cheddar cheese and set aside.
2. In a bowl, combine the mozzarella cheese with the cream cheese and heat in a microwave for 1 minute. Stir in the garlic powder, salt, flour, black pepper, onion powder, and egg. Knead the dough well, split into 4 pieces, and flatten each into a circle.
3. Set the chicken mixture into 4 ramekins, top each with a dough circle, and cook in the oven at 370 F for 25 minutes.

Nutrition:

Calories 563

Fat 44.6g

Net Carbs 7.7g

Protein 36g

Flying Jacob Casserole

Preparation Time: 15 minutes

Cooking Time: 20-25 minutes

Servings: 6

Ingredients:

- 1 pc Grilled Chicken
- 2 tbsp. Butter
- 225 g Diced bacon
- 250 g Mushrooms
- 475 ml Cream
- 125 ml hot chili sauce
- 1 tsp. Seasoning curry
- Salt and black pepper to taste
- 125 g Peanuts
- Salad
- 175 g Spinach
- 2 pcs Tomato

Directions:

1. Preheat the oven to 400 ° F.
2. Chop the mushrooms into small pieces then fry in oil with bacon. Salt and pepper to taste.
3. Separate the chicken meat from the bones and chop it into small pieces.
4. Put these pieces of chicken in a mold for baking, oiled. Add mushrooms and bacon.
5. Beat the cream until soft peaks. Put chili sauce, curry, and salt and pepper to taste.
6. Pour the chicken into the resulting mixture.
7. Bake in the oven for at least 20-25 minutes until the dish will get a pleasant golden color. Sprinkle toasted and chopped nuts on top. Serve with salad.

Nutrition:

Carbohydrates: 11 g

Fats: 80 g

Proteins: 40 g

Calories: 912

BBQ Chicken Zucchini Boats

Preparation Time: 10 minutes

Cooking Time: 15-20 minutes

Servings: 4

Ingredients:

- 3 Zucchini halved
- 1 lb. cooked Chicken breast
- .5 cup BBQ sauce
- .33 cup Shredded Mexican cheese
- 1 Avocado, sliced
- .5 cup Halved cherry tomatoes
- .25 cup Diced green onions
- 3 tbsp. Keto-friendly ranch dressing
- Also Needed: 9x13 casserole dish

Directions:

1. Set the oven to reach 350° Fahrenheit.
2. Using a knife, cut the zucchini in half. Discard the seeds. Make the boat by carving out of the center. Place the zucchini flesh side up into the casserole dish.
3. Discard and cut the skin and bones from the chicken. Shred and add the chicken in with the barbeque sauce. Toss to coat all the chicken fully.
4. Fill the zucchini boats with the mixture using about .25 to .33 cup each.
5. Sprinkle with Mexican cheese on top.
6. Bake for approximately 15 minutes. (If you would like it tenderer; bake for an additional 5 to 10 minutes to reach the desired tenderness.)
7. Remove from the oven. Top it off with avocado, green onion, tomatoes, and a drizzle of dressing. Serve.

Nutrition:

Calories: 212

Net Carbs: 9 g

Total Fat Content: 11 g

Protein: 19 g

Cashew Chicken Curry

Preparation Time: 15 minutes

Cooking Time: 25 minutes

Servings: 4

Ingredients:

- 1 cups Cauliflower
- 2 large fresh tomatoes
- 1 medium Red onion
- 2 cups Cucumber
- 2 tbsp. Coconut oil
- 1 tbsp. & .5 tsp. Yellow curry powder - divided
- Sea salt & Black pepper (as desired)
- .66 cup Roasted - salted cashews (
- 1.lb Breasts of chicken, 4 small
- 1 large Egg white
- For the Garnish:
- Freshly chopped fresh mint
- Minced fresh cilantro
- Also Needed: Food processor & Rimmed baking sheet

Directions:

1. Chop the cauliflower into florets and quarter the tomatoes. Roughly chop the onion and thinly slice the cucumber into halves. Take off the skin and bones from the chicken.
2. Heat the oven to 425° Fahrenheit.
3. Toss the quartered tomatoes, cauliflower florets, and onion into a mixing container. Melt the coconut oil and sprinkle using 1.5 teaspoons of curry powder. Mix until well.
4. Prepare on a baking sheet in one layer. Dust with pepper and salt to your liking. Add the rest of the curry powder and cashews into a food processor. Pulse leaving a few chunks for texture.
5. Pat to remove the moisture from the chicken breasts using a paper towel.

6. Put the egg white and cashews into two shallow plates.
7. Dredge the chicken through the egg white. Shake off any excess, and press into the cashews.
8. Flip and lightly press the other side into the cashews.
9. Put the chicken breast onto a small cooling rack that fits on your sheet pan (one with legs is preferred, so it sits over the veggies).
10. Continue the process with the remaining chicken. Place the cooling rack over a sheet pan (over the top of the veggies).
11. Bake the chicken to reach an internal temperature of 165° Fahrenheit (14-15 min.). Once it's done, toss the fresh cucumbers onto the pan. Garnish with mint and cilantro.

Nutrition:

Calories: 364

Net Carbs: 14 g

Total Fat Content: 18 g

Protein: 34 g

Creamy Chicken & Greens

Preparation Time: 10 minutes

Cooking Time: 20 minutes

Servings: 4

Ingredients:

- 1 lb. Chicken thighs – skins on
- 1 cup. Chicken stock
- 1 cup. Cream
- 2 tbsp. Coconut oil
- 1 tsp. Italian herbs
- 2 cups Dark leafy greens
- Pepper & Salt (your preference)
- 2 tbsp. Coconut flour
- 2 tbsp. Melted butter

Directions:

1. On the stovetop, add oil in a skillet using the med-high temperature setting.
2. Remove the bones from the chicken and dust using salt and pepper. Fry the chicken until done.
3. Make the sauce by adding the butter to a saucepan. Whisk in the flour to form a thick paste. Slowly, whisk in the cream. Once it boils, mix in the herbs.
4. Transfer the chicken to the counter and add the stock.
5. Deglaze the pan, and whisk the cream sauce. Toss in the greens until thoroughly coated with the sauce.
6. Arrange the thighs on the greens, warm up, and serve.

Nutrition:

Calories: 446

Net Carbs: 3 g

Total Fat Content: 38 g

Protein: 18 g

Curry Chicken Lettuce Wraps

Preparation Time: 15 minutes

Cooking Time: 10 minutes

Servings: 5

Ingredients:

- 2 Minced garlic cloves
- .25 cups Minced onion
- 1 lb. Chicken thighs – skinless & boneless
- 2 tbsp. Ghee
- 1 tsp. Black pepper
- 2 tsp. Curry powder
- 1.5 tsp. Salt
- 1 cup Riced cauliflower
- 5-6 Lettuce leaves
- Keto-friendly sour cream (as desired - count the carbs)

Directions:

1. Mince the garlic and onions. Set aside for now.
2. Pull out the bones and skin from the chicken and dice into one-inch pieces.
3. On the stovetop, add 2 tbsp. of ghee to a skillet and melt. Toss in the onion and

sauté until browned. Fold in the chicken and sprinkle with the garlic, pepper, and salt.
4. Cook for eight minutes. Stir in the remainder of the ghee, riced cauliflower, and curry. Stir until well mixed.
5. Prepare the lettuce leaves and add the mixture.
6. Serve with a dollop of cream.

Nutrition:

Calories: 554

Net Carbs: 7 g

Total Fat Content: 36 g

Protein: 50 g

Nacho Chicken Casserole

Preparation Time: 15 minutes

Cooking Time: 25 minutes

Servings: 6

Ingredients:

- 1 medium Jalapeño pepper
- 1.75lb. Chicken thighs
- Pepper and salt (to taste)
- 2 tbsp. Olive oil
- 1.5tsp. Chili seasoning
- 4 oz. Cheddar cheese
- 4 oz. Cream cheese
- 3 tbsp. Parmesan cheese
- 1 cup Green chilies and tomatoes
- .25 cup Sour cream
- 1 pkg. Frozen cauliflower
- Also Needed: Immersion blender

Directions:

1. Warm the oven to reach 375° Fahrenheit.
2. Slice the jalapeño into pieces and set aside.
3. Cutaway the skin and bones from the chicken. Chop it and sprinkle using the pepper and salt. Prepare in a skillet using a portion of olive oil on the med-high temperature setting until browned.
4. Mix in the sour cream, cream cheese, and ¾ of the cheddar cheese. Stir until melted and combined well. Place in the tomatoes and chilies. Stir then put it all to a baking dish.
5. Cook the cauliflower in the microwave. Blend in the rest of the cheese with the immersion blender until it resembles mashed potatoes. Season as desired.
6. Spread the cauliflower concoction over the casserole and sprinkle with the peppers. Bake approximately 15 to 20 minutes.

Nutrition:

Calories: 426

Net Carbs: 4.3 g

Total Fat Content: 32.2 g

Protein: 31 g

Pesto & Mozzarella Chicken Casserole

Preparation Time: 10 minutes

Cooking Time: 25-30 minutes

Servings: 8

Ingredients:

- Cooking oil (as needed)
- 2 lb. Grilled & cubed chicken breasts
- 8 oz. Cubed mozzarella
- 8 oz. Cream cheese
- 8 oz. Shredded mozzarella
- .25 cup Pesto
- .25 to .5 cup Heavy cream

Directions:

1. Warm the oven to 400° Fahrenheit. Spritz a casserole dish with a spritz of cooking oil spray.
2. Combine the pesto, heavy cream, and softened cream cheese.
3. Add the chicken and cubed mozzarella into the greased dish.
4. Sprinkle the chicken using the shredded mozzarella. Bake for 25-30 minutes.

Nutrition:

Calories: 451

Net Carbs: 3 g

Total Fat Content: 30 g

Protein: 38 g

Rotisserie Chicken & Cabbage Shreds

Preparation Time: 10 minutes

Cooking Time: 0 minutes

Servings: 2

Ingredients:

- .5 of 1 Red onion
- 7 oz. Fresh green cabbage
- 1 lb. Precooked rotisserie chicken
- .5 cup Keto-friendly mayo
- 1 tbsp. Olive oil
- Pepper & Salt

Direction:

1. Use a sharp kitchen knife to shred the cabbage and slice the onion into thin slices.
2. Place the chicken on a platter, add the mayo, and a drizzle of oil. Dust using salt and pepper. Serve.

Nutrition:

Calories: 423

Net Carbs: 6 g

Total Fat Content: 35 g

Protein: 17 g

Chicken Quiche

Preparation Time: 15 minutes

Cooking Time: 50 minutes

Servings: 6

Ingredients:

- 16 oz. almond flour
- 7 medium eggs
- Salt and ground black pepper to taste
- 2 tbsp. coconut oil
- 1 lb. ground chicken
- 2 small zucchini, grated
- 1 tsp dried oregano
- 1 tsp fennel seeds
- ½ cup heavy cream

Directions:

1. Place almond flour, 1 egg, salt, and coconut oil in blender or food processor and blend.
2. Grease pie pan and pour the dough in it. Press well on the bottom.
3. Preheat pan on medium heat and toss ground chicken, cook for 2 minutes, set aside.
4. In a medium bowl, whisk together 6 eggs, zucchini, oregano, salt, pepper, fennel seeds, and heavy cream.
5. Add chicken to egg mixture and stir well.
6. Preheat oven to 350 F.
7. Pour egg mixture into pie pan and place in oven. Cook for 40 minutes.
8. Let it cool and slice. Serve.

Nutrition:

Calories

295

Carbs 3.95g

Fat 24g

Protein 19g

Chicken Parmigiana

Preparation Time: 15 minutes

Cooking Time: 26 minutes

Servings: 4

Ingredients:

- 1 large organic egg, beaten
- ½ cup of superfine blanched almond flour
- ¼ cup Parmesan cheese, grated
- ½ teaspoon dried parsley
- ½ teaspoon paprika
- ½ teaspoon garlic powder

- Salt and ground black pepper, as required
- 4 -6-ounces grass-fed skinless, boneless chicken breasts, pounded into a ½-inch thickness
- ¼ cup olive oil
- 1½ cups marinara sauce
- 4 ounces mozzarella cheese, thinly sliced
- 2 tablespoons fresh parsley, chopped

Directions:

1. Preheat the oven to 375 degrees F.
2. Add the beaten egg into a shallow dish.
3. Place the almond flour, Parmesan, parsley, spices, salt, and black pepper in another shallow dish and mix well.
4. Dip each chicken breast into the beaten egg and then coat with the flour mixture.
5. Heat the oil in a deep skillet over medium-high heat and fry the chicken breasts for about 3 minutes per side.
6. Using a slotted spoon, moved the chicken breasts onto a paper towel-lined plate to drain.
7. At the bottom of a casserole, put about ½ cup of marinara sauce and spread evenly.
8. Arrange the chicken breasts over marinara sauce in a single layer.
9. Top with the remaining marinara sauce, followed by mozzarella cheese slices.
10. Bake for about at least 20 minutes or until done completely.
11. Take off from the oven and serve hot with the garnishing of fresh parsley.

Nutrition:

Calories: 542

Net Carbs: 5.7g

Carbohydrate: 9g

Fiber: 3.3g

Protein: 54.2g

Fat: 33.2g

Sugar: 3.8g

Sodium: 609mg

Vodka Duck Fillets

Preparation Time: 5 minutes

Cooking Time: 15 minutes

Servings: 4

Ingredients:

- 1 tablespoon lard, room temperature
- 4 duck fillets
- 4 green onions, chopped
- Salt and cayenne pepper, to taste
- 1 teaspoon mixed peppercorns
- 1 ½ cups turkey stock
- 3 tablespoons Worcestershire sauce
- 2 ounces vodka
- 1/2 teaspoon ground bay leaf
- 1/2 cup sour cream

Directions:

1. Melt the lard in a skillet that is preheated over medium-high heat. Sear the duck fillets, turning once, for 4 to 6 minutes.
2. Now, add the remaining ingredients, except for the sour cream, to the skillet. Cook, partially covered, for a further 7 minutes.
3. Serve warm, garnished with sour cream. Bon appétit!

Nutrition:

351 Calories

24.7g Fat

6.6g Carbs

22.1g Protein

Baked Chicken Meatballs - Habanero & Green Chili

Preparation Time: 10 minutes

Cooking Time: 25 minutes

Servings: 15

Ingredients:

- 1 pound ground chicken
- 1 poblano pepper
- 1 habanero pepper
- 1 jalapeno pepper
- 1/2 cup cilantro

- 1 tbsp. vinegar
- 1 tbsp. olive oil
- salt to taste

Directions:

1. Preheat broiler to 400 degrees Fahrenheit.
2. In an enormous blending bowl, join chicken, minced peppers, cilantro, salt, and vinegar with your hands. Structure 1-inch meatballs with the blend
3. Coat every meatball with olive oil, at that point, place on a rimmed heating sheet or meal dish.
4. Heat for 25 minutes

Nutrition:

Calories 54

Fat 3g

Carbs 5g

Protein 5g

BBQ Chicken Liver and Hearts

Preparation Time: 15 minutes

Cooking Time: 20 minutes

Servings: 4

Ingredients:

- 1 lb. chicken hearts
- 1 lb. chicken livers
- sea salt
- black pepper
- bamboo skewers

Directions:

1. The liver and hearts defrost and bring to room temperature.
2. The heart's extreme top parts can be evacuated with a sharp blade.
3. Meanwhile, set up the BBQ - we utilize just charcoals; however, you can utilize gas, and bring to prescription/high warmth.
4. Presently string the hearts on the sticks, 5 to 7 each, contingent upon their size.
5. After cleaning the livers, focusing not to break or smash them, lay level on an adaptable barbecuing bushel
6. Season both liver and hearts with ocean salt and naturally ground dark pepper.
7. The livers will generally stick on the barbecue and effectively break separated currently set on the flame broil and cook until the ideal doneness is come to.

Nutrition:

Calories 361

Fat 28g

Carbs 4.5g

Protein 23g

Buffalo Balls

Preparation Time: 10 minutes

Cooking Time: 40 minutes

Servings: 18

Ingredients:

- For the Meatballs:
- 1lb ground chicken or turkey
- 1/4 cup almond flour
- 2 oz. cream cheese softened
- 1 egg
- 2 tbsp. chopped celery
- 3 tbsp. crumbled blue cheese
- 1/4 tsp black pepper
- For the Sauce:
- 1/2 stick (4 oz.) unsalted butter
- 1/2 cup Frank's Red Hot

Directions:

1. In a medium bowl, put all the meatballs ingredients then mix. Form into about 1 inch balls.
2. Set it on a greased cookie sheet (with sides) and bake at 350°F for at least 10 minutes.
3. To make the sauce: put the Frank's and butter in a small saucepan on medium heat, or place in a microwave-safe bowl for 2 minutes on high.
4. After 10 minutes, remove balls from the oven and dunk carefully in the buffalo sauce.
5. Return onto the cookie sheet and bake for another 12 minutes. If you have a leftover

sauce, you could pour it over the meatballs and bake for another 3 to 4 minutes if you want them saucy.

Nutrition:

Calories: 331

Fat: 28g

Carbs: 2g

Protein: 17g

Turkey Chili

Preparation Time: 5 minutes

Cooking Time: 30 minutes

Servings: 2

Ingredients:

- 1 ounce jalapeno pepper
- 1 ounce red bell pepper (or other colors)
- 3 ounces zucchini
- 1 ½ tablespoon olive oil
- 5 ounces ground turkey
- 1 cup water or as needed
- 1 ½ ounces cauliflower rice
- 1 ½ tablespoons sour cream
- 4 tablespoons shredded cheddar cheese
- ¼ teaspoon pepper
- 1 teaspoon paprika
- 1/3 teaspoon onion powder or garlic powder (optional)
- ¼ teaspoon ground cumin (optional)
- Salt to taste

Directions:

1. Chop the red bell pepper, jalapeno pepper, and zucchini into smaller, bite-sized pieces. Feel free to slice jalapeno pepper into larger pieces if you want to avoid them and control the spiciness in your mouth later on.
2. Take a large stewing pot, add the olive oil, and put it on medium heat. Put the ground turkey and cook it until it becomes brown. Use a spatula to break it up.
3. Mix bell pepper, jalapeno, and zucchini with turkey. Put a cover on your pot and let your mixture cook on a low heat for approximately 5 minutes or until you see that vegetables became a little bit softer.
4. Season everything and add water. Stir the chili.
5. Cover your pot once again and bring your mixture to a simmer. Continue to stir it for about 10 more minutes.
6. Add the cauliflower rice. Remove the cover and keep cooking at the low heat.
7. Fill approximately ½ of a cup with the liquid you remove from the pot. Place it into a clean bowl and mix it with the sour cream.
8. Bring the thickened liquid back to the pot. Stir your ingredients once again and let your chili simmer for 5 more minutes for it to thicken a little bit more.
9. While serving this meal, fill 2 bowls and top each of those with 2 tablespoons of cheddar cheese.

Nutrition:

Calories: 378

Total Carbs: 6,3g

Fiber: 2g

Net Carbs: 4,3g

Fat: 30g

Protein: 23g

Beef with Carrot & Broccoli

Preparation Time: 15 minutes

Cooking Time: 14 minutes

Servings: 4

Ingredients:

- 2 tbsp. coconut oil, divided
- 2 medium garlic cloves, minced
- 1 lb. beef sirloin steak, sliced into thin strips
- Salt, to taste
- ¼ cup chicken broth

- 2 tsp. fresh ginger, grated
- 1 tbsp. Ground flax seeds
- ½ tsp. Red pepper flakes, crushed
- ¼ tsp. freshly ground black pepper
- 1 large carrot, peeled and sliced thinly
- 2 cups broccoli florets
- 1 medium scallion, sliced thinly

Directions:
1. In a skillet, warm 1 tbsp. of oil on medium-high heat.
2. Put garlic and sauté approximately 1 minute.
3. Add beef and salt and cook for at least 4-5 minutes or till browned.
4. Using a slotted spoon, transfer the beef in a bowl.
5. Take off the liquid from the skillet.
6. In a bowl, put together broth, ginger, flax seeds, red pepper flakes, and black pepper then mix.
7. In the same skillet, warm remaining oil on medium heat.
8. Put the carrot, broccoli, and ginger mixture then cook for at least 3-4 minutes or till desired doneness.
9. Mix in beef and scallion then cook for around 3-4 minutes.

Nutrition:

Calories: 412

Fat: 13g

Carbohydrates: 28g

Fiber: 9g

Protein: 35g

Beef with Mushroom & Broccoli

Preparation Time: 15 minutes

Cooking Time: 12 minutes

Servings: 4

Ingredients:

- For Beef Marinade:
- 1 garlic clove, minced
- 1 (2-inch piece fresh ginger, minced
- Salt, to taste
- Freshly ground black pepper, to taste
- 3 tbsp. white wine vinegar
- ¾ cup beef broth
- 1 lb. flank steak, trimmed and sliced into thin strips
- For Vegetables:
- 2 tbsp. coconut oil, divided
- 2 minced garlic cloves
- 3 cups broccoli rabe, chopped
- 4 oz. shiitake mushrooms halved
- 8 oz. cremini mushrooms, sliced

Directions:
1. For marinade in a bowl, put together all ingredients except beef then mix.
2. Add beef and coat with marinade.
3. Bring in the fridge to marinate for at least 15 minutes.
4. In the skillet, warm oil on medium-high heat.
5. Take off beef from the bowl, reserving the marinade.
6. Put beef and garlic and cook for about 3-4 minutes or till browned.
7. Using a slotted spoon, transfer the beef in a bowl.
8. In the same skillet, put the reserved marinade, broccoli, and mushrooms and cook for at least 3-4 minutes.
9. Stir in beef and cook for at least 3-4 minutes.

Nutrition:

Calories: 417

Fat: 10g

Carbohydrates: 23g

Fiber: 11g

Protein: 33g

Citrus Beef with Bok Choy

Preparation Time: 15 minutes

Cooking Time: 11 minutes

Servings: 4

Ingredients:

- For Marinade:
- 2 minced garlic cloves
- 1 (1-inch piece fresh ginger, grated
- 1/3 cup fresh orange juice
- ½ cup coconut aminos
- 2 tsp. fish sauce
- 2 tsp. Sriracha
- 1¼ lb. sirloin steak, sliced thinly

For Veggies:

- 2 tbsp. coconut oil, divided
- 3-4 wide strips of fresh orange zest
- 1 jalapeño pepper, sliced thinly
- ½ pound string beans stemmed and halved crosswise
- 1 tbsp. arrowroot powder
- ½ pound Bok choy, chopped
- 2 tsp. sesame seeds

Directions:

1. For marinade in a big bowl, put together garlic, ginger, orange juice, coconut aminos, fish sauce, and Sriracha then mix.
2. Put the beef and coat with marinade.
3. Place in the fridge to marinate for around a couple of hours.
4. In a skillet, warm oil on medium-high heat.
5. Add orange zest and sauté approximately 2 minutes.
6. Take off the beef from a bowl, reserving the marinade.
7. In the skillet, add beef and increase the heat to high.
8. Stir fry for at least 2-3 minutes or till browned.
9. With a slotted spoon, transfer the beef and orange strips right into a bowl.
10. With a paper towel, wipe out the skillet.
11. In a similar skillet, heat remaining oil on medium-high heat.
12. Add jalapeño pepper and string beans and stir fry for about 3-4 minutes.
13. Meanwhile, add arrowroot powder in reserved marinade and stir to mix.
14. In the skillet, add marinade mixture, beef, and Bok choy and cook for about 1-2 minutes.
15. Serve hot with garnishing of sesame seeds.

Nutrition:

Calories: 398

Fat: 11g

Carbohydrates: 20g

Fiber: 6g

Protein: 34g

Beef with Zucchini Noodles

Preparation Time: 15 minutes

Cooking Time: 9 minutes

Servings: 4

Ingredients:

- 1 teaspoon fresh ginger, grated
- 2 medium garlic cloves, minced
- ¼ cup coconut aminos
- 2 tablespoons fresh lime juice
- 1½ pound NY strip steak, trimmed and sliced thinly
- 2 medium zucchinis, spiralized with Blade C
- Salt, to taste
- 3 tablespoons essential olive oil
- 2 medium scallions, sliced
- 1 teaspoon red pepper flakes, crushed
- 2 tablespoons fresh cilantro, chopped

Directions:

1. In a big bowl, mix together ginger, garlic, coconut aminos, and lime juice.
2. Add beef and coat with marinade generously.
3. Refrigerate to marinate for approximately 10 minutes.
4. Place zucchini noodles over a large paper towel and sprinkle with salt.
5. Keep aside for around 10 minutes.
6. In a big skillet, heat oil on medium-high heat.
7. Add scallion and red pepper flakes and sauté for about 1 minute.
8. Add beef with marinade and stir fry for around 3-4 minutes or till browned.
9. Add zucchini and cook for approximately 3-4 minutes.

10. Serve hot with all the topping of cilantro.

Nutrition:

Calories: 434

Fat: 17g

Carbohydrates: 23g

Fiber: 12g

Protein: 29g

Beef with Asparagus & Bell Pepper

Preparation Time: 15 minutes

Cooking Time: 13 minutes

Servings: 4-5

Ingredients:

- 4 garlic cloves, minced
- 3 tablespoons coconut aminos
- 1/8 teaspoon red pepper flakes, crushed
- 1/8 teaspoon ground ginger
- Freshly ground black pepper, to taste
- 1 bunch asparagus, trimmed and halved
- 2 tablespoons olive oil, divided
- 1-pound flank steak, trimmed and sliced thinly
- 1 red bell pepper, seeded and sliced
- 3 tablespoons water
- 2 teaspoons arrowroot powder

Directions:

1. In a bowl, mix together garlic, coconut aminos, red pepper flakes, crushed, ground ginger, and black pepper. Keep aside.
2. In a pan of boiling water, cook asparagus for about 2 minutes.
3. Drain and rinse under cold water.
4. In a substantial skillet, heat 1 tablespoon of oil on medium-high heat.
5. Add beef and stir fry for around 3-4 minutes.
6. With a slotted spoon, transfer the beef in a bowl.
7. In a similar skillet, heat remaining oil on medium heat.
8. Add asparagus and bell pepper and stir fry for approximately 2-3 minutes.
9. Meanwhile, in the bowl, mix together water and arrowroot powder.
10. Stir in beef, garlic mixture, and arrowroot mixture, and cook for around 3-4 minutes or till desired thickness.

Nutrition:

Calories: 399

Fat: 17g

Carbohydrates: 27g

Fiber: 8g

Protein: 35g

Spiced Ground Beef

Preparation Time: 10 minutes

Cooking Time: 22 minutes

Servings: 5

Ingredients:

- 2 tablespoons coconut oil
- 2 whole cloves
- 2 whole cardamoms
- 1 (2-inch piece cinnamon stick
- 2 bay leaves
- 1 teaspoon cumin seeds
- 2 onions, chopped
- Salt, to taste
- ½ tablespoon garlic paste
- ½ tablespoon fresh ginger paste
- 1-pound lean ground beef
- 1½ teaspoons fennel seeds powder
- 1 teaspoon ground cumin
- 1½ teaspoons red chili powder
- 1/8 teaspoon ground turmeric
- Freshly ground black pepper, to taste
- 1 cup coconut milk
- ¼ cup water
- ¼ cup fresh cilantro, chopped

Directions:

1. In a sizable pan, heat oil on medium heat.
2. Add cloves, cardamoms, cinnamon stick, bay leaves, and cumin seeds and sauté for about 20-a few seconds.

3. Add onion and 2 pinches of salt and sauté for about 3-4 minutes.
4. Add garlic-ginger paste and sauté for about 2 minutes.
5. Add beef and cook for about 4-5 minutes, entering pieces using the spoon.
6. Cover and cook approximately 5 minutes.
7. Stir in spices and cook, stirring for approximately 2-2½ minutes.
8. Stir in coconut milk and water and cook for about 7-8 minutes.
9. Season with salt and take away from heat.
10. Serve hot using the garnishing of cilantro.

Nutrition:

Calories: 444

Fat: 15g

Carbohydrates: 29g

Fiber: 11g

Protein: 39g

Ground Beef with Cabbage

Preparation Time: 10 minutes

Cooking Time: 15 minutes

Servings: 6

Ingredients:

- 1 tbsp. olive oil
- 1 onion, sliced thinly
- 2 teaspoons fresh ginger, minced
- 4 garlic cloves, minced
- 1-pound lean ground beef
- 1½ tablespoons fish sauce
- 2 tablespoons fresh lime juice
- 1 small head purple cabbage, shredded
- 2 tablespoons peanut butter
- ½ cup fresh cilantro, chopped

Directions:

1. In a huge skillet, warm oil on medium heat.
2. Add onion, ginger, and garlic and sauté for about 4-5 minutes.
3. Add beef and cook for approximately 7-8 minutes, getting into pieces using the spoon.
4. Drain off the extra liquid in the skillet.
5. Stir in fish sauce and lime juice and cook for approximately 1 minute.
6. Add cabbage and cook approximately 4-5 minutes or till desired doneness.
7. Stir in peanut butter and cilantro and cook for about 1 minute.
8. Serve hot.

Nutrition:

Calories: 402

Fat: 13g

Carbohydrates: 21g

Fiber: 10g

Protein: 33g

Ground Beef with Veggies

Preparation Time: 15 minutes

Cooking Time: 20 minutes

Servings: 2-4

Ingredients:

- 1-2 tablespoons coconut oil
- 1 red onion, sliced
- 2 red jalapeño peppers, seeded and sliced
- 2 minced garlic cloves
- 1-pound lean ground beef
- 1 small head broccoli, chopped
- ½ of head cauliflower, chopped
- 3 carrots, peeled and sliced
- 3 celery ribs, sliced
- Chopped fresh thyme, to taste
- Dried sage, to taste
- Ground turmeric, to taste
- Salt, to taste
- Freshly ground black pepper, to taste

Directions:

1. In a huge skillet, melt coconut oil on medium heat.
2. Add onion, jalapeño peppers and garlic and sauté for about 5 minutes.
3. Add beef and cook for around 4-5 minutes, entering pieces using the spoon.

4. Add remaining ingredients and cook, occasionally stirring for about 8-10 min.
5. Serve hot.

Nutrition:

Calories: 453

Fat: 17g

Carbohydrates: 26g

Fiber: 8g,

Protein: 35g

Ground Beef with Cashews & Veggies

Preparation Time: 15 minutes

Cooking Time: 15 minutes

Servings: 4

Ingredients:

- 1½ pound lean ground beef
- 1 tablespoon garlic, minced
- 2 tablespoons fresh ginger, minced
- ¼ cup coconut aminos
- Salt, to taste
- Freshly ground black pepper, to taste
- 1 medium onion, sliced
- 1 can water chestnuts, drained and sliced
- 1 large green bell pepper, sliced
- ½ cup raw cashews, toasted

Directions:

1. Heat a nonstick skillet on medium-high heat.
2. Add beef and cook for about 6-8 minutes, breaking into pieces with all the spoon.
3. Add garlic, ginger, coconut aminos, salt, and black pepper and cook approximately 2 minutes.
4. Put the vegetables and cook approximately 5 minutes or till desired doneness.
5. Stir in cashews and immediately remove from heat.
6. Serve hot.

Nutrition:

Calories: 452

Fat: 20g

Carbohydrates: 26g

Fiber: 9g

Protein: 36g

Ground Beef with Greens & Tomatoes

Preparation Time: 15 minutes

Cooking Time: 15 minutes

Servings: 4

Ingredients:

- 1 tbsp. organic olive oil
- ½ of white onion, chopped
- 2 garlic cloves, chopped finely
- 1 jalapeño pepper, chopped finely
- 1-pound lean ground beef
- 1 teaspoon ground coriander
- 1 teaspoon ground cumin
- ½ teaspoon ground turmeric
- ½ teaspoon ground ginger
- ½ teaspoon ground cinnamon
- ½ teaspoon ground fennel seeds
- Salt, to taste
- Freshly ground black pepper, to taste
- 8 fresh cherry tomatoes, quartered
- 8 collard greens leaves, stemmed and chopped
- 1 teaspoon fresh lemon juice

Directions:

1. In a huge skillet, warm oil on medium heat.
2. Put onion and sauté for approximately 4 minutes.
3. Add garlic and jalapeño pepper and sauté for approximately 1 minute.
4. Add beef and spices and cook approximately 6 minutes breaking into pieces while using spoon.
5. Stir in tomatoes and greens and cook, stirring gently for about 4 minutes.
6. Stir in lemon juice and take away from heat.

Nutrition:

Calories: 432

Fat: 16g

Carbohydrates: 27g

Fiber: 12g

Protein: 39g

Beef & Veggies Chili

Preparation Time: 15 minutes

Cooking Time: 1 hour

Servings: 6-8

Ingredients:

- 2 pounds lean ground beef
- ½ head cauliflower, chopped into large pieces
- 1 onion, chopped
- 6 garlic cloves, minced
- 2 cups pumpkin puree
- 1 teaspoon dried oregano, crushed
- 1 teaspoon dried thyme, crushed
- 1 teaspoon ground cumin
- 1 teaspoon ground turmeric
- 1-2 teaspoons chili powder
- 1 teaspoon paprika
- 1 teaspoon cayenne pepper
- ¼ teaspoon red pepper flakes, crushed
- Salt, to taste
- Freshly ground black pepper, to taste
- 1 (26 oz.) can tomatoes, drained
- ½ cup water
- 1 cup beef broth

Directions:

1. Heat a substantial pan on medium-high heat.
2. Add beef and stir fry for around 5 minutes.
3. Add cauliflower, onion, and garlic and stir fry for approximately 5 minutes.
4. Add spices and herbs and stir to mix well.
5. Stir in remaining ingredients and provide to a boil.
6. Reduce heat to low and simmer, covered approximately 30-45 minutes.
7. Serve hot.

Nutrition:

Calories: 453

Fat: 10g

Carbohydrates: 20g

Fiber: 8g

Protein: 33g

Ground Beef & Veggies Curry

Preparation Time: 15 minutes

Cooking Time: 36 minutes

Servings: 6-8

Ingredients:

- 2-3 tablespoons coconut oil
- 1 cup onion, chopped
- 1 garlic clove, minced
- 1-pound lean ground beef
- 1½ tablespoons curry powder
- 1/8 teaspoon ground ginger
- 1/8 teaspoon ground cinnamon
- 1/8 teaspoon ground turmeric
- Salt, to taste
- 2½-3 cups tomatoes, chopped finely
- 2½-3 cups fresh peas shelled
- 2 sweet potatoes, peeled and chopped

Directions:

1. In a sizable pan, melt coconut oil on medium heat.
2. Add onion and garlic and sauté for around 4-5 minutes.
3. Add beef and cook for about 4-5 minutes.
4. Add curry powder and spices and cook for about 1 minute.
5. Stir in tomatoes, peas, and sweet potato and bring to your gentle simmer.
6. Simmer covered approximately 25 minutes.

Nutrition:

Calorie: 432

Fat: 16g

Carbohydrates: 21g

Fiber: 11g

Protein: 36g

Spicy & Creamy Ground Beef Curry

Preparation Time: 15 minutes

Cooking Time: 32 minutes

Servings: 4

Ingredients:

- 1-2 tablespoons coconut oil
- 1 teaspoon black mustard seeds
- 2 sprigs curry leaves
- 1 Serrano pepper, minced
- 1 large red onion, chopped finely
- 1 (1-inch) fresh ginger, minced
- 4 garlic cloves, minced
- 1 teaspoon ground coriander
- 1 teaspoon ground cumin
- ½ teaspoon ground turmeric
- ¼ teaspoon red chili powder
- Salt, to taste
- 1-pound lean ground beef
- 1 potato, peeled and chopped
- 3 medium carrots, peeled and chopped
- ¼ cup water
- 1 (14 oz.) can coconut milk
- Salt, to taste
- Freshly ground black pepper, to taste
- Chopped fresh cilantro, for garnishing

Directions:

1. In a big pan, melt coconut oil on medium heat.
2. Add mustard seeds and sauté for about thirty seconds.
3. Add curry leaves and Serrano pepper and sauté approximately half a minute.
4. Add onion, ginger, and garlic and sauté for about 4-5 minutes.
5. Add spices and cook for about 1 minute.
6. Add beef and cook for about 4-5 minutes.
7. Stir in potato, carrot, and water and provide with a gentle simmer.
8. Simmer, covered for around 5 minutes.
9. Stir in coconut milk and simmer for around fifteen minutes.
10. Stir in salt and black pepper and remove from heat.
11. Serve hot while using garnishing of cilantro.

Nutrition:

Calories: 432

Fat: 14g

Carbohydrates: 22g

Fiber: 8g

Protein: 39g

Curried Beef Meatballs

Preparation Time: 20 minutes

Cooking Time: 22 minutes

Servings: 6

Ingredients:

- For Meatballs:
- 1-pound lean ground beef
- 2 organic eggs, beaten
- 3 tablespoons red onion, minced
- ¼ cup fresh basil leaves, chopped
- 1 (1-inch fresh ginger piece, chopped finely
- 4 garlic cloves, chopped finely
- 3 Thai bird's eye chilies, minced
- 1 teaspoon coconut sugar
- 1 tablespoon red curry paste
- Salt, to taste
- 1 tablespoon fish sauce
- 2 tablespoons coconut oil
- For Curry:
- 1 red onion, chopped
- Salt, to taste
- 4 garlic cloves, minced
- 1 (1-inch) fresh ginger piece, minced
- 2 Thai bird's eye chilies, minced
- 2 tablespoons red curry paste
- 1 (14 oz.) coconut milk
- Salt, to taste
- Freshly ground black pepper, to taste

- Lime wedges, for

Directions:

1. For meatballs in a huge bowl, put all together the ingredients except oil and mix till well combined.
2. Make small balls from the mixture.
3. In a huge skillet, melt coconut oil on medium heat.
4. Add meatballs and cook for about 3-5 minutes or till golden brown all sides.
5. Transfer the meatballs right into a bowl.
6. In the same skillet, add onion and a pinch of salt and sauté for around 5 minutes.
7. Add garlic, ginger, and chilies, and sauté for about 1 minute.
8. Add curry paste and sauté for around 1 minute.
9. Add coconut milk and meatballs and convey to some gentle simmer.
10. Reduce the warmth to low and simmer, covered for around 10 minutes.
11. Serve using the topping of lime wedges.

Nutrition:

Calories: 444

Fat: 15g

Carbohydrates: 20g

Fiber: 2g

Protein: 37g

Beef Meatballs in Tomato Gravy

Preparation Time: 20 minutes

Cooking Time: 37 minutes

Servings: 4

Ingredients:

- For Meatballs:
- 1-pound lean ground beef
- 1 organic egg, beaten
- 1 tablespoon fresh ginger, minced
- 1 garlic oil, minced
- 2 tablespoons fresh cilantro, chopped finely
- 2 tablespoons tomato paste
- 1/3 cup almond meal
- 1 tablespoon ground cumin
- Pinch of ground cinnamon
- Salt, to taste
- Freshly ground black pepper, to taste
- ¼ cup coconut oil
- For Tomato Gravy:
- 2 tablespoons coconut oil
- ½ small onion, chopped
- 2 garlic cloves, chopped
- 1 teaspoon fresh lemon zest, grated finely
- 2 cups tomatoes, chopped finely
- Pinch of ground cinnamon
- 1 teaspoon red pepper flakes, crushed
- ¾ cup chicken broth
- Salt, to taste
- Freshly ground black pepper, to taste
- ¼ cup fresh parsley, chopped

Directions:

1. For meatballs in a sizable bowl, add all ingredients except oil and mix till well combined.
2. Make about 1-inch sized balls from the mixture.
3. In a substantial skillet, melt coconut oil on medium heat.
4. Add meatballs and cook for approximately 3-5 minutes or till golden brown all sides.
5. Transfer the meatballs into a bowl.
6. For gravy in a big pan, melt coconut oil on medium heat.
7. Add onion and garlic and sauté for approximately 4 minutes.
8. Add lemon zest and sauté approximately 1 minute.
9. Add tomatoes, cinnamon, red pepper flakes, and broth and simmer approximately 7 minutes.
10. Stir in salt, black pepper, and meatballs and reduce the warmth to medium-low.
11. Simmer for approximately twenty minutes.
12. Serve hot with all the garnishing of parsley.

Nutrition:

Calories: 404

Fat: 11g

Carbohydrates: 27g

Fiber: 4g

Protein: 38g

Pork with Lemongrass

Preparation Time: 10 minutes

Cooking Time: 30 minutes

Servings: 4

Ingredients:

- 4 pork chops
- 2 tablespoons olive oil
- 2 spring onions, chopped
- A pinch of salt and black pepper
- ½ cup vegetable stock
- 1 stalk lemongrass, chopped
- 2 tablespoons coconut aminos
- 2 tablespoons cilantro, chopped

Directions:

1. Warm a pan with the oil on medium-high heat, add the spring onions, and the meat and brown for 5 minutes.
2. Add the rest of the ingredients, toss, and cook everything over medium heat for 25 minutes.
3. Divide the mix between plates and serve.

Nutrition:

Calories 290

Fat 4

Fiber 6

Carbs 8

Protein 14

Pork with Olives

Preparation Time: 10 minutes

Cooking Time: 40 minutes

Servings: 4

Ingredients:

- 1 yellow onion, chopped
- 4 pork chops
- 2 tablespoons olive oil
- 1 tablespoon sweet paprika
- 2 tablespoons balsamic vinegar
- ¼ cup kalamata olives, pitted and chopped
- 1 tablespoon cilantro, chopped
- Pinch of Sea Salt
- Pinch black pepper

Directions:

1. Warm a pan with the oil on medium heat; add the onion and sauté for 5 minutes.
2. Add the meat and brown for a further 5 minutes.
3. Put the rest of the ingredients, toss, cook over medium heat for 30 minutes, divide between plates and serve.

Nutrition:

Calories 280

Fat 11

Fiber 6

Carbs 10

Protein 21

Pork Chops with Tomato Salsa

Preparation Time: 10 minutes

Cooking Time: 15 minutes

Servings: 4

Ingredients:

- 4 pork chops
- 1 tablespoon olive oil
- 4 scallions, chopped
- 1 teaspoon cumin, ground
- ½ tablespoon hot paprika
- 1 teaspoon garlic powder
- Pinch of sea salt
- Pinch of black pepper
- 1 small red onion, chopped
- 2 tomatoes, cubed
- 2 tablespoons lime juice
- 1 jalapeno, chopped
- ¼ cup cilantro, chopped
- 1 tablespoon lime juice

Directions:

1. Warm a pan with the oil on medium heat, add the scallions and sauté for 5 minutes.
2. Add the meat, cumin paprika, garlic powder, salt, and pepper, toss, cook for 5 minutes on each side, and divide between plates.
3. In a bowl, combine the tomatoes with the remaining ingredients, toss, divide next to the pork chops and serve.

Nutrition:

Calories 313

Fat 23.7

Fiber 1.7

Carbs 5.9

Protein 19.2

Mustard Pork Mix

Preparation Time: 10 minutes

Cooking Time: 35 minutes

Servings: 4

Ingredients:

- 2 shallots, chopped
- 1 pound pork stew meat, cubed
- 2 garlic cloves, minced
- 2 tablespoons olive oil
- ¼ cup Dijon mustard
- 2 tablespoons chives, chopped
- 1 teaspoon cumin, ground
- 1 teaspoon rosemary, dried
- Pinch of sea salt
- Pinch black pepper

Directions:

1. Warm a pan with the oil on medium-high heat, add the shallots and sauté for 5 minutes.
2. Put the meat and brown for a further 5 minutes.
3. Put the rest of the ingredients, toss, and cook on medium heat for 25 minutes more.
4. Divide the mix between plates and serve.

Nutrition:

Calories 280

Fat 14.3

Fiber 6

Carbs 11.8

Protein 17

Pork with Chili Zucchinis and Tomatoes

Preparation Time: 10 minutes

Cooking Time: 35 minutes

Servings: 4

Ingredients:

- 2 tomatoes, cubed
- 2 pounds pork stew meat, cubed
- 4 scallions, chopped
- 2 tablespoons olive oil
- 1 zucchini, sliced
- Juice of 1 lime
- 2 tablespoons chili powder
- ½ tablespoons cumin powder
- Pinch of sea salt
- Pinch black pepper

Directions:

1. Warm a pan with the oil on medium heat, add the scallions and sauté for 5 minutes.
2. Add the meat and brown for 5 minutes more.
3. Add the tomatoes and the other ingredients, toss, cook over medium heat for 25 minutes more, divide between plates and serve.

Nutrition:

Calories 300

Fat 5

Fiber 2

Carbs 12

Protein 14

Pork with Thyme Sweet Potatoes

Preparation Time: 10 minutes

Cooking Time: 35 minutes

Servings: 4

Ingredients:

- 2 sweet potatoes, cut into wedges
- 4 pork chops
- 3 spring onions, chopped
- 1 tablespoon thyme, chopped
- 2 tablespoons olive oil
- 4 garlic cloves, minced
- Pinch of sea salt
- Pinch black pepper
- ½ cup vegetable stock
- ½ tablespoon chives, chopped

Directions:

1. In a roasting pan, combine the pork chops with the potatoes and the other ingredients, toss gently and cook at 390 degrees F for 35 minutes.
2. Divide everything between plates and serve.

Nutrition:

Calories 210

Fat 12.2

Fiber 5.2

Carbs 12

Protein 10

Pork with Pears and Ginger

Preparation Time: 10 minutes

Cooking Time: 35 minutes

Servings: 4

Ingredients:

- 2 green onions, chopped
- 2 tablespoons avocado oil
- 2 pounds pork roast, sliced
- ½ cup coconut aminos
- 1 tablespoon ginger, minced
- 2 pears, cored and cut into wedges
- ¼ cup vegetable stock
- 1 tablespoon chives, chopped

Directions:

1. Warm a pan with the oil on medium heat, add the onions, and the meat and brown for 2 minutes on each side.
2. Add the rest of the ingredients, toss gently, and bake at 390 degrees F for 30 minutes.
3. Divide the mix between plates and serve.

Nutrition:

Calories 220

Fat 13.3

Fiber 2

Carbs 16.5

Protein 8

Parsley Pork and Artichokes

Preparation Time: 10 minutes

Cooking Time: 35 minutes

Servings: 4

Ingredients:

- 2 tbsp. balsamic vinegar
- 1 cup canned artichoke hearts, drained
- 2 tbsp. olive oil
- 2 lb. pork stew meat, cubed
- 2 tbsp. parsley, chopped
- 1 tsp. cumin, ground
- 1 tsp. turmeric powder
- 2 garlic cloves, minced
- Pinch of sea salt
- Pinch black pepper

Directions:

1. Warm a pan with the oil on medium heat, add the meat and brown for 5 minutes.
2. Add the artichokes, the vinegar, and the other ingredients, toss, cook over medium heat for 30 minutes, divide between plates and serve.

Nutrition:

Calories 260

Fat 5

Fiber 4

Carbs 11

Protein 20

Pork with Mushrooms and Cucumbers

Preparation Time: 10 minutes

Cooking Time: 25 minutes

Servings: 4

Ingredients:

- 2 tablespoons olive oil
- ½ teaspoon oregano, dried
- 4 pork chops
- 2 garlic cloves, minced
- Juice of 1 lime
- ¼ cup cilantro, chopped
- Pinch of sea salt
- Pinch black pepper
- 1 cup white mushrooms, halved
- 2 tablespoons balsamic vinegar

Directions:

1. Warm a pan with the oil on medium heat, add the pork chops and brown for 2 minutes on each side.
2. Put the rest of the ingredients, toss, cook on medium heat for 20 minutes, divide between plates and serve.

Nutrition:

Calories 220

Fat 6

Fiber 8

Carbs 14.2

Protein 20

Oregano Pork

Preparation Time: 10 minutes

Cooking Time: 8 hours

Servings: 4

Ingredients:

- 2 pounds pork roast, sliced
- 2 tablespoons oregano, chopped
- ¼ cup balsamic vinegar
- 1 cup tomato paste
- 1 tablespoon sweet paprika
- 1 teaspoon onion powder
- 2 tablespoons chili powder
- 2 garlic cloves, minced
- A pinch of salt and black pepper

Directions:

1. In your slow cooker, combine the roast with the oregano, the vinegar, and the other ingredients, toss, put the lid on and cook on Low for 8 hours.
2. Divide everything between plates and serve.

Nutrition:

Calories 300

Fat 5

Fiber 2

Carbs 12,

Protein 24

Creamy Pork and Tomatoes

Preparation Time: 10 minutes

Cooking Time: 35 minutes

Servings: 4

Ingredients:

- 2 pounds pork stew meat, cubed

- 2 tablespoons avocado oil
- 1 cup tomatoes, cubed
- 1 cup coconut cream
- 1 tablespoon mint, chopped
- 1 jalapeno pepper, chopped
- Pinch of sea salt
- Pinch of black pepper
- 1 tablespoon hot pepper
- 2 tablespoons lemon juice

Directions:

1. Warm a pan with the oil over medium heat, add the meat and brown for 5 minutes.
2. Add the rest of the ingredients, toss, cook over medium heat for 30 minutes more, divide between plates and serve.

Nutrition:

Calories 230

Fat 4

Fiber 6

Carbs 9

Protein 14

Pork with Balsamic Onion Sauce

Preparation Time: 10 minutes

Cooking Time: 35 minutes

Servings: 4

Ingredients:

- 1 yellow onion, chopped
- 4 scallions, chopped
- 2 tablespoons avocado oil
- 1 tablespoon rosemary, chopped
- 1 tablespoon lemon zest, grated
- 2 pounds pork roast, sliced
- 2 tablespoons balsamic vinegar
- ½ cup vegetable stock
- Pinch of sea salt
- Pinch black pepper

Directions:

1. Warm a pan with the oil on medium heat, add the onion, and the scallions and sauté for 5 minutes.
2. Add the rest of the ingredients except the meat, stir, and simmer for 5 minutes.
3. Add the meat, toss gently, cook over medium heat for 25 minutes, divide between plates and serve.

Nutrition:

Calories 217

Fat 11

Fiber 1

Carbs 6

Protein 14

Ground Pork Pan

Preparation Time: 5 minutes

Cooking Time: 15 minutes

Servings: 4

Ingredients:

- 2 garlic cloves, minced
- 2 red chilies, chopped
- 2 tablespoons olive oil
- 2 pounds pork stew meat, ground
- 1 red bell pepper, chopped
- 1 green bell pepper, chopped
- 1 tomato, cubed
- ½ cup mushrooms, halved
- Pinch of sea salt
- Pinch black pepper
- 1 tablespoon basil, chopped
- 2 tablespoons coconut aminos

Directions:

1. Warm a pan with the oil on medium heat, add the garlic, chilies, bell peppers, tomato, and the mushrooms and sauté for 5 minutes.
2. Add the meat and the rest of the ingredients, toss, cook over medium heat for 10 minutes more, divide between plates and serve.

Nutrition:

Calories 200

Fat 3

Fiber 5

Carbs 7

Protein 17

Baked Pork Chops with Cashew

Preparation Time: 10 minutes

Cooking Time: 25 minutes

Servings: 4

Ingredients:

- 4 pork chops
- 2 eggs, whisked
- ½ cup cashew meal
- 1/3 cup sunflower seeds, minced
- 2 teaspoons garlic powder
- A pinch of salt and black pepper
- 1½ teaspoon smoked paprika
- 1 teaspoon chipotle chili powder

Directions:

1. In a bowl, mix the cashew meal with sunflower seeds, garlic powder, salt, pepper, paprika, and chili powder. Dip the pork chops in whisked eggs, then in cashew mix and place them on a lined baking sheet and bake at 400 degrees F for 25 minutes. Divide between plates and serve.
2. Enjoy!

Nutrition:

Calories 251

Fat 12

Fiber 4

Carbs 7

Protein 16

Cranberry Pork

Preparation Time: 10 minutes

Cooking Time: 8 hours

Servings: 4

Ingredients:

- 1 ½ pound pork roast
- ½ teaspoon fresh grated ginger
- 1 tablespoon coconut flour
- A pinch of mustard powder
- A pinch of salt and black pepper
- ½ cup cranberries
- ¼ cup water
- Juice of ½ lemon
- 2 garlic cloves, minced

Directions:

1. In your slow cooker, mix the roast with the ginger, flour, mustard, salt, pepper, cranberries, water, lemon juice, and garlic. Cover then cook on low temperature for at least 8 hours. Slice and divide everything between plates and serve.
2. Enjoy!

Nutrition:

Calories 261

Fat 4

Fiber 8

Carbs 9

Protein 17

Pork Tenderloin with Date Gravy and Mustard

Preparation Time: 10 minutes

Cooking Time: 40 minutes

Servings: 6

Ingredients:

- 1 ½ pound pork tenderloin
- 2 tablespoons veggie stock
- 1/3 cup dates, pitted
- ¼ teaspoon onion powder
- ¼ teaspoon smoked paprika

- 2 tablespoons mustard
- ¼ cup coconut aminos
- Salt and black pepper to the taste

Directions:

1. In your food processor, mix dates with the stock, coconut aminos, mustard, paprika, salt, pepper, and onion powder and blend well. Put pork tenderloin in a baking dish, drizzle the date sauce all over, toss and bake in the oven at 400 degrees F for 40 minutes. Divide between plates and serve.
2. Enjoy!

Nutrition:

Calories 270

Fat 8

Fiber 5

Carbs 13

Protein 24

Creamy Coconut Pork Mix

Preparation Time: 10 minutes

Cooking Time: 25 minutes

Servings: 4

Ingredients:

- 12 mushrooms, sliced
- 1 shallot, chopped
- 1 pound pork meat, cubed
- 2 garlic cloves, minced
- 2 tablespoons olive oil
- ¼ cup Dijon mustard
- 1 ¼ cup coconut cream
- 2 tablespoons chopped parsley
- Pinch of sea salt
- Pinch of black pepper

Directions:

1. Warm a pan with the oil on medium-high heat, add the pork, season with salt and pepper and cook for 4 minutes on each side. Add garlic and shallots, stir and cook for 3 minutes. Add mushrooms, coconut cream, mustard, parsley, salt, and black pepper. Stir, cook for 6 minutes more, divide everything into bowls and serve.

Enjoy!

Nutrition:

Calories 280

Fat 12

Fiber 6

Carbs 10

Protein 14

Pork Kabobs with Bell Peppers

Preparation Time: 10 minutes

Cooking Time: 12 minutes

Servings: 4

Ingredients:

- 2 red bell peppers, chopped
- 2 pounds pork, cubed
- 1 red onion, chopped
- 1 zucchini, sliced
- Juice of 1 lime
- 2 tablespoons chili powder
- 2 tablespoon hot sauce
- ½ tablespoons cumin powder
- ¼ cup olive oil
- ¼ cup salsa
- Pinch of sea salt
- Pinch of black pepper

Directions:

1. In a bowl, whisk the salsa with lime juice, oil, hot sauce, chili powder, cumin, salt, and black pepper. Arrange the meat, bell peppers, zucchini, and onion onto skewers then brush them with the salsa. Place them on the preheated grill over medium-high heat and cook them for 6 minutes on each side. Divide between plates and serve.
2. Enjoy!

Nutrition:

Calories 300

Fat 5

Fiber 2

Carbs 12

Protein 14

Pork and Leeks

Preparation Time: 10 minutes

Cooking Time: 1 hour and 15 minutes

Servings: 4

Ingredients:

- 2 pounds pork, cubed
- 2 carrots, chopped
- 3 leek, chopped
- 1 celery stalk, chopped
- 1 teaspoon black peppercorns
- 2 yellow onions, chopped
- 1 tablespoon chopped parsley
- 2 cups coconut cream
- 1 teaspoon mustard
- A pinch of salt and black pepper

Directions:

1. Put the pork in a pot, add peppercorns, leeks, carrots, celery, onions, and water to cover. Bring to a boil over medium heat and cook for 1 hour stirring often. Add cream, mustard, salt, and pepper, stir, cook for 15 minutes, divide into bowls and serve with parsley on top.
2. Enjoy!

Nutrition:

Calories 250

Fat 7

Fiber 7

Carbs 18

Protein 18

Almond Cinnamon Beef Meatballs

Preparation Time: 10 minutes

Cooking Time: 25 minutes

Servings: 8

Ingredients:

- 2 lbs. ground beef
- 3 eggs
- ½ cup fresh parsley, minced
- 1 tsp cinnamon
- 1 ½ tsp dried oregano
- 2 tsp cumin
- 1 tsp garlic, minced
- 1 cup almond flour
- 1 medium onion, grated
- 1 tsp pepper
- 2 tsp salt

Directions:

1. Set the oven to 400 F.
2. Put all together ingredients into the mixing bowl and mix until well combined.
3. Make small meatballs from mixture and place on a greased baking tray and bake for 20-25 minutes.
4. Serve and enjoy.

Nutrition:

Calories 325

Fat 16 g

Carbohydrates 6 g

Sugar 2 g

Protein 40 g

Cholesterol 54 mg

Creamy Beef Stroganoff

Preparation Time: 10 minutes

Cooking Time: 20 minutes

Servings: 4

Ingredients:

- 1 lb beef strips
- 3/4 cup mushrooms, sliced
- 1 small onion, chopped
- 1 tbsp. butter
- 2 tbsp. olive oil
- 2 tbsp. green onion, chopped
- 1/4 cup sour cream

- 1 cup chicken broth
- Pepper
- Salt

Directions:

1. Add meat in bowl and coat with 1 teaspoon oil, pepper and salt.
2. Heat remaining oil in a pan.
3. Add meat to the pan and cook until golden brown on both sides.
4. Transfer meat in bowl and set aside.
5. Add butter in the same pan.
6. Add onion and cook until onion softened.
7. Add mushrooms and sauté until the liquid is absorbed.
8. Add broth and cook until the sauce thickened.
9. Add sour cream, green onion, and meat and stir well.
10. Cook over medium-high heat for 3-4 minutes.
11. Serve and enjoy.

Nutrition:

Calories 345

Fat 20 g

Carbohydrates 3 g

Sugar 2 g

Protein 35 g

Cholesterol 115 mg

Spicy Beef

Preparation Time: 10 minutes

Cooking Time: 4 Hours

Servings: 6

Ingredients:

- 2 lbs. beef chuck, sliced
- 1 1/2 tsp garlic powder
- 1 cup beef broth
- 1/2 onion, sliced
- 3 bell pepper, chopped
- 1 tbsp. sriracha sauce
- 1/2 cup parsley, chopped
- 1/2 tsp pepper
- 1 1/2 tsp salt

Directions:

1. Place meat into the crockpot.
2. Top with onion and bell pepper.
3. Season with garlic powder, pepper, and salt.
4. Mix together sriracha and broth and pour over meat.
5. Cover and cook on high for 4 hours.
6. Garnish with parsley and serve.

Nutrition:

Calories 326

Fat 12 g

Carbohydrates 6 g

Sugar 3 g

Protein 48 g

Cholesterol 66 mg

Beef Stuffed Cabbage

Preparation Time: 20 minutes

Cooking Time: 1 hour and 15 minutes

Servings: 6-8

Ingredients:

- 1 medium head cabbage
- 1 pound ground beef
- 1 cup cooked brown rice
- 1 organic, free-range egg
- 1 tablespoon dried parsley flakes
- 1/2 teaspoon garlic powder
- 2 celery stalks with leaves
- 1 1/2 cup gluten-free tomato sauce
- 1 tablespoon apple cider vinegar
- 1 tablespoon raw honey

Directions:

1. In a hotpot placed over high heat, add 2 quarts water and cabbage and bring to a boil for 15 minutes, or until outer leaves are tender. Drain the cabbage and allow it to cool completely. Using a paring knife, remove the outer core of the cabbage.

2. Mix together the beef, rice, egg, parsley flakes, garlic powder, and celery in a large
3. Bowl.
4. Stuff the center of each cabbage leaf with 1/3 cup of the beef mixture. Fold sides over, tucking in the sides of the leaf.
5. Pile up the stuffed cabbage leaves in a large pot over medium-low heat, placing the larger leaves on the bottom. Add the tomato sauce, Vinegar, honey, and enough water to cover.
6. Simmer for an hour, or until cabbage is very tender. Add tomato sauce as needed.

Nutrition:

Calories: 208 kcal

Protein: 19.22 g

Fat: 10.05 g

Carbohydrates: 10.6 g

Hot Chicken Meatballs

Preparation Time: 5 minutes

Cooking Time: 21 minutes

Servings: 2

Ingredients:

- 1 pound ground chicken
- Salt and black pepper, to taste
- 2 tablespoons yellow mustard
- ½ cup almond flour
- ¼ cup mozzarella cheese, grated
- ¼ cup hot sauce
- 1 egg

Directions:

1. Preheat oven to 4000F and line a baking tray with parchment paper.
2. In a bowl, combine the chicken, black pepper, mustard, flour, mozzarella cheese, salt, and egg. Form meatballs and arrange them on the baking tray.
3. Cook for 16 minutes, then pour over the hot sauce and bake for 5 more minutes.

Nutrition:

Calories: 487

Fat: 35g

Net Carbs: 4.3g,

Protein: 31.5g

Keto Chicken Enchaladas

Preparation Time: 10 minutes

Cooking Time: 25 minutes

Servings: 6

Ingredients:

- 2 cups gluten-free enchilada sauce
- Chicken
- 1 tablespoon Avocado oil
- 4 cloves Garlic (minced)
- 3 cups Shredded chicken (cooked)
- ¼ cup Chicken broth
- ¼ cup fresh cilantro (chopped)
- Assembly
- 12 Coconut tortillas
- 3/4 cup Colby jack cheese (shredded)
- ¼ cup Green onions (chopped)

Direction:

1. Warm oil at medium to high heat in a large pan. Add the chopped garlic and cook until fragrant for about a minute.
2. Add rice, 1 cup enchilada sauce (half the total), chicken, and coriander. Simmer for 5 minutes.
3. In the meantime, heat the oven to 3750 F. Grease a 9x13 baking dish.
4. In the middle of each tortilla, place ¼ cup chicken mixture. Roll up and place seam side down in the baking dish.
5. Pour the remaining cup enchilada sauce over the enchiladas. Sprinkle with shredded cheese.
6. Bake for 10 to 12 minutes Sprinkle with green onions.

Nutrition:

Calories: 349

Fat: 19g

Net Carbs: 9g

Protein: 31g

Home-Style Chicken Kebab

Preparation Time: 10 minutes

Cooking Time: 10 minutes

Servings: 2

Ingredients:

- 2 Roma tomatoes, chopped
- 1 pound chicken thighs, boneless, skinless and halved
- 2 tablespoons olive oil
- 1/2 cup Greek-style yogurt
- 1 ½ ounce Swiss cheese, sliced

Directions:

1. Place the chicken thighs, yogurt, tomatoes, and olive oil in a glass storage container. You can add in mustard seeds, cinnamon, and sumac if desired.
2. Cover then place in the fridge to marinate for 3 to 4 hours.
3. Thread the chicken thighs onto skewers, creating a thick log shape. Grill the kebabs over medium-high heat for 3 or 4 minutes on each side.
4. Use an instant-read thermometer to check the doneness of meat; it should read about 165 degrees F.
5. Top with the cheese; continue to cook for 4 minutes or until cheesy is melted. Enjoy!

Nutrition:

498 Calories

23.2g Fat

6.2g Carbs

61g Protein

1.7g Fiber

Traditional Hungarian Gulyás

Preparation Time: 10 minutes

Cooking Time: 1 hour and 10 minutes

Servings: 4

Ingredients:

- 1/2 cup celery ribs, chopped
- 1 ripe tomato, pureed
- 1 tablespoon spice mix for goulash
- 2 (1-ounce) slices bacon, chopped
- 1/2 pound duck legs, skinless and boneless

Directions:

1. Heat a heavy-bottomed pot over the medium-high flame; then, fry the bacon for about 3 minutes. Stir in the duck legs and continue to cook until they are nicely browned on all sides.
2. Shred the meat and discard the bones. Set aside.
3. In the pan drippings, sauté the celery for about 3 minutes, stirring with a wide spatula. Add in pureed tomatoes and spice mix for goulash; add in the reserved bacon and meat.
4. Pour 2 cups of water or chicken broth into the pot.
5. Place heat to medium-low, cover, and simmer for 50 minutes more or until everything is cooked thoroughly. Serve warm and enjoy!

Nutrition:

363 Calories

22.3g Fat

5.1g Carbs

33.2g Protein

1.4g Fiber

Greek Chicken Stifado

Preparation Time: 10 minutes

Cooking Time: 35 minutes

Servings: 2

Ingredients:

- 2 ounces bacon, diced
- 1 teaspoon poultry seasoning mix
- 2 vine-ripe tomatoes, pureed
- 3/4 pound whole chicken, boneless and chopped
- 1/2 medium-sized leek, chopped

Directions:

1. Cook the bacon in the preheated skillet over medium-high heat. Fold in the chicken and continue to cook for 5 minutes more until it is no longer pink; set aside.
2. In the same skillet, sauté the leek until it has softened or about 4 minutes. Stir in the poultry seasoning mix and 2 cups of water or chicken broth.
3. Now, reduce the heat to medium-low and continue to simmer for 15 to 20 minutes.
4. Add in tomatoes along with the reserved meat. Continue to cook for a further 13 minutes or until cooked through. Bon appétit!

Nutrition:

352 Calories

14.3g Fat

5.9g Carbs

44.2g Protein

2.4g Fiber

Tangy Chicken with Scallions

Preparation Time: 10 minutes

Cooking Time: 40 minutes

Servings: 4

Ingredients:

- 3 tablespoons butter, melted
- 1 pound chicken drumettes
- 2 tablespoons white wine
- 1 garlic clove, sliced
- 1 tablespoon fresh scallions, chopped

Directions:

1. Arrange the chicken drumettes on a foil-lined baking pan. Brush with melted butter.
2. Add in the garlic and wine. Spice with salt and black pepper to taste. Bake in the preheated oven at 400 degrees F for about 30 minutes or until internal temperature reaches about 165 degrees F.
3. Serve garnished with scallions and enjoy!

Nutrition:

209 Calories

12.2g Fat

0.4g Carbs

23.2g Protein

1.9g Fiber

Double Cheese Italian Chicken

Preparation Time: 10 minutes

Cooking Time: 20 minutes

Servings: 2

Ingredients:

- 2 chicken drumsticks
- 2 cups baby spinach
- 1 teaspoon Italian spice mix
- 1/2 cup cream cheese
- 1 cup Asiago cheese, grated

Directions:

1. In a saucepan, heat 1 tbsp. of oil over medium-high heat. Sear the chicken drumsticks for 7 to 8 minutes or until nicely browned on all sides; reserve.
2. Pour in 1/2 cup of chicken bone broth; add in spinach and continue to cook for 5 minutes more until spinach has wilted.
3. Add in Italian spice mix, cream cheese, Asiago cheese, and reserved chicken drumsticks; partially cover and continue to cook for 5 more minutes. Serve warm.

Nutrition:

589 Calories

46g Fat

5.8g Carbs

37.5g Protein

2g Fiber

Middle Eastern Shish Kebab

Preparation Time: 10 minutes

Cooking Time: 20 minutes

Servings: 5

Ingredients:

- 2 pounds chicken tenders, cut into bite-sized cubes
- 1/2 cup ajran
- 1 tablespoon mustard
- 1/2 cup tomato sauce
- Turkish spice mix

Directions:

1. Place chicken tenders with the remaining ingredients in a ceramic dish. Cover and let it marinate for 4 hours in your refrigerator.
2. Thread chicken tenders onto skewers and place them on the preheated grill until golden brown on all sides approximately 15 minutes.
3. Serve immediately and enjoy!

Nutrition:

274 Calories

10.7g Fat

3.3g Carbs

39.3g Protein

0.8g Fiber

Capocollo and Garlic Chicken

Preparation Time: 10 minutes

Cooking Time: 40 minutes

Servings: 5

Ingredients:

- 2 pounds chicken drumsticks, skinless and boneless, butterflied
- 10 thin slices of capocollo
- 1 garlic clove, peeled and halved
- Coarse sea salt, to taste
- Ground black pepper, to taste
- 1/2 teaspoon smoked paprika

Directions:

1. Rub garlic halves over the surface of chicken drumsticks. Season with paprika, salt, and black pepper.
2. Place a slice of capocollo on each chicken drumsticks and roll them up; secure with kitchen twine.
3. Bake in the oven at 410°F for 30 to 35 minutes until your chicken begins to brown. Bon appétit!

Nutrition:

485 Calories

33.8g Fat

3.6g Carbs

39.2g Protein

1g Fiber

Cheesy Mexican-Style Chicken

Preparation Time: 10 minutes

Cooking Time: 25 minutes

Servings: 6

Ingredients:

- 1 ½ pounds chicken breasts, cut into bite-sized cubes
- 2 ripe tomatoes, pureed
- 4 ounces sour cream
- 6 ounces Cotija cheese, crumbled
- 1 Mexican chili pepper, finely chopped

Directions:

1. Preheat your oven to 390 degrees F.
2. In a saucepan, heat 2 tablespoons of olive oil over medium-high heat. Cook the chicken breasts for about 10 minutes, frequently stirring to ensure even cooking.
3. Then, add in Mexican chili pepper and cook until it has softened.
4. Add in the pureed tomatoes and continue to cook, partially covered, for 4 to 5 minutes—season with the Mexican spice mix. Transfer the mixture to a lightly greased baking dish.
5. Top with the sour cream and Cotija cheese. Bake in the preheated oven for about 15 minutes or until hot and bubbly. Enjoy!

Nutrition:

354 Calories

23.2g Fat

6g Carbs

29.3g Protein

0.6g Fiber

Asian Saucy Chicken

Preparation Time: 10 minutes

Cooking Time: 15 minutes

Servings: 4

Ingredients:

- 1 tablespoon sesame oil
- 4 chicken legs
- 1/4 cup Shaoxing wine
- 2 tablespoons brown erythritol
- 1/4 cup spicy tomato sauce

Directions:

1. Heat the sesame oil in a wok at medium-high heat. Fry the chicken until golden in color; reserve.
2. Add Shaoxing wine to deglaze the pan.
3. Add in erythritol and spicy tomato sauce, and bring the mixture to a boil. Then, immediately reduce the heat to medium-low.
4. Let it simmer for about 10 minutes until the sauce coats the back of a spoon. Add the chicken back to the wok.
5. Continue to cook until the chicken is sticky and golden or about 4 minutes. Enjoy!

Nutrition:

367 Calories

14.7g Fat

3.5g Carbs

51.2g Protein

1.1g Fiber

VEGETABLES AND VEGAN RECIPES

Lentils with Tomatoes and Turmeric

Preparation Time: 10 minutes

Cooking Time: 10 minutes

Servings: 4

Ingredients:

- 2 tbsp. Extra Olive Virgin Oil, plus extra for garnish
- 1 Onion, finely chopped
- 1 tbsp. Ground turmeric
- 1 tsp. Garlic powder
- 1 (14 oz.) can Lentils, drained
- 1 (14 oz.) can Chopped tomatoes, drained
- ½ tsp. Sea salt
- ¼ tsp. Freshly ground black pepper

Directions:

1. In a huge pot on medium-high heat, warm the olive oil until it shimmers.
2. Add the onion and turmeric, and cook for about 5 minutes, occasionally stirring, until soft.
3. Add the garlic powder, lentils, tomatoes, salt, and pepper. Cook for 5 minutes, stirring occasionally. Serve garnished with additional olive oil, if desired

Nutrition:

Calories: 24

Total Fat: 8g

Total Carbs: 34g

Sugar: 5g

Fiber: 15g

Protein: 12g

Sodium 243mg

Whole-Wheat Pasta with Tomato-Basil Sauce

Preparation Time: 15 minutes

Cooking Time: 10 minutes

Servings: 4

Ingredients:

- 2 tbsp. Extra Olive virgin oil
- 1 Onion, minced
- 6 Garlic cloves, minced
- 2 (28 oz.) can crushed tomatoes, undrained
- ½ tsp. Sea salt
- ¼ tsp. Ground black pepper
- ¼ cup Basil leaves, chopped
- 1 (8 oz.) Package whole-wheat pasta

Directions:

1. In a huge pot on medium-high heat, warm the olive oil until it shimmers.
2. Add the onion. Cook for about 5 minutes, occasionally stirring, until soft.
3. Add the garlic. Cook for 30 seconds, stirring constantly.
4. Stir in the tomatoes, salt, and pepper. Bring it to a simmer. Reduce the heat to medium and cook for 5 minutes, stirring occasionally.
5. Pull it out from the heat then stir in the basil. Toss with the pasta.

Nutrition:

Calories: 330

Total Fat: 8g

Total Carbs: 56g

Sugar: 24g

Fiber: 17g

Protein: 14g

Sodium: 1,000mg

Fried Rice with Kale

Preparation Time: 10 minutes

Cooking Time: 12 minutes

Servings: 4

Ingredients:

- 2 tbsp. Extra olive virgin oil
- 8 oz. Tofu, chopped
- 6 Scallion, white and green parts, thinly sliced
- 2 cups Kale, stemmed and chopped
- 3 cups Cooked brown rice
- ¼ cup Stir fry sauce

Directions:

1. In a huge skillet on medium-high heat, warm the olive oil until it shimmers.
2. Add the tofu, scallions, and kale. Cook for 5 to 7 minutes, frequently stirring, until the vegetables are soft.
3. Add the brown rice and stir-fry sauce. Cook for 3 to 5 minutes, occasionally stirring, until heated through.

Nutrition:

Calories: 301

Total Fat: 11g

Total Carbs: 36g

Sugar: 1g

Fiber: 3g

Protein: 16g

Sodium: 2,535mg

Nutty and Fruity Garden Salad

Preparation Time: 10 minutes

Cooking Time: 0 minutes

Servings: 2

Ingredients:

- 6 cups baby spinach
- ½ cup chopped walnuts, toasted
- 1 ripe red pear, sliced
- 1 ripe persimmon, sliced
- 1 teaspoon garlic minced
- 1 shallot, minced
- 1 tablespoon extra-virgin olive oil
- 2 tablespoons fresh lemon juice
- 1 teaspoon wholegrain mustard

Directions:

1. Mix well garlic, shallot, oil, lemon juice, and mustard in a large salad bowl.
2. Add spinach, pear, and persimmon. Toss to coat well.
3. To serve, garnish with chopped pecans.

Nutrition:

Calories 332

Total Fat 21g

Saturated Fat 2g

Total Carbs 37g

Net Carbs 28g

Protein 7g

Sugar: 20g

Fiber 9g

Sodium 75mg

Potassium 864mg

Roasted Root Vegetables

Preparation Time: 10 minutes

Cooking Time: 1 hour and 30 minutes

Servings: 6

Ingredients:

- 2 tbsp. olive oil
- 1 head garlic, cloves separated and peeled
- 1 large turnip, peeled and cut into ½-inch pieces
- 1 medium-sized red onion, cut into ½-inch pieces
- 1 ½ lb. beets, trimmed but not peeled, scrubbed and cut into ½-inch pieces
- 1 ½ lb. Yukon gold potatoes, unpeeled, cut into ½-inch pieces
- 2 ½ lbs. butternut squash, peeled, seeded, cut into ½-inch pieces

Directions:

1. Grease 2 rimmed and large baking sheets. Preheat oven to 425oF.

2. In a huge bowl, mix all ingredients thoroughly.
3. Into the two baking sheets, evenly divide the root vegetables, spread in one layer.
4. Season generously with pepper and salt.
5. Place it into the oven, then roast for at least 1 hour and 15 minutes or until golden brown and tender.
6. Remove from the oven and let it cool for at least 15 minutes before serving.

Nutrition:

Calories 278

Total Fat 5g,

Saturated Fat 1g

Total Carbs 57g

Net Carbs 47g

Protein 6g

Sugar: 15g

Fiber 10g

Sodium 124mg

Potassium 1598mg

Stir-Fried Brussels sprouts and Carrots

Preparation Time: 10 minutes

Cooking Time: 15 minutes

Servings: 6

Ingredients:

- 1 tbsp. cider vinegar
- 1/3 cup water
- 1 lb. Brussels sprouts halved lengthwise
- 1 lb. carrots cut diagonally into ½-inch thick lengths
- 3 tbsp. olive oil, divided
- 2 tbsp. chopped shallot
- ½ tsp pepper
- ¾ tsp salt

Directions:

1. On medium-high fire, place a nonstick medium fry pan and heat 2 tbsp. oil.
2. Ass shallots and cook until softened, around one to two minutes while occasionally stirring.
3. Add pepper salt, Brussels sprouts, and carrots. Stir fry until vegetables start to brown on the edges, around 3 to 4 minutes.
4. Add water, cook, and cover.
5. After 5 to 8 minutes, or when veggies are already soft, add remaining butter.
6. If needed, season with more pepper and salt to taste.
7. Turn off fire, transfer to a platter, serve and enjoy.

Nutrition:

Calories 98

Total Fat 4g

Saturated Fat 2g

Total Carbs 14g

Net Carbs 9g

Protein 3g

Sugar: 5g

Fiber 5g

Sodium 357mg

Potassium 502mg

Curried Veggies and Poached Eggs

Preparation Time: 10 minutes

Cooking Time: 50 minutes

Servings: 4

Ingredients:

- 4 large eggs
- ½ tsp white vinegar
- 1/8 tsp crushed red pepper – optional
- 1 cup water
- 1 14-oz can chickpeas, drained
- 2 medium zucchinis, diced

- ½ lb. sliced button mushrooms
- 1 tbsp. yellow curry powder
- 2 cloves garlic, minced
- 1 large onion, chopped
- 2 tsp extra virgin olive oil

Directions:

1. On medium-high fire, place a large saucepan and heat oil.
2. Sauté onions until tender around four to five minutes.
3. Put the garlic and continue sautéing for another half minute.
4. Add curry powder, stir and cook until fragrant around one to two minutes.
5. Add mushrooms, mix, cover, and cook for 5 to 8 minutes or until mushrooms are tender and have released their liquid.
6. Add red pepper if using, water, chickpeas, and zucchini. Mix well to combine and bring to a boil.
7. Once boiling, reduce fire to a simmer, cover, and cook until zucchini is tender around 15 to 20 minutes of simmering.
8. Meanwhile, in a small pot filled with 3-inches deep water, bring to a boil on a high fire.
9. When boiling, lower the heat temperature to a simmer and add vinegar.
10. Slowly add one egg, slipping it gently into the water. Allow to simmer until egg is cooked, around 3 to 5 minutes.
11. Take off the egg using a slotted spoon and transfer to a plate, one plate one egg.
12. Repeat the process with remaining eggs.
13. Once the veggies are done cooking, divide evenly into 4 servings and place one serving per plate of the egg.
14. Serve and enjoy.

Nutrition:

Calories 254

Total Fat 9g

Saturated Fat 2g

Total Carbs 30g

Net Carbs 21g

Protein 16g

Sugar: 7g

Fiber 9g

Sodium 341mg

Potassium 480mg

Braised Kale

Preparation Time: 10 minutes

Cooking Time: 15 minutes

Servings: 3

Ingredients:

- 2 to 3 tbsp. water
- 1 tbsp. coconut oil
- ½ sliced red pepper
- 2 stalk celery (sliced to ¼-inch thick)
- 5 cups of chopped kale

Directions:

1. Heat a pan over medium heat.
2. Add coconut oil and sauté the celery for at least five minutes.
3. Add the kale and red pepper.
4. Add a tablespoon of water.
5. Let the vegetables wilt for a few minutes. Add a tablespoon of water if the kale starts to stick to the pan.
6. Serve warm.

Nutrition:

Calories 61

Total Fat 5g

Saturated Fat 1g

Total Carbs 3g

Net Carbs 2g

Protein 1g

Sugar: 1g

Fiber 1g

Sodium 20mg

Potassium 185mg

Braised Leeks, Cauliflower and Artichoke Hearts

Preparation Time: 10 minutes

Cooking Time: 10 minutes

Servings: 4

Ingredients:

- 2 tbsp. coconut oil
- 2 garlic cloves, chopped
- 1 ½ cup artichoke hearts
- 1 ½ cups chopped leeks
- 1 ½ cups cauliflower flowerets

Directions:

1. In a skillet, warm oil on medium-high heat temperature.
2. Put the garlic and sauté for one minute. Add the vegetables and constantly stir until the vegetables are cooked.
3. Serve with roasted chicken, fish or pork.

Nutrition:

Calories 111

Total Fat 7g

Saturated Fat 1g

Total Carbs 12g

Net Carbs 8g

Protein 3g

Sugar: 2g

Fiber 4g

Sodium 65mg

Potassium 305mg

Celery Root Hash Browns

Preparation Time: 10 minutes

Cooking Time: 10 minutes

Servings: 4

Ingredients:

- 4 tbsp. coconut oil
- ½ tsp sea salt
- 2 to 3 medium celery roots

Directions:

1. Scrub the celery root clean and peel it using a vegetable peeler.
2. Grate the celery root in a manual grater.
3. In a skillet, add oil and heat it over medium heat.
4. Place the grated celery root on the skillet and sprinkle with salt.
5. Let it cook for 10 minutes on each side or until the grated celery turns brown.
6. Serve warm.

Nutrition:

Calories 160

Total Fat 14g

Saturated Fat 3g

Total Carbs 10g

Net Carbs 7g

Protein 1.5g

Sugar: 0g

Fiber 3g

Sodium 314mg

Potassium 320mg

Braised Carrots 'n Kale

Preparation Time: 10 minutes

Cooking Time: 10 minutes

Servings: 2

Ingredients:

- 1 tablespoon coconut oil
- 1 onion, sliced thinly
- 5 cloves of garlic, minced
- 3 medium carrots, sliced thinly
- 10 ounces of kale, chopped
- ½ cup water
- Salt and pepper to taste
- A dash of red pepper flakes

Directions:
1. Warm oil in a skillet over medium flame and sauté the onion and garlic until fragrant.
2. Toss in the carrots and stir for 1 minute. Add the kale and water. Season with salt and pepper to taste.
3. Close the lid and allow to simmer for 5 minutes.
4. Sprinkle with red pepper flakes.
5. Serve and enjoy.

Nutrition:

Calories 161

Total Fat 8g

Saturated Fat 1g

Total Carbs 20g

Net Carbs 14g

Protein 8g

Sugar: 6g

Fiber 6g

Sodium 63mg

Potassium 900mg

Stir-Fried Gingery Veggies

Preparation Time: 10 minutes

Cooking Time: 10 minutes

Servings: 4

Ingredients:

- 1 tablespoon oil
- 3 cloves of garlic, minced
- 1 onion, chopped
- 1 thumb-size ginger, sliced
- 1 tablespoon water
- 1 large carrots, peeled and julienned and seedless
- 1 large green bell pepper, julienned and seedless
- 1 large yellow bell pepper, julienned and seedless
- 1 large red bell pepper, julienned and seedless
- 1 zucchini, julienned
- Salt and pepper to taste

Directions:
1. Heat oil in a nonstick saucepan over a high flame and sauté the garlic, onion, and ginger until fragrant.
2. Stir in the rest of the ingredients.
3. Keep on stirring for at least 5 minutes until vegetables are tender.
4. Serve and enjoy.

Nutrition:

Calories 70

Total Fat 4g

Saturated Fat 1g

Total Carbs 9g

Net Carbs 7g

Protein 1g

Sugar: 4g

Fiber 2g

Sodium 273mg

Potassium 263mg

Cauliflower Fritters

Preparation Time: 10 minutes

Cooking Time: 15 minutes

Servings: 6

Ingredients:

- 1 large cauliflower head, cut into florets
- 2 eggs, beaten
- ½ teaspoon turmeric
- ½ teaspoon salt
- ¼ teaspoon black pepper
- 1 tablespoon coconut oil

Directions:
1. Put the cauliflower florets in a pot with water and bring to a boil. Cook until

tender, around 5 minutes of boiling. Drain well.
2. Place the cauliflower, eggs, turmeric, salt, and pepper into the food processor.
3. Pulse until the mixture becomes coarse.
4. Transfer into a bowl. Using your hands, form six small flattened balls and place in the fridge for at least 1 hour until the mixture hardens.
5. Warm the oil in a nonstick pan and fry the cauliflower patties for 3 minutes on each side.
6. Serve and enjoy.

Nutrition:

Calories 53

Total Fat 6g

Saturated Fat 2g

Total Carbs 2

Net Carbs 1g

Protein 3g

Sugar: 1g

Fiber 1g

Sodium 228mg

Potassium 159mg

Stir-Fried Squash

Preparation Time: 10 minutes

Cooking Time: 10 minutes

Servings: 4

Ingredients:

- 1 tablespoon olive oil
- 3 cloves of garlic, minced
- 1 butternut squash, seeded and sliced
- 1 tablespoon coconut aminos
- 1 tablespoon lemon juice
- 1 tablespoon water
- Salt and pepper to taste

Directions:

1. Heat oil over medium flame and sauté the garlic until fragrant.
2. Stir in the squash for another 3 minutes before adding the rest of the ingredients.
3. Close the lid and allow to simmer for 5 more minutes or until the squash is soft.
4. Serve and enjoy.

Nutrition:

Calories 83

Total Fat 3g

Saturated Fat 0.5g

Total Carbs 14g

Net Carbs 12g

Protein 2g

Sugar: 1g

Fiber 2g

Sodium 8mg

Potassium 211mg

Cauliflower Hash Brown

Preparation Time: 10 minutes

Cooking Time: 20 minutes

Servings: 6

Ingredients:

- 4 eggs, beaten
- ½ cup coconut milk
- ½ teaspoon dry mustard
- Salt and pepper to taste
- 1 large head cauliflower, shredded

Directions:

1. Place all together ingredients in a mixing bowl and mix until well combined.
2. Place a nonstick fry pan and heat over medium flame.
3. Add a large dollop of cauliflower mixture in the skillet.

4. Fry one side for 3 minutes, flip and cook the other side for a minute, like a pancake. Repeat process to remaining ingredients.
5. Serve and enjoy.

Nutrition:

Calories 102

Total Fat 8g

Saturated Fat 1g

Total Carbs 4g

Net Carbs 3g

Protein 5g

Sugar: 2g

Fiber 1g

Sodium 63mg

Potassium 251mg

Sweet Potato Puree

Preparation Time: 10 minutes

Cooking Time: 15 minutes

Servings: 5

Ingredients:

- 2 pounds sweet potatoes, peeled
- 1 ½ cups water
- 5 Medjool dates, pitted and chopped

Directions:

1. Place water and potatoes in a pot.
2. Close the lid and boil for at least 15 minutes until the potatoes are soft.
3. Drain the potatoes and place them in a food processor together with the dates.
4. Pulse until smooth.
5. Serve and enjoy.

Nutrition:

Calories 172

Total Fat 0.2g

Saturated Fat 0g

Total Carbs 41g

Net Carbs 36g

Protein 3g

Sugar: 14g

Fiber 5g

Sodium 10mg

Potassium 776mg

Curried Okra

Preparation Time: 10 minutes

Cooking Time: 12 minutes

Servings: 4

Ingredients:

- 1 lb. small to medium okra pods, trimmed
- ¼ tsp curry powder
- ½ tsp kosher salt
- 1 tsp finely chopped serrano chile
- 1 tsp ground coriander
- 1 tbsp. canola oil
- ¾ tsp brown mustard seeds

Direction:

1. On medium-high fire, place a large and heavy skillet and cook mustard seeds until fragrant, around 30 seconds.
2. Add canola oil. Add okra, curry powder, salt, chile, and coriander. Sauté for a minute while stirring every once in a while.
3. Cover and cook low fire for at least 8 minutes. Stir occasionally.
4. Uncover, increase the fire to medium-high and cook until okra is lightly browned, around 2 minutes more.
5. Serve and enjoy.

Nutrition:

Calories 78

Total Fat 6g

Saturated Fat 0.7

Total Carbs 6g

Net Carbs 3g

Protein 2g

Sugar: 3g

Fiber 3g

Sodium 553mg

Potassium 187mg

Vegetable Potpie

Preparation Time: 10 minutes

Cooking Time: 10 minutes

Servings: 8

Ingredients:

- 1 recipe pastry for double-crust pie
- 2 tbsp. cornstarch
- 1 tsp ground black pepper
- 1 tsp kosher salt
- 3 cups vegetable broth
- 1 cup fresh green beans, snapped into ½ inch
- 2 cups cauliflower florets
- 2 stalks celery, sliced ¼ inch wide
- 2 potatoes, peeled and diced
- 2 large carrots, diced
- 1 clove garlic, minced
- 8 oz. mushroom
- 1 onion, chopped
- 2 tbsp. olive oil

Directions:

1. In a large saucepan, sauté garlic in oil until lightly browned, add onions and continue sautéing until soft and translucent.
2. Add celery, potatoes, and carrots and sauté for 3 minutes.
3. Add vegetable broth, green beans, and cauliflower and bring to a boil. Slow fire and simmer until vegetables are slightly tender. Season with pepper and salt.
4. Mix ¼ cup water and cornstarch in a small bowl. Stir until the mixture is smooth and has no lumps. Then pour into the vegetable pot while mixing constantly.
5. Continue mixing until soup thickens, around 3 minutes. Remove from fire.
6. Meanwhile, roll out pastry dough and place on an oven-safe 11x7 baking dish. Pour the vegetable filling and then cover with another pastry dough. Seal and flute the edges of the dough and prick the top dough with a fork in several places.
7. Bake the dish in a preheated oven of 425oF for 30 minutes or until the crust has turned a golden brown.

Nutrition:

Calories 202

Total Fat 10g

Saturated Fat 2g

Total Carbs 26g

Net Carbs 23g

Protein 4g

Sugar: 3g

Fiber 3g

Sodium 466m

Potassium 483mg

Grilled Eggplant Roll-Ups

Preparation Time: 5 minutes

Cooking Time: 3 minutes

Servings: 8

Ingredients:

- 1 tomato
- 2 tbsps. chopped fresh basil
- 2 tbsps. olive oil
- 4 oz. mozzarella cheese
- 1 eggplant, sliced

Directions:

1. Thinly slice the tomato and mozzarella and reserve.
2. Rub the eggplant slices with olive oil and grill them in a skillet for 3 minutes per side.
3. Lay a slice of cheese and tomato on top of each zucchini.
4. Sprinkle basil and black pepper and grill for 3 minutes to soften the cheese.
5. Remove the slices and set them on a plate.
6. Roll each of the slices before serving.
7. Enjoy.

Nutrition:

Calories: 50 kcal

Protein: 6.12 g

Fat: 0.92 g

Carbohydrates: 5.14 g

Eggplant Gratin

Preparation Time: 10 minutes

Cooking Time: 40 minutes

Servings: 6

Ingredients:

- ¾ c. Gruyere cheese
- ½ tsp. black pepper
- 1 c. heavy cream
- 2 sliced eggplant
- 3 tbsps. Olive oil
- ½ c. tomato sauce
- ½ tsp. salt
- 3 oz. crumbled feta cheese
- 1 tsp. Chopped thyme
- ¼ c. chopped fresh basil
- 1 tbsp. chopped chives

Directions:

1. Heat the oven to about 3750F.
2. Cover the slices of eggplant with salt, pepper, and olive oil and bake them for 20 minutes on a baking pan.
3. Meanwhile, put feta cheese and heavy cream in a pot and boil them.
4. Remove the pot from heat and add chives and thyme, then stir before setting aside.
5. Spread the tomato sauce on a medium-sized pan and lay the eggplant slices over it.
6. Cover eggplant slices with basil and Gruyere cheese.
7. Add another layer of the remaining eggplant and cover it with the heavy cream mixture.
8. Bake for about 20 minutes and serve.

Nutrition:

Calories: 217 kcal

Protein: 8.37 g

Fat: 15.47 g

Carbohydrates: 13.66 g

Veggie Stuffed Peppers

Preparation Time: 5 minutes

Cooking Time: 0 minutes

Servings: 6

Ingredients:

- 1 c. quartered cherry tomatoes
- 1 tsp. black pepper
- 3 tbsps. Dijon mustard
- ¼ c. chopped fresh parsley
- 3 halved green bell peppers
- ½ peeled and sliced cucumber
- 1 bunch sliced scallions
- 2 tbsps. rice wine vinegar
- ½ tsp. Salt
- ½ c. Greek yogurt
- 4 diced celery stalks

Directions:

1. In a medium bowl, combine salt, pepper, yogurt, rice wine vinegar, and mustard.
2. Add cucumbers, celery, tomatoes, and scallions and combine well.
3. Stuff the mix into the pepper halves.
4. Add the chopped parsley to garnish.
5. Serve immediately and enjoy

Nutrition:

Calories: 41 kcal

Protein: 2.49 g

Fat: 1.78 g

Carbohydrates: 4.3 g

Cheesy Gratin Zucchini

Preparation Time: 15 minutes

Cooking Time: 45 minutes

Servings: 9

Ingredients:

- Spray oil
- ½ c. heavy cream
- 1 tsp. rosemary
- 1 tsp. turmeric
- 1 tsp. black pepper
- 2 tbsps. olive oil
- 1 peeled and sliced small white onion
- 4 c. sliced raw zucchini
- 1 tbsp. garlic powder
- 2 c. shredded pepper jack cheese
- ½ tsps. salt

Directions:

1. Heat the oven to about 3750F.
2. Grease the baking tray with cooking oil
3. Add a third of the zucchini and onion slices on the pan and sprinkle seasonings and half of the pepper jack cheese.
4. Add one more layer of zucchini slices, and onion then season with pepper, salt, and the remaining pepper jack cheese.
5. Lay on the remaining zucchini slices and onions.
6. Microwave garlic powder, butter, and heavy cream for a minute to melt the butter and mix well.
7. Pour the mixture over the top layer of slices
8. Bake uncovered for 45 minutes
9. Serve and enjoy

Nutrition:

Calories: 151 kcal

Protein: 8.49 g

Fat: 12.08 g

Carbohydrates: 2.49 g

Caprese Tomatoes with Basil Dressing

Preparation Time: 10 minutes

Cooking Time: 30 minutes

Servings: 4

Ingredients:

- 1 tsp. minced garlic
- 2 tbsps. Olive oil
- ½ tsp. black pepper
- 1 tbsp. olive oil
- 2 tbsps. Balsamic vinegar
- ½ tsp. ground thyme
- 2 tbsps. lemon juice
- 1 ½ tbsps. Dried basil
- ½ tsp. salt
- 1 tbsp. Garlic powder
- ½ tsp. salt
- 4 thin mozzarella cheese slices

Directions:

1. Heat the oven to 3500F.
2. Cut the core end of the tomatoes then slice each tomato in half.
3. Put the tomato halves on a cookie sheet with the inside up.
4. Add a coating of pepper, salt, balsamic vinegar, olive oil mixture to each of the halves
5. Bake the tomato halves for about 25 minutes
6. Lay one of the thin mozzarella cheese slices on each tomato bottom half and bake for 5 minutes more.
7. Put crushed basil on each of the tomatoes and place the top half back on the bottom half.
8. Drizzle the dressing over the tomatoes before serving.
9. Enjoy.

Nutrition:

Calories: 66 kcal

Protein: 2.17 g

Fat: 4.98 g

Carbohydrates: 3.92 g

Korean Barbecue Tofu

Preparation Time: 10 minutes

Cooking Time: 15 minutes

Servings: 3

Ingredients:

- 1 tbsps. olive oil
- 2 tsp onion powder
- 4 garlic cloves, minced
- 2 tsp dry mustard
- 3 tbsp. brown sugar
- ½ cup soy sauce
- 1 ½ lb. firm tofu, sliced to ¼-inch cubes

Directions:

1. In a re-sealable bag, mix all ingredients except for tofu and oil. Mix well until sugar is dissolved.
2. Add sliced tofu and slowly turn bag to mix. Seal bag and place flatly inside the ref for an hour.
3. After an hour, turn the bag to the other side and marinate for another hour.
4. To cook, in a nonstick fry pan, heat oil on medium-high fire. Add tofu and stir fry until sides are browned.
5. Serve and enjoy.

Nutrition:

Calories 437

Fat 25g

Carbs 23g

Protein 40g

Fiber 6g

Fruit Bowl with Yogurt Topping

Preparation Time: 15 minutes

Cooking Time: 0 minutes

Servings: 6

Ingredients:

- ¼ cup golden brown sugar
- 2/3 cup minced fresh ginger
- 1 16-oz Greek yogurt
- ¼ tsp ground cinnamon
- 2 tbsp. honey
- ½ cup dried cranberries
- 3 navel oranges
- 2 large tangerines
- 1 pink grapefruit, peeled

Directions:

1. Into sections, break tangerines and grapefruit.
2. Slice tangerine sections in half and grapefruit sections into thirds. Place all sliced fruits and its juices in a large bowl.
3. Peel oranges, remove the pith, slice into ¼-inch thick rounds, and then cut into quarters. Transfer to the bowl of fruit along with juices. In a bowl, add cinnamon, honey, and ¼ cup of cranberries. Place in the ref for an hour. In a medium bowl, mix ginger and yogurt. Place on top of the fruit bowl, drizzle with remaining cranberries and brown sugar.
4. Serve and enjoy.

Nutrition:

Calories 171 Fat 1g

Carbs 35g

Protein 9g

Fiber 3g

Collard Green Wrap

Preparation Time: 10 minutes

Cooking Time: 0 minutes

Servings: 4

Ingredients:

- ½ block feta, cut into 4 (1-inch thick) strips (4-oz)
- ½ cup purple onion, diced
- ½ medium red bell pepper, julienned
- 1 medium cucumber, julienned
- 4 large cherry tomatoes, halved
- 4 large collard green leaves, washed
- 8 whole kalamata olives, halved

Sauce **Ingredients:**

- 1 cup low-fat plain Greek yogurt
- 1 tablespoon white vinegar

- 1 teaspoon garlic powder
- 2 tablespoons minced fresh dill
- 2 tablespoons olive oil
- 2.5-ounces cucumber, seeded and grated (¼-whole)
- Salt and pepper to taste

Directions:

1. Make the sauce first: make sure to squeeze out all the excess liquid from the cucumber after grating. In a small bowl, put all together the sauce ingredients and mix thoroughly then refrigerate.
2. Prepare and slice all wrap ingredients.
3. On a flat surface, spread one collard green leaf. Spread 2 tablespoons of Tzatziki sauce in the middle of the leaf.
4. Layer ¼ of each of the tomatoes, feta, olives, onion, pepper, and cucumber. Place them on the center of the leaf, like piling them high instead of spreading them.
5. Fold the leaf-like you would a burrito. Repeat process for remaining ingredients.
6. Serve and enjoy.

Nutrition:

Calories 463

Fat 31g

Carbs 31g

Protein 20g

Fiber 7g

Zucchini Garlic Fries

Preparation Time: 10 minutes

Cooking Time: 20 minutes

Servings: 6

Ingredients:

- ¼ teaspoon garlic powder
- ½ cup almond flour
- 2 large egg whites, beaten
- 3 medium zucchinis, sliced into fry sticks
- Salt and pepper to taste

Directions:

1. Set the oven to 400F.
2. Mix all together the ingredients in a bowl until the zucchini fries are well coated.
3. Place fries on the cookie sheet and spread evenly.
4. Put in the oven and cook for 20 minutes.
5. Halfway through cooking time, stir-fries.

Nutrition:

Calories 11

Fat 0.1g,

Carbs 1g

Protein1.5 g

Fiber 0.5g

Mashed Cauliflower

Preparation Time: 10 minutes

Cooking Time: 10 minutes

Servings: 3

Ingredients:

- 1 cauliflower head
- 1 tablespoon olive oil
- ½ tsp salt
- ¼ tsp dill
- Pepper to taste
- 2 tbsp. low-fat milk

Directions:

1. Place a small pot of water to a boil.
2. Chop cauliflower in florets.
3. Add florets to boiling water and boil uncovered for 5 minutes. Turn off fire and let it sit for 5 minutes more.
4. In a blender, add all ingredients except for cauliflower and blend to mix well.
5. Drain cauliflower well and add it to a blender. Puree until smooth and creamy.
6. Serve and enjoy.

Nutrition:

Calories 78

Fat 5g

Carbs 6g

Protein 2g

Fiber 2g

Stir-Fried Eggplant

Preparation Time: 10 minutes

Cooking Time: 10 minutes

Servings: 2

Ingredients:

- 1 tablespoon coconut oil
- 2 eggplants, sliced into 3-inch in length
- 4 cloves of garlic, minced
- 1 onion, chopped
- 1 teaspoon ginger, grated
- 1 teaspoon lemon juice, freshly squeezed
- ½ tsp salt
- ½ tsp pepper

Directions:

1. Heat oil in a nonstick saucepan.
2. Pan-fry the eggplants for 2 minutes on all sides.
3. Add the garlic and onions until fragrant, around 3 minutes.
4. Stir in the ginger, salt, pepper, and lemon juice.
5. Add a ½ cup of water and bring to a simmer. Cook until eggplant is tender.

Nutrition:

Calories 232

Fat 8g

Carbs 41g

Protein 7g

Fiber 18g

Sautéed Garlic Mushrooms

Preparation Time: 10 minutes

Cooking Time: 10 minutes

Servings: 4

Ingredients:

- 1 tablespoon olive oil
- 3 cloves of garlic, minced
- 16 ounces fresh brown mushrooms, sliced
- 7 ounces fresh shiitake mushrooms, sliced
- ½ tsp salt
- ½ tsp pepper or more to taste

Directions:

1. Place a nonstick saucepan on medium-high fire and heat pan for a minute.
2. Add oil and heat for 2 minutes.
3. Stir in garlic and sauté for a minute.
4. Add remaining ingredients and stir fry until soft and tender, around 5 minutes.
5. Turn off fire, let mushrooms rest while the pan is covered for 5 minutes.
6. Serve and enjoy.

Nutrition:

Calories 95

Fat 4g

Carbs 14g

Protein 3g,

Fiber 4g

Stir-Fried Asparagus and Bell Pepper

Preparation Time: 10 minutes

Cooking Time: 10 minutes

Servings: 6

Ingredients:

- 1 tablespoon olive oil
- 4 cloves of garlic, minced
- 1-pound fresh asparagus spears, trimmed
- 2 large red bell peppers, seeded and julienned
- ½ teaspoon thyme
- 5 tablespoons water
- ½ tsp salt
- ½ tsp pepper or more to taste

Directions:

1. Place a nonstick saucepan on high fire and heat pan for a minute.

2. Add oil and heat for 2 minutes.
3. Stir in garlic and sauté for a minute.
4. Add remaining ingredients and stir fry until soft and tender, around 6 minutes.
5. Turn off fire, let veggies rest while the pan is covered for 5 minutes.

Nutrition:

Calories 45

Fat 2g

Carbs 5g, Net

Protein 2g

Fiber 2g

Wild Rice with Spicy Chickpeas

Preparation Time: 15 minutes

Cooking Time: 60 minutes

Servings: 6-7

Ingredients:

- 1 Cup basmati rice
- 1 Cup wild rice
- Salt & pepper to taste
- 4tbsp Olive oil
- 1tbsp Garlic powder
- 2tsp cumin powder
- ¼ Cup sunflower oil
- 3 Cups chickpeas
- 1tsp Flour
- 1tsp Curry powder
- 3tsp Paprika powder
- 1tsp Dill
- 3tbsp parsley (chopped)
- 1 Medium onion (thinly sliced)
- 2 Cups currants

Directions:

1. For cooking wild rice, fill the half pot with water and bring it to boil. Put the rice and let it simmer for at least 40 minutes.
2. Take olive in the pot and heat it on medium flame. Now add cumin powder, salt, and water and bring it to boil. Then add basmati rice and cook for 20 minutes.
3. Leave rice for cooking and prepare spicy chickpeas. Heat 2tbsp of olive oil in the pan and toss chickpeas, garlic powder, salt & pepper, cumin, and paprika powder in it.
4. In another pan, cook onion with sunflower oil until it is golden brown and add flour.
5. Mix flour and onion with your hands.
6. For serving, place both types of rice in a bowl with spicy chickpeas and fry the onion. Garnish it with parsley and herbs.

Nutrition:

Calories: 647 kcal

Protein: 25.43 g

Fat: 25.72 g

Carbohydrates: 88.3 g

Cashew Pesto & Parsley with veggies

Preparation Time: 15 minutes

Cooking Time: 10 minutes

Servings: 3-4

Ingredients:

- 3 Zucchini (sliced)
- 8 Soaked bamboo skewers
- 2 Red capsicums
- ¼Cup olive oil
- 750grams Eggplant
- 4 Lemon cheeks

For Serving

- Couscous salad

For Preparing Cashew Pesto

- ½Cup cashew (roasted)
- ½ Cup parsley
- 2 Cup grated parmesan
- 2tbsp Lime juice
- ¼Cup olive oil

Directions:

1. Toss capsicum, eggplant, and zucchini with oil and salt and thread it onto skewers.

2. Cook bamboo sticks for 6-8 minutes on a barbecue grill pan on medium heat.
3. Also, grill lemon cheeks from both sides.
4. For preparing cashew pesto, combine all ingredients in the food processor and blend.
5. For serving, place grill skewers in a plate with grill lemon slices and drizzle some cashew pesto over it.

Nutrition:

Calories: 666 kcal

Protein: 23.96 g

Fat: 48.04 g

Carbohydrates: 41.4 g

Spicy Chickpeas with Roasted Vegetables

Preparation Time: 10 minutes

Cooking Time: 25 minutes

Servings: 2-3

Ingredients:

- 1 Large carrot (peeled)
- 2tbsp Sunflower oil
- 1 Cauliflower head
- 1tbsp ground cumin
- ½ Red onions (diced)
- 1 Red pepper (deseeded)
- 400g Can chickpeas

Directions:

1. Line a large baking tine in the preheated oven (at 240C).
2. Cut all the vegetables and toss with salt, pepper, and onion.
3. In a bowl, whisk olive oil, pepper, and cumin powder.
4. Add all veggies in the bowl and toss.
5. Transfer vegetables on baking tin and baked it almost for 15 minutes.
6. Now add chickpeas and stir.
7. Return to the oven and bake it for the next 10 minutes.
8. Serve it with toast bread.

Nutrition:

Calories: 348 kcal

Protein: 14.29 g

Fat: 15.88 g

Carbohydrates: 40.65 g

Special Vegetable Kitchree

Preparation Time: 10 minutes

Cooking Time: 46 minutes

Servings: 5-6

Ingredients:

- ½Cup brown grain rice
- 1 Cup dry lentil or split peas
- 1tsp Sea salt, cumin powder, ground turmeric, ground fenugreek, and ground coriander
- 3tbsp Coconut oil
- 1tbsp Ginger
- 5 Cups vegetable stock
- 1 Cup baby spinach
- 1 Medium Zucchini (roughly chopped)
- 1 Small crown broccoli (chopped)
- Greek Yogurt (for serving)

Directions:

1. In a saucepan, warm the coconut oil on medium flame and add ginger, cumin, coriander, fennel seeds, fenugreek, and turmeric and cook it for 1 minute.
2. Now add lentils and brown rice in the spices and stir. Pour the vegetable stock in it and simmer for 40 minutes.
3. Add broccoli in the tender rice and lentils and cook for another 5 minutes. Now add other vegetables and stir for 10 minutes.
4. For serving, pour some Greek yogurt over vegetable kitcheree and serve hot.

Nutrition:

Calories: 1728 kcal

Protein: 4.13 g

Fat: 190.35 g

Carbohydrates: 17.31 g

Mashed Sweet Potato Burritos

Preparation Time: 15 minutes

Cooking Time: 60 minutes

Servings: 4

Ingredients:

- 4 Tortillas
- 1 Avocado
- 1tsp Capsicum, paprika powder, and oregano
- Salt & pepper as needed
- ½Cup sour cream
- 1 Can diced tomato
- 2 Sweet Potatoes (mashed)
- 2 Garlic cloves (minced)
- 1tbsp Cumin powder
- Fresh cilantro or parsley

Directions:

1. Before mashing roast sweet potatoes for 45 minutes in an already preheated (at 160°C) oven.
2. Cook onion in a frying pan with oil on medium heat. Add garlic cloves and cook for 1 minute.
3. Add 1 tin of tomatoes and leave it to simmer for 10 minutes. In halfway through, add salt & pepper, paprika, cumin powder, and black beans.
4. After 5 minutes, add avocado in it.
5. Now make burritos, mix one scoop of mashed potatoes with avocado filling.
6. Wrap your tortilla and grill it in the oven at 200C for 30seconds.
7. Serve it with sour cream and hot sauce.

Nutrition:

Calories: 442 kcal

Protein: 12.05 g

Fat: 15.43 g

Carbohydrates: 66.85 g

Zucchini & Pepper Lasagna

Preparation Time: 10 minutes

Cooking Time: 60 minutes

Servings: 1

Ingredients:

- ½ pack Soft Tofu
- ½ pack Firm Tofu
- ½ Box Wholegrain Lasagna Sheet
- 1 cup Baby spinach
- 1 cup Almond milk
- ¼ tsp. Garlic powder
- ½ cup Lemon Juice
- 1 ½
- tbsp. Fresh basil, chopped
- 1 can Chopped Tomato
- Pinch ground black pepper
- 1 Zucchini, diced
- 1 Red pepper, diced (optional)

Directions:

1. Set the oven to 325°F.
2. In a blender, process the soft and firm tofu, garlic powder, almond milk, basil, lemon juice, and pepper until smooth.
3. Toss in the spinach and zucchini for the last 30 seconds.
4. Put about 1/3 of the chopped tomatoes at the bottom of an oven dish.
5. Top the sauce with 1/3 of the lasagna sheets and then 1/3 of the spinach/tofu mixture.
6. Repeat the layers finishing with the chopped tomatoes on top.
7. Cook for at least 1 hour, up to the pasta sheets are soft.
8. Serve with a lovely side salad and enjoy.

Nutrition:

Calories: 337 kcal

Protein: 19.17 g

Fat: 15.29 g

Carbohydrates: 37.01 g

Toasted Cumin Crunch

Preparation Time: 10 minutes

Cooking Time: 1 minute

Servings: 1

Ingredients:

- 1 tbsp. Ground cumin seeds (Use pestle and mortar or Blender)
- 2 tbsp. Extra virgin olive oil
- 1 tsp. Crack black peppercorns
- ½ tsp. Cumin seeds, whole
- 1 tsp. Cilantro, finely chopped
- 1/2 Jalapeno, finely chopped
- 2 cups Green Cabbage, sliced
- 2 cups Carrots, grated
- ½ cup of Cilantro, chopped
- 3 tbsp. Lime Juice

Directions:

1. Get a large saucepan, and then heat the oil over medium heat.
2. Cook the peppercorns, coriander, and the whole cumin seeds for about a minute until browned.
3. Add in the jalapeno and then cook for another 45 seconds until tender.
4. Add in then the carrots and the cabbage, cooking for about 5 minutes or until the cabbage starts to soften.
5. Add in the crushed cumin seeds and cook for 30 seconds before taking off the heat and then stirring in the lime juice and the cilantro.
6. Serve warm.

Nutrition:

Calories: 377 kcal

Protein: 12.77 g

Fat: 20.54 g

Carbohydrates: 41.82 g

Spicy Vegetable Burgers

Preparation Time: 2 minutes

Cooking Time: 15 minutes

Servings: 2

Ingredients:

- 1 pack Extra firm tempeh
- 1 tsp. Red chili flakes
- 1 Red pepper, diced (optional)
- 1/2 Red Onion, diced
- 1/2 cup Baby spinach
- 1 tbsp. Olive Oil
- 2 100% Wholegrain Bun (optional)

Directions:

1. Heat the broiler on medium-high heat.
2. Marinate the tempeh in oil and red chili flakes.
3. In a skillet, warm a little bit of oil on medium heat.
4. Sauté the onion in the skillet for 6-7 minutes or until caramelized.
5. Stir in the pepper and baby spinach for a further 3-4 minutes.
6. Broil the tempeh for around 4 minutes on each side.
7. Lay down the tempeh in the buns and then add the caramelized onion, spinach, and diced peppers.
8. Serve immediately while hot with a side of arugula.

Nutrition:

Calories: 833 kcal

Protein: 14.1 g

Fat: 54.47 g

Carbohydrates: 73.01 g

Chickpea Shawarma Dip

Preparation Time: 10 minutes

Cooking Time: 20 minutes

Servings: 4

Ingredients:

- 2 tablespoons fresh lemon juice
- 1 teaspoon curry powder
- 2 teaspoons extra virgin olive oil
- 3/4 teaspoon salt
- 1/2 teaspoon ground cumin
- 3 cloves garlic, minced

- 1 chicken breast without skin and boneless 500 g, cut into strips
- Cooking spray
- 4 pits (6 inches)
- 1 cup sliced romaine lettuce
- 8 slices of tomato 1/4 inch thick.

Directions:

1. Preheat the grill over medium-high heat.
2. To prepare the chicken, combine the first 6 ingredients in a medium bowl.
3. Add the chicken to the well-stretched bowl until covered.
4. Let stand at room temperature for 20 minutes.
5. Screw 2 chicken strips into each of the 8 skewers.
6. Place the kebabs on a spray-covered grill rack to cook about 4 minutes on each side or until done.
7. Place the pitas on the grill rack
8. Leave on the grill 1 minute on each side or until lightly toasted
9. Place 1 pita on each of 4 plates
10. Cover each serving with 1/4 cup of lettuce, 2 slices of tomato and 4 pieces of chicken

Nutrition:

Calories: 45 kcal

Protein: 2.36 g

Fat: 2.76 g

Carbohydrates: 3.22 g

Light Mushroom Risotto

Preparation Time: 10 minutes

Cooking Time: 35 minutes

Servings: 4

Ingredients:

- 500g medium potatoes
- 300 g of mushrooms
- 250 g of arborous rice or carnaroli
- 1 onion
- 1 clove garlic
- 1 l of vegetable broth
- 1 glass of white wine
- 50 g of Parmesan cheese
- 4 tablespoons of olive oil
- A sprig of parsley
- Salt and pepper

Directions:

1. Heat the vegetable broth. Put the vegetable broth to heat. Wash the parsley, potatoes, dry it, reserve some whole leaves for decorating, and chopping the rest. Grate the Parmesan cheese.
2. Poach the garlic and onion. Peel and clean the garlic and onion and chop them. In a casserole with olive oil, beat them for about 5 minutes or so over low heat.
3. Skip the mushrooms. Meanwhile, clean the mushrooms. Leave a few whole pieces for decoration and the rest of the pieces in small pieces. Add them all to the casserole and sauté everything around five more minutes.
4. Incorporate the rice. Once you have sautéed the mushrooms with the onion and garlic, remove the ones that you had left whole and reserve them. Add the rice to the pan, arborous rice or carnaroli, and then sauté everything together for another 5 minutes, stirring constantly.
5. Make the risotto. Pour the glass of white wine and a broth of broth, and cook for 15 minutes, stirring frequently, and adding broth as the rice absorbs it.
6. Complete the risotto. After the indicated time, add the cheese, parsley, salt and pepper to taste, and the rest of the broth and cook for three more minutes, stirring vigorously. Let stand for 2 minutes and serve.

Nutrition:

Calories: 111

Total Fat: 2g

Carbohydrates: 19g

Fiber: 0 g

Sugar: 18 g

Vegetable Pie

Preparation Time: 10 minutes

Cooking Time: 40 minutes

Servings: 6-8

Ingredients:

- 1 red pepper (you can make it green)
- 1 bunch parsley
- 1/2 grated carrot
- 6 mushrooms cut it into slices
- 6 eggs
- 1 tablespoon oil
- 1 teaspoon salt, one pepper and a small cup of bread crumbs

Directions:

1. First of all, put to heat the oven to 180F.
2. You must cut everything in small squares (parsley) the carrot, the mushrooms cut in sheets ah, and use natural, but everything is to your liking you can use the pot.
3. Once you have everything cut, put a small piece of oil and put it in a pan to brown (all the vegetables).
4. Once the vegetables are golden brown, put the six eggs in a bowl, salt, pepper, and bread crumbs.
5. Put the vegetables in the mold (or muffin molds) to taste and the time of each one, pour the ingredients of the bowl and put it in the oven for 35 or 40 minutes.
6. Serve and enjoy.

Nutrition:

Calories: 127 kcal

Protein: 7.81 g

Fat: 9.74 g

Carbohydrates: 1.77 g

Turmeric Nachos

Preparation Time: 5 minutes

Cooking Time: 20-30 minutes

Servings: 2-3

Ingredients:

- 1 cup Cornmeal
- ½ cup Flour
- 1/4 teaspoon turmeric powder
- 1/4 teaspoon Aji wine
- Water as needed
- 2 tablespoons Oil

Directions:

1. Put cornmeal and flour in a bowl.
2. Add salt, turmeric powder, and aji wine.
3. Mix everything very well.
4. Now knead the dough firmly with warm water.
5. Cover the dough and leave it for 10-15 minutes to harden.
6. Grease your hands with a small amount of oil and knead the dough again.
7. Make a ball with the dough.
8. Take the ball and round it.
9. Push it a little and place it on the rolling board.
10. It grows a little like Chapati.
11. After placing the poor, stab it with the help of a fork.
12. Then cut in half from the center and repeat the process.
13. TIPS
14. Heat the oil in a deep pan and fry nachos over medium heat.
15. After this, lift the tip continuously. Stir until golden.
16. On the other hand, chips from other dough balls are also prepared.
17. When finished, drain the chip on the paper to remove excess oil. Allow the tip to cool completely.
18. Then put the fries on a plate and put the grated cheese, finely chopped onion, finely chopped tomatoes, and mayonnaise on top of the fries.

Nutrition:

Calories: 378 kcal

Protein: 8.03 g

Fat: 12.22 g

Carbohydrates: 57.66 g

Rucola Salad

Preparation Time: 10 minutes

Cooking Time: 0 minutes

Servings: 2

Ingredients:

- 4 teaspoons fresh lemon juice
- 4 teaspoons walnut oil
- low sodium salt and freshly ground pepper
- 6 cups rucola leaves and tender stems (about 6 ounces)
- Garlic powder to taste

Directions:

1. Put the lemon juice into a bowl. Gradually whisk in the oil. Season with low sodium salt and pepper.
2. Add the greens, toss until evenly dressed, and serve at once. This is delicious, and feel free to add tomatoes or grated carrot and onion slices.
3. Substitution: Any mild green, such as lamb's lettuce, will do.

Nutrition:

Calories: 163 kcal

Protein: 9.16 g

Fat: 12.94 g

Carbohydrates: 5.92 g

Tasty Spring Salad

Preparation Time: 10 minutes

Cooking Time: 0 minutes

Servings: 2

Ingredients:

- 5 cups of any salad greens in the season of your choice
- Dressing:
- 125 mL (1/2 cup) olive oil
- 45 mL (3 tbsp.) lemon juice
- 15 mL (1 tbsp.) pure mustard powder
- 45 mL (3 tbsp.) capers, minced (optional)
- low sodium salt
- Pepper

Directions:

1. Combine salad greens and any other raw vegetables of choice.
2. Combine oil, lemon juice, and mustard. Mix well.
3. Add capers, low sodium salt, and pepper to taste.
4. Pour dressing over salad, toss and serve.

Nutrition:

Calories: 2140 kcal

Protein: 4.8 g

Fat: 234.59 g

Carbohydrates: 3.96 g

Pure Delish Spinach Salad

Preparation Time: 10 minutes

Cooking Time: 0 minutes

Servings: 2

Ingredients:

- 2 bunches fresh spinach
- 1 bunch scallions, chopped
- juice of 1 lemon
- 1/4 tbsp. olive oil
- pepper to taste
- optional: rice vinegar to taste

Directions:

1. Wash spinach well. Drain and chop.
2. After a few minutes, squeeze excess water.
3. Add scallions, lemon juice, oil, and pepper.

Nutrition:

Calories: 157 kcal

Protein: 13.6 g

Fat: 6.86 g

Carbohydrates: 16.7 g

Sexy Salsa Salad

Preparation Time: 10 minutes

Cooking Time: 0 minutes

Servings: 2

Ingredients:

- 1 bunch of cilantro
- 5-6 Roma tomatoes
- 1 small yellow or red onion
- 1 small chili pepper
- 2 ripe avocados.
- Handful of rucola leaf

Directions:

1. Chop cilantro, diced tomatoes, diced onion, finely dice chili pepper, diced avocado.
2. After dicing each ingredient, add to a large bowl. Add rucola to bowl.
3. When finished, toss.

Nutrition:

Calories: 433 kcal

Protein: 10.66 g

Fat: 33.22 g

Carbohydrates: 32.46 g

Jalapeno Salsa

Preparation Time: 10 minutes + fridge time

Cooking Time: 0 minutes

Servings: 2

Ingredients:

- 1 jalapeno pepper seeded and chopped fine
- 2 large ripe tomatoes, peeled and chopped
- 1 medium onion, minced
- 2 tbsp. olive oil
- juice of 1 lemon
- 1/2 tsp dried oregano
- pepper to taste

Directions:

1. Combine all ingredients and mix well.
2. Refrigerate covered until ready to eat.

Nutrition:

Calories: 238 kcal

Protein: 6.03 g

Fat: 17.78 g

Carbohydrates: 16.65 g

Lentil Curry

Preparation Time: 10 minutes

Cooking Time: 16 minutes

Servings: 2

Ingredients:

- 1½ cups of filtered water
- ½ cup of split red lentils
- ½ tablespoon of olive oil
- ½ teaspoon of ginger paste
- ½ teaspoon of curry powder
- ¼ teaspoon of red pepper flakes, crushed
- Salt
- 1 tablespoon of freshly squeezed lemon juice

Directions:

1. Put water and lentils in a microwave-safe bowl and microwave it for around 14 minutes.
2. Remove the new bowl from your microwave and stir it.
3. Cover the bowl and set it aside.
4. Put oil in another microwave-safe bowl and heat it for a few seconds.
5. Add the remaining ingredients (except the lemon juice) and microwave it for another minute (stir after 30 seconds.)
6. Add the oil mixture and fresh lemon juice to a bowl containing lentils and stir. Serve immediately.

Nutrition:

Calories: 205

Fats: 4.2g

Carbs: 29.7g

Sugar: 1.2g

Proteins: 12.6g

Sodium: 82mg

Lentils in Tomato Sauce

Preparation Time: 10 minutes

Cooking Time: 20 minutes

Servings: 4

Ingredients:

- For the Tomato Puree:
- 1 cup of tomatoes, chopped
- 1 garlic clove, chopped
- A (1-inch) piece of fresh ginger (chopped)
- 1 green chili, chopped
- ¼ cup of filtered water
- For the Lentils:
- 1 cup of red lentils
- 3 cups of filtered water
- 1 tablespoon of olive oil
- ½ medium-sized onions (white,) chopped finely
- ½ teaspoon of ground cumin
- ½ teaspoon of red pepper cayenne
- ¼ teaspoon of ground turmeric
- ¼ cup of fresh parsley leaves, chopped

Directions:

1. .For the tomato paste: put all ingredients into a blender and pulse. Set the puree aside.
2. Put three servings of water and lentils in a large pan and let it boil on high heat.
3. Lessen the temperature to medium-low and simmer (covered) for 15 minutes or until they tenderize. Drain the lentils.
4. Heat oil on a large skillet over medium heat and sauté the onion for 2-3 minutes.
5. Add the spices and sauté for another minute.
6. Add the tomato puree and cook for 4-5 minutes while stirring continuously.
7. Add the lentils and cook for 4-5 minutes or until you attain the desired doneness.
8. Serve hot while garnished with parsley.

Nutrition:

Calories: 219

Fats: 4.3g

Carbs: 32.9g

Sugar: 2.9g

Proteins: 13.2g

Sodium: 9mg

Black Eyed-Peas Curry

Preparation Time: 10 minutes

Cooking Time: 15 minutes

Servings: 3

Ingredients:

- 1 teaspoon of olive oil
- 1 red bell pepper (seeded and chopped)
- ¼ cup of shallot, chopped
- 2 teaspoons of fresh ginger, minced
- 3 garlic cloves, minced
- 1 fresh green chili, chopped finely
- 1 tablespoon of fresh thyme, chopped
- 2 bay leaves
- 2 teaspoons of curry powder
- ½ teaspoon of ground cumin
- 1 (16-ounce) can of black-eyed peas (drained and rinsed)
- ¾ cup of filtered water
- ¾ cup of unsweetened coconut milk
- 1 teaspoon of raw honey
- A tablespoon of fresh lime juice
- Salt and ground black pepper
- 2 tablespoons of fresh parsley, chopped

Directions:

1. In a pan, warm the heat on medium heat. Sauté chopped bell pepper and shallots for 4-5 minutes.
2. Add ginger, garlic, green chili, thyme, bay leaves, curry powder, and cumin. Sauté them for one minute.
3. Add the black-eyed peas, water, coconut milk, and honey to the mixture and let it boil.
4. Cover the pan then cook for at least 5 minutes.
5. Add lime juice, salt, and black pepper. Stir and cook for 1 minute.
6. Remove the food from heat and discard the bay leaves.
7. Serve hot while garnished with parsley.

Nutrition:

Calories: 282

Fats: 15.9g

Carbs: 30.4g

Sugar: 4.1g

Proteins: 9.8g,

Sodium: 98mg

Vegan Meatballs

Preparation Time: 20 minutes.

Cooking Time: 48 minutes.

Serves: 4

Ingredients:

- 1 cup cooked quinoa
- 1 (15-ounce) can black beans
- 2 tablespoons water
- 3 garlic cloves, minced
- 1/2 cup shallot, diced
- 1/4 teaspoon salt
- 2 1/2 teaspoon fresh oregano
- 1/2 teaspoon red pepper flake
- 1/2 teaspoon fennel seeds
- 1/2 cup vegan parmesan cheese, shredded
- 2 tablespoons tomato paste
- 3 tablespoons fresh basil, chopped
- 2 tablespoons Worcestershire sauce

Direction:

1. At 350 degrees F, preheat your oven.
2. Spread the beans in a baking sheet and bake for 15 minutes.
3. Meanwhile, sauté garlic, shallots and water to a skillet for 3 minutes.
4. Transfer to the food processor along with fennel, red pepper flakes, baked beans, oregano and salt.
5. Blend these ingredients just until incorporated.
6. Stir in quinoa, and rest of the ingredients then mix evenly.
7. Make golf-ball sized meatballs out of this mixture.
8. Pread these meatballs in a grease baking sheet and bake for 20-30 minutes until brown.
9. Flip the meatballs once cooked half way through.
10. Serve warm.

Nutrition

Calories 338

Fat 24g

Sodium 620mg

Carbs 58.3g

Fiber 2.4g

Protein 5.4g

Tofu Fried Rice

Preparation Time: 10 minutes.

Cooking Time: 13 minutes.

Serves: 4

Ingredients:

- •1 package baked tofu
- •4 cup cauliflower rice
- •1 cup frozen peas
- •1 cup carrots, shredded
- •1 teaspoon onion powder
- •1 teaspoon garlic powder
- •1/2 cup soy sauce
- •1/4 cup scallions, chopped
- •Salt and black pepper to taste

Direction:

1. Sauce tofu with peas, carrots, garlic powder, soy sauce, scallions, black pepper and salt in a cooking pan for 10 minutes.
2. Stir in cauliflower rice and mix well.
3. Cover and cook for 3 minutes on medium heat.
4. Serve warm.

Nutrition:

Calories 378

Fat 3.8g

Sodium 620mg

Carbs 13.3g

Fiber 2.4g

Protein 5.4g

Corn Chowder

Preparation Time: 15 minutes.

Cooking Time: 28 minutes.

Serves: 8

Ingredients:

- 4 cups vegetable broth
- 8 cups corn
- 1 whole yellow onion, diced
- 1 tablespoon chili powder
- 1 teaspoon salt
- 4 cups water
- 1/4 cup nutritional yeast
- 1/4 lime juiced
- 1/4 cup cilantro

Direction:

1. Add vegetable broth, onion, corn and chili powder to a cooking pot.
2. Cook for 8 minutes with occasional stirring.
3. Remove 1/3 of this cooking mixture and keep it aside.
4. Add water to the rest and cook for 20 minutes on a simmer.
5. Puree the cooked corn soup until smooth.
6. Stir in lime juice, yeast, and remaining corn mixture.
7. Serve warm with cilantro on top. Enjoy.

Nutrition:

Calories 341

Fat 24g

Sodium 547mg

Carbs 36.4g

Fiber 1.2g

Sugar 1g

Protein 10.3g

Asian Slaw

Preparation Time: 15 minutes.

Cooking Time: 0 minutes.

Serves: 4

Ingredients:

Salad:

- 2 cups green cabbage, shredded
- 1/2 cup carrots, shredded
- 1/2 cup cilantro, chopped
- 1/2 cup bell peppers, sliced
- 1/2 cup peanuts, crushed
- Avocado slices

Dressing:

- 2 tablespoons peanut butter
- 1 teaspoon agave syrup
- 1 tablespoon soy sauce
- 1 teaspoon white wine vinegar
- 1 teaspoon lime juice
- 1 tablespoon water
- Salt and black pepper to taste

Direction:

1. First, mix all the dressing ingredients in a salad bowl.
2. Stir in rest of the slaw ingredients and mix well.
3. Serve.

Nutrition:

Calories 318

Fat 15.7g

Sodium 124mg

Carbs 27g

Fiber 0.1g

Sugar 0.3g

Protein 4.9g

Spinach Alfredo Soup

Preparation Time: 15 minutes.

Cooking Time: 23 minutes.

Serves: 6

Ingredients:

- 2 cups cauliflower florets
- 1/2 teaspoon garlic, minced
- 1 teaspoon olive oil
- ½ cup cottage cheese
- 9 ounces shredded cheese
- 6 wedges Light Laughing Cow cheese
- ½ teaspoon salt
- ¼ teaspoon black pepper
- 1 cup cashew milk
- 26 ounces frozen Spinach
- 3 tablespoon Parmesan cheese, shredded
- 18 ounces yogurt

Direction:

1. Boil cauliflower in a cooking pan filled with water for 10 minutes.
2. Transfer the cauliflower florets to a blender along with 1 cup cooking liquid.
3. Puree this mixture and keep it aside.
4. Sauté garlic with olive oil in a suitable pan for 3 minutes.
5. Transfer to the cauliflower and add all these cheese, black pepper, milk and salt.
6. Blend these ingredients together until smooth.
7. Return the mixture to the saucepan and add one more cup of cooking liquid.
8. Cook the soup to a boil then add spinach and cook for 10 minutes.
9. Serve warm.

Serving Suggestion: Serve the soup with cauliflower rice.

Variation Tip: Add broccoli florets to the soup as well.

Nutrition:

Calories 314

Fat 2.2g

Sodium 276mg

Carbs 27.7g

Fiber 0.9g

Protein 8.8g

Artichoke Stuffed Mushroom

Preparation Time: 15 minutes.

Cooking Time: 20 minutes.

Serves: 8

Ingredients:

- 8 (1/2 ounces) Portobello Mushroom, caps
- Filling ingredients:
- 1/4 cup alfredo sauce
- 2 wedges light laughing cow cheese
- 1 teaspoon garlic, minced
- 1 egg
- 4 ounces cheese, shredded
- 1-1/2 cup light cottage cheese
- 1/2 cup hearts of palm, diced
- 1 cup spinach, shredded
- 4 tablespoons parmesan, shredded

Direction:

1. Mix all the filling ingredients in a suitable bowl.
2. Divide this mixture in the mushroom caps.
3. Place these stuffed caps in a greased baking sheet.
4. Bake them for 20 minutes at 350 degrees F in the oven.
5. Serve warm.

Nutrition:

Calories 324

Fat 5g

Sodium 432mg

Carbs 13.1g

Fiber 0.3g

Protein 5.7g

Asparagus with Garlic

Preparation Time: 15 minutes.

Cooking Time: 45 minutes.

Serves: 4

Ingredients:

- 1 lb. thick asparagus spears, trimmed and chopped
- ½ cup garlic cloves, peeled and chopped
- 3 tablespoons olive oil

- Salt and black pepper, to taste

Direction:
1. Mix asparagus with garlic, olive oil, black pepper and salt in a bowl.
2. Cover and marinate for 30 minutes.
3. Meanwhile, at 450 degrees F, preheat your oven.
4. Spread the asparagus in a baking sheet.
5. Roast them for 15 minutes in the preheated oven.
6. Serve warm.

Nutrition:

Calories 136

Fat 10g

Sodium 249mg

Carbs 8g

Fiber 2g

Protein 4g

Avocado Tomato Salad

Preparation Time: 15 minutes.

Cooking Time: 14 minutes.

Serves: 2

Ingredients:
- 2 ripe avocados
- 2 ripe beefsteak tomatoes
- 2 tablespoons lemon juice
- 3 tablespoons cilantro, chopped
- Salt and black pepper to taste

Direction:
1. Peel the avocados, remove their pits and cut into cubes.
2. Transfer the avocados to a salad bowl.
3. Stir in tomatoes, lemon juice, cilantro, black pepper and salt.
4. Mix well and serve fresh.

Nutrition:

Calories 151

Fat 9g

Sodium 412mg

Carbs 43g

Fiber 0.3g

Protein 3g

Feta and Pesto Wrap

Preparation Time: 15 minutes

Cooking Time: 10 minutes

Servings: 4

Ingredients:
- 8 ounces (250 g) smoked salmon fillet, thinly sliced
- 1 cup (150 g) feta cheese
- 8 (15 g) Romaine lettuce leaves
- 4 (6-inch) pita bread
- 1/4 cup (60 g) basil pesto sauce

Directions:
1. Place 1 pita bread on a plate. Top with lettuce, salmon, feta cheese, and pesto sauce. Fold or roll to enclose filling. Repeat the procedure for the remaining ingredients.
2. Serve and enjoy.

Nutrition:

Calories 408

Fat 2

Carbs 1

Protein 11

Cheese and Onion on Bagel

Preparation Time: 15 minutes

Cooking Time: 10 minutes

Servings: 4

Ingredients:
- 8 ounces (250 g) smoked salmon fillet, thinly sliced
- 1/2 cup (125 g) cream cheese
- 1 medium (110 g) onion, thinly sliced
- 4 bagels (about 80g each), split

- 2 tablespoons (7 g) fresh parsley, chopped
- Freshly ground black pepper to taste

Directions:
1. Spread the cream cheese on each bottom's half of bagels. Top with salmon and onion, season with pepper, sprinkle with parsley, and then cover with bagel tops.
2. Serve and enjoy.

Nutrition:

Calories: 34

Carbs: 0g

Fat: 1g

Protein: 5g

Zucchini Ravioli

Preparation Time: 20 minutes.

Cooking Time: 30 minutes.

Serves: 6

Ingredients:
- 1 1/4 lbs. zucchini
- 1 cup part-skim ricotta
- 1/4 cup parmesan
- 1 egg
- 1/4 cup fresh spinach, chopped
- 2 tablespoons fresh basil, chopped
- 1/4 teaspoon nutmeg
- 1/4 teaspoon salt
- 1/8 teaspoons black pepper
- 1 1/2 cups jarred marinara sauce
- 2/3 cup mozzarella, shredded
- 2 tablespoons parmesan, shredded
- 2 teaspoons olive oil
- 1/2 teaspoon black pepper
- Fresh basil, to garnish

Direction:
1. At 375 degrees F, preheat your oven.
2. Cut the whole zucchini into thin strips using a potato peeler to get 60 slices.
3. Mix black pepper, spinach, egg, salt, nutmeg, basil, spinach, parmesan and ricotta in a bowl.
4. Spread marinara sauce in a 9x13 inches baking dish.
5. Place two zucchini slices on a working surface in a cross.
6. Add a tablespoon filling at the center of this cross and wrap the zucchini slices around.
7. Place the wraps in the casserole dish and drizzle olive oil, black pepper, salt and remaining cheese on top.
8. Bake the ravioli for 30 minutes in the preheated oven.
9. Serve warm.

Nutrition:

Calories 338 Fat 24g

Sodium 620mg

Carbs 58.3g

Fiber 2.4g

Sugar 1.2g

Protein 5.4g

Cauliflower Salad

Preparation Time: 5 minutes.

Cooking Time: 0 minutes.

Serves: 4

Ingredients:
- 4 cups cauliflower florets
- 1 tablespoon Tuscan fantasy seasoning
- 1/4 cup apple cider vinegar

Direction:
1. Toss cauliflower with seasoning and apple cider vinegar in a bowl.
2. Serve.

Nutrition:

Calories 93

Fat 3g

Sodium 510mg

Carbs 12g

Fiber 3g

Protein 4g

Tofu Spinach Sauté

Preparation Time: 10 minutes.

Cooking Time: 10 minutes.

Serves: 4

Ingredients:

- 1/4 cup onion, chopped
- 1/4 cup button mushrooms, chopped
- 8 ounces tofu, pressed and chopped
- 3 teaspoons nutritional yeast
- 1 teaspoon liquid aminos
- 4 cups baby spinach
- 4 grape tomatoes, chopped
- Cooking spray

Direction:

1. Sauté mushrooms and onion with oil in a skillet for 3 minutes.
2. Stir in tofu and sauté for 3 minutes.
3. Add liquid aminos and yeast then mix well.
4. Stir in tomatoes and spinach then sauté for 4 minutes.
5. Serve warm.

Nutrition:

Calories 378

Fat 3.8g

Sodium 620mg

Carbs 13.3g

Fiber 2.4g

Protein 5.4g

Zucchini Lasagna

Preparation Time: 15 minutes.

Cooking Time: 24 minutes.

Serves: 4

Ingredients:

- 6 ounces crumbled tofu
- 1 garlic clove, minced
- 1 tablespoon dried parsley flakes
- 1 tablespoon dried basil
- 1/8 teaspoons salt
- 1 can diced tomatoes, drained
- 3/4 cup 1% cottage cheese, shredded
- 3 ounces mozzarella cheese, shredded
- 1 tablespoon dried parsley flakes
- 2 tablespoons egg, beaten
- 2 small zucchini squash

Direction:

1. At 350 degrees F, preheat your oven.
2. Cut the whole zucchini into thin slices using a potato peeler.
3. Sauté tofu with garlic, parsley, basil, and salt in a cooking pan until golden brown.
4. Stir in tomatoes, egg and parsley then cook for 4 minutes.
5. Spread a layer of thin zucchini slices at the bottom of a casserole dish.
6. Top these slices with half of the tofu mixture.
7. Mix cottage cheese with mozzarella cheese in bowl.
8. Drizzle 1/3 of the cheese mixture over the tofu filling.
9. Repeat the zucchini layer and top it with the remaining tofu mixture.
10. .Add 1/3 of the cheese mixture and add another layer of zucchini on top.
11. Drizzle remaining cheese on top and bake for 20 minutes in the oven,
12. .Serve warm.

Nutrition: Calories 304

Fat 31g

Sodium 834mg

Carbs 21.4g

Fiber 0.2g

Protein 4.6g

Vegetable and Egg Casserole

Preparation Time: 15 minutes.

Cooking Time: 30 minutes.

Serves: 6

Ingredients:

- 6 eggs
- 1 cup egg whites
- 1 ¼ cup cheese, shredded

- 16 ounces bag frozen spinach
- 2 cups mushrooms, sliced
- 1 bell pepper, diced

Direction:

1. At 350 degrees F, preheat your oven.
2. Beat egg with egg whites, cheese, spinach, mushrooms and bell pepper in a bowl.
3. Spread this egg mixture into a casserole dish.
4. Bake this casserole for 30 minutes in the oven.
5. Serve warm.

Nutrition:

Calories 341

Fat 24g

Sodium 547mg

Carbs 36.4g

Fiber 1.2g

Protein 10.3g

Green Buddha Bowl

Preparation Time: 15 minutes.

Cooking Time: 0 minutes.

Serves: 2

Ingredients:

- 1 tablespoon olive oil
- 1 lb. brussels sprouts, trimmed and halved
- Salt and black pepper, to taste
- 2 cups cooked quinoa
- 1 cup red apple, chopped
- ¼ cup pepitas
- 1 avocado, sliced
- 1 ½ cups arugula
- ½ cup of mayo
- ¾ cup plain Greek yogurt
- 1 teaspoon ground mustard
- ¼ cup Pompeian White Balsamic Vinegar
- ½ teaspoon salt
- 1 tablespoon fresh basil, chopped
- 1 garlic clove, minced

Direction:

1. Mix quinoa with apple and the rest of the ingredients in a salad bowl.
2. Serve.
3. Serving Suggestion: Serve the bowl with spaghetti squash.
4. Variation Tip: Add some edamame beans to the bowl.

Nutrition:

Calories 318

Fat 15.7g

Sodium 124mg

Carbs 27g

Fiber 0.1g

Protein 4.9g

Spaghetti Squash

Preparation Time: 15 minutes.

Cooking Time: 45 minutes.

Serves: 4

Ingredients:

- •1 spaghetti squash
- •1 pinch black pepper
- •1 tablespoon olive oil
- •1 tablespoon Pecorino Romano, shredded

Direction:

1. At 425 degrees F, preheat your oven.
2. Cut the spaghetti squash in half, remove its seeds and place in a baking sheet.
3. Drizzle black pepper, and olive oil on top, then bake for 45 minutes.
4. Scrap the squash flesh with a fork and add to the serving plate.
5. Drizzle pecorino Romano on top.
6. Serve.

Nutrition

Calories 324

Fat 5g

Sodium 432mg

Carbs 13.1g

Fiber 0.3g

Protein 5.7g

Roasted Green Beans and Mushrooms

Preparation Time: 15 minutes.

Cooking Time: 25 minutes.

Serves: 4

Ingredients:

- •8 ounces mushrooms, cleaned and halved
- •1 lb. green beans, halved
- •8 whole garlic cloves, halved
- •2 tablespoons olive oil
- •1 tablespoon balsamic vinegar
- •Salt and black pepper, to taste

Direction:

1. At 450 degrees F, preheat your oven.
2. Spread a foil sheet in a baking tray.
3. Add mushrooms, garlic and green beans to the baking sheet.
4. Mix balsamic vinegar with olive oil in a small bowl and pour over the veggies.
5. Drizzle black pepper and salt on top then bake for 25 minutes.
6. Serve warm.
7. Serving Suggestion: Serve the veggies with toasted bread slices.
8. Variation Tip: Add boiled zucchini pasta to the mixture.

Nutrition:

Calories 136

Fat 10g

Sodium 249mg

Carbs 8g

Fiber 2g

Protein 4g

Mexican Cauliflower Rice

Preparation Time: 15 minutes.

Cooking Time: 14 minutes.

Serves: 4

Ingredients:

- 1 head cauliflower, riced
- 1 tablespoon olive oil
- 1 medium white onion, diced
- 2 garlic cloves, minced
- 1 jalapeno, seeded and minced
- 3 tablespoons tomato paste
- 1 teaspoon of sea salt
- 1 teaspoon cumin
- 1/2 teaspoon paprika
- 3 tablespoons fresh cilantro, chopped
- 1 tablespoon lime juice

Direction:

1. Grate the cauliflower in a food processor.
2. Sauté onion with oil in a skillet over medium-high heat for 6 minutes.
3. Stir in jalapeno and garlic, then sauté for 2 minutes.
4. Add paprika, cumin, salt, and tomato paste, then sauté for 1 minute.
5. Stir in cauliflower rice and the rest of the ingredients and cook for 5 minutes.
6. Add cilantro and lime juice in the top.
7. Serve.

Nutrition:

Calories 351

Fat 19g

Sodium 412mg

Carbs 43g

Fiber 0.3g

Protein 23g

Quick Collard Greens

Preparation Time: 8 minutes

Cooking Time: 7 minutes

Servings: 2

Ingredients:

- 10-ounces collard greens
- 1 ½ tablespoons extra-virgin olive oil
- ¼ teaspoon fine sea salt
- Two cloves' garlic, pressed or minced
- Pinch of red pepper flakes
- A couple lemon wedges – for serving

Direction:
1. For preparing the collard:
2. Slice the thick center rib out of each collard green.
3. Stack the rib-less green and roll up into a cigar-like shape.
4. Cut "cigar" thinly to prepare long strands.
5. Place the skillet on the stove over a medium-high flame, and then add olive oil.
6. When shimmering, add the salt and all collard green.
7. Stir well until all greens are coated with oil and cook for half-minute.
8. Stir well and cook for half-minute more until dark green, greens are wilted, and brown on the edges. It will take three to six minutes.
9. When done, add red pepper flakes and garlic. Cook for half-minute until fragrant.
10. Remove from pan and also remove from flame.
11. Split cooked collard on the serving plate.
12. Serve with a lemon wedge.

Nutrition:

Calories 140

Fat 11.4g

Sodium 289.6mg

Carbohydrates 8.8g

Fiber 5.7g

Sugar 0.7g

Protein 4.5g

FISH AND SEAFOOD RECIPES

Lemon-Caper Trout with Caramelized Shallots

Preparation Time: 10 minutes

Cooking Time: 20 minutes

Servings: 2

Ingredients:

- For the Shallots
- 2 shallots, thinly sliced
- 1 teaspoon ghee
- Dash salt
- For the Trout
- 1 tablespoon plus 1 teaspoon ghee, divided
- 2 (4-ounce) trout fillets
- ¼ cup freshly squeezed lemon juice
- 3 tablespoons capers
- ¼ teaspoon salt
- Dash freshly ground black pepper
- 1 lemon, thinly sliced

Directions:

1. To make the Shallot:
2. In a huge skillet on medium heat, cook the shallots, ghee, and salt for 20 minutes, stirring every 5 minutes, until the shallots have fully wilted and caramelized.
3. To make the Trout:
4. While the shallots cook, in another large skillet over medium heat, heat 1 teaspoon of ghee.
5. Add the trout fillets. Cook for at least 3 minutes each side, or until the center is flaky. Transfer to a plate and set aside.
6. In the skillet used for the trout, add the lemon juice, capers, salt, and pepper. Bring it to a simmer. Whisk in the remaining 1 tablespoon of ghee. Spoon the sauce over the fish.
7. Garnish the fish with the lemon slices and caramelized shallots before serving.

Nutrition:

Calories: 399

Total Fat: 22g

Saturated Fat: 10g

Cholesterol: 46mg

Carbohydrates: 17g

Fiber: 2g

Protein: 21g

Shrimp Scampi

Preparation Time: 10 minutes

Cooking Time: 15 minutes

Servings: 4

Ingredients:

- ¼ cup Extra Olive Oil
- 1 Onion, Finely Chopped
- 1 Red Bell Pepper, Chopped
- 1½ Pound Shrimp, Peeled and Tails Removed
- 6 Garlic Cloves, Minced
- 2 Lemon Juices
- 2 Lemon Zest
- ½ tsp. Sea Salt
- ⅛ tsp. Freshly Ground Black Pepper

Directions:

1. In a huge nonstick skillet on medium-high heat, warm the olive oil until it shimmers.
2. Add the onion and red bell pepper. Cook for about 6 minutes, occasionally stirring, until soft.
3. Add the shrimp and cook for about 5 minutes until pink.
4. Add the garlic. Cook for 30 seconds, stirring constantly.
5. Add the lemon juice and zest, salt, and pepper. Simmer for 3 minutes.

Nutrition:

Calories: 345

Total Fat: 16

Total Carbs: 10g

Sugar: 3g

Fiber: 1g

Protein: 40g

Sodium: 424mg

Shrimp with Spicy Spinach

Preparation Time: 10 minutes

Cooking Time: 15 minutes

Servings: 4

Ingredients:

- ¼ cup Extra Olive Oil. divided
- 1½ Pound Peeled Shrimp
- 1 tsp. Sea Salt, divided
- 4 cups Baby fresh Spinach
- 6 Garlic cloves, minced
- ½ cup Freshly Squeezed Orange Juice
- 1 tbsp. Sriracha Sauce
- ⅛ tsp. Freshly ground black pepper

Directions:

1. In a huge nonstick skillet on medium-high heat, heat 2 tablespoons of the olive oil until it shimmers.
2. Add the shrimp and ½ teaspoon salt. Cook for at least 4 minutes, occasionally stirring, until the shrimp are pink. Transfer the shrimp to a plate, tent with aluminum foil to keep warm, and set aside.
3. Put back the skillet to the heat and heat the remaining 2 tablespoons of olive oil until it shimmers.
4. Add the spinach. Cook for 3 minutes, stirring.
5. Add the garlic. Cook for 30 seconds, stirring constantly.
6. In a small bowl, put and mix together the orange juice, Sriracha, remaining ½ teaspoon of salt, and pepper. Add this to the spinach and cook for 3 minutes. Serve the shrimp with the spinach on the side.

Nutrition:

Calories: 317

Total Fat: 16

Total Carbs: 7g

Sugar: 3

Fiber: 1g

Protein: 38g

Sodium: 911mg

Shrimp with Cinnamon Sauce

Preparation Time: 10 minutes

Cooking Time: 10 minutes

Servings: 4

Ingredients:

- 2 tbsp. Extra Virgin Olive Oil
- 1½ Pound Peeled Shrimp
- 2 tbsp. Dijon Mustard
- 1 cup No Salt Added Chicken Broth
- 1 tsp. Ground Cinnamon
- 1 tsp. Onion Powder
- ½ tsp. Sea Salt
- ¼ tsp. Freshly Ground Black Pepper

Directions:

1. In a huge nonstick skillet at medium-high heat, heat the olive oil until it shimmers.
2. Add the shrimp. Cook for at least 4 minutes, occasionally stirring, until the shrimp is opaque.
3. In a small bowl, whisk the mustard, chicken broth, cinnamon, onion powder, salt, and pepper. Pour this into the skillet and continue to cook for 3 minutes, stirring occasionally.

Nutrition:

Calories: 270

Total Fat: 11g

Total Carbs: 4g

Sugar: 1g

Fiber: 1g

Protein: 39g

Sodium: 664mg

Pan-Seared Scallops with Lemon-Ginger Vinaigrette

Preparation Time: 10 minutes

Cooking Time: 7 minutes

Servings: 4

Ingredients:

- 2 tbsp. Extra Virgin Olive Oil
- 1½ Pound Sea Scallop
- ½ tsp. Sea Salt
- ⅛ tsp. Freshly Ground Black Pepper
- ¼ cup Lemon Ginger Vinaigrette

Directions:

1. In a huge nonstick skillet at medium-high heat, heat the olive oil until it shimmers.
2. Season the scallops with pepper and salt and add them to the skillet. Cook for at least 3 minutes per side until just opaque.
3. Serve with the vinaigrette spooned over the top.

Nutrition:

Calories: 280

Total Fat: 16

Total Carbs: 5g

Sugar: 1g

Fiber: 0g

Protein: 29g

Sodium: 508mg

Manhattan-Style Salmon Chowder

Preparation Time: 10 minutes

Cooking Time: 15 minutes

Servings: 4

Ingredients:

- ¼ cup Extra Virgin Olive Oil
- 1 Red Bell Pepper, Chopped
- 1 Pound Skinless Salmon. Pin Bones removed, chopped into ½ inch
- 2 (28 oz.) Cans Crushed Tomatoes, 1 Drained, 1 undrained
- 6 cups No salt added chicken broth
- 2 cups diced (1/2 inch) Sweet Potato
- 1 tsp. Onion Powder
- ½ tsp. Sea Salt
- ¼ tsp. Freshly Ground Black Pepper

Directions:

1. Add the red bell pepper and salmon. Cook for at least 5 minutes, occasionally stirring, until the fish is opaque and the bell pepper is soft.
2. Stir in the tomatoes, chicken broth, sweet potatoes, onion powder, salt, and pepper. Place to a simmer then lower the heat to medium. Cook for at least 10 minutes, occasionally stirring, until the sweet potatoes are soft.

Nutrition:

Calories: 570

Total Fat: 42

Total Carbs: 55g

Sugar: 24g

Fiber: 16g

Protein: 41g

Sodium: 1,249mg

Roasted Salmon and Asparagus

Preparation Time: 5 minutes

Cooking Time: 15 minutes

Servings: 4

Ingredients:

- 1 pound Asparagus Spears, trimmed
- 2 tbsp. Extra Virgin Olive Oil
- 1 tsp. Sea Salt, divide
- 1½ pound Salmon, cut into 4 fillets
- ⅛ tsp. freshly ground cracked black pepper
- 1 Lemon, zest, and slice

Directions:

1. Preheat the oven to 425°F.
2. Stir the asparagus with the olive oil then put ½ teaspoon of the salt. Place in a single layer in the bottom of a roasting pan.
3. Season the salmon with the pepper and the remaining ½ teaspoon of salt. Put skin-side down on top of the asparagus.
4. Sprinkle the salmon and asparagus with the lemon zest and place the lemon slices over the fish.
5. Roast at the oven for at least 12 to 15 minutes until the flesh is opaque.

Nutrition:

Calories: 308

Total Fat: 18g

Total Carbs: 5g

Sugar: 2g

Fiber: 2g

Protein: 36g

Sodium: 545mg

Citrus Salmon on a Bed of Greens

Preparation Time: 10 minutes

Cooking Time: 19 minutes

Servings: 4

Ingredients:

- ¼ cup Extra Virgin Olive Oil, divided
- 1½ pound Salmon
- 1 tsp. Sea Salt, divided
- ½ tsp. Freshly ground black pepper, divided
- 1 Lemon Zest
- 6 cups Swiss Chard, stemmed and chopped
- 3 Garlic cloves, chopped
- 2 Lemon Juice

Directions:

1. In a huge nonstick skillet at medium-high heat, heat 2 tablespoons of the olive oil until it shimmers.
2. Season the salmon with ½ teaspoon of the salt, ¼ teaspoon of the pepper, and the lemon zest. Put the salmon to the skillet, skin-side up, and cook for about 7 minutes until the flesh is opaque. Flip the salmon and cook for at least 3 to 4 minutes to crisp the skin. Set aside on a plate, cover using aluminum foil.
3. Put back the skillet to the heat, add the remaining 2 tablespoons of olive oil, and heat it until it shimmers.
4. Add the Swiss chard. Cook for about 7 minutes, occasionally stirring, until soft.
5. Add the garlic. Cook for 30 seconds, stirring constantly.
6. Sprinkle in the lemon juice, the remaining ½ teaspoon of salt, and the remaining ¼ teaspoon of pepper. Cook for 2 minutes.
7. Serve the salmon on the Swiss chard.

Nutrition:

Calories: 363

Total Fat: 25

Total Carbs: 3g

Sugar: 1g

Fiber: 1g

Protein: 34g

Sodium: 662mg

Orange and Maple-Glazed Salmon

Preparation Time: 15 minutes

Cooking Time: 15 minutes

Servings: 4

Ingredients:

- 2 Orange Juice
- 1 Orange Zest
- ¼ cup Pure maple syrup
- 2 tbsp. Low Sodium Soy Sauce
- 1 tsp. Garlic Powder
- 4 4-6 oz. Salmon Fillet, Pin bones removed

Directions:

1. Preheat the oven to 400°F.
2. In a small, shallow dish, whisk the orange juice and zest, maple syrup, soy sauce, and garlic powder.
3. Put the salmon pieces, flesh-side down, into the dish. Let it marinate for 10 minutes.
4. Transfer the salmon, skin-side up, to a rimmed baking sheet and bake for about 15 minutes until the flesh is opaque.

Nutrition:

Calories: 297

Total Fat: 11

Total Carbs: 18g

Sugar: 15g

Fiber: 1g

Protein: 34g

Sodium: 528mg

Salmon Ceviche

Preparation Time: 10 minutes +20 resting time

Cooking Time: 0 minutes

Servings: 4

Ingredients:

- 1 pound Salmon, skinless & boneless, cut into bite-size pieces
- ½ cup Fresh squeezed lime juice
- 2 Tomatoes, diced
- ¼ cup Fresh Cilantro Leaves, chopped
- 1 Jalapeno Pepper, seeded and diced
- 2 tbsp. Extra Virgin Olive Oil
- ½ tsp. Sea Salt

Directions:

1. In a medium bowl, put and stir together the salmon and lime juice. Let it marinate for 20 minutes.
2. Stir in the tomatoes, cilantro, jalapeño, olive oil, and salt.

Nutrition:

Calories: 222

Total Fat: 14g

Total Carbs: 3g

Sugar: 2g

Fiber: 1g

Protein: 23g

Sodium: 288mg

Cod with Ginger and Black Beans

Preparation Time: 10 minutes

Cooking Time: 15 minutes

Servings: 4

Ingredients:

- 2 tbsp. Extra Virgin Olive Oil
- 4 (6 oz.) Cod Fillets
- 1 tbsp. Grated fresh ginger
- 1 tsp. Sea Salt, divided
- ¼ tsp. Freshly ground black pepper
- 5 Garlic cloves, minced
- 1 (14 oz.) Can Black Beans, drained
- ¼ cup Fresh Cilantro Leaves, chopped

Directions:

1. In a huge nonstick skillet at medium-high heat, heat the olive oil until it shimmers.
2. Season the cod with the ginger, ½ teaspoon of the salt, and the pepper. Put it in the hot oil then cook for at least 4 minutes per side until the fish is opaque. Take off the cod from the pan and set it aside on a platter, tented with aluminum foil.
3. Put back the skillet to the heat and add the garlic. Cook for 30 seconds, stirring constantly.
4. Stir in the black beans and the rest ½ teaspoon of salt. Cook for 5 minutes, stirring occasionally.
5. Stir in the cilantro and spoon the black beans over the cod.

Nutrition:

Calories: 419

Total Fat: 2g

Total Carbs: 33g

Sugar: 1g

Fiber: 8g

Protein: 50g

Sodium: 605mg

Rosemary-Lemon Cod

Preparation Time: 5 minutes

Cooking Time: 10 minutes

Servings: 4

Ingredients:

- 2 tbsp. Extra Virgin Olive Oil
- 1½ pound Cod, Skin and Bone Removed, cut into 4 fillets
- 1 tbsp. Fresh Rosemary Leaves, chopped
- ½ tsp. Ground black pepper, or more to taste
- ½ tsp. Sea Salt
- 1 Lemon Juice

Directions:

1. In a huge nonstick skillet at medium-high heat, heat the olive oil until it shimmers.
2. Season the cod with the rosemary, pepper, and salt. Put the fish to the skillet and cook for 3 to 5 minutes per side until opaque.
3. Pour the lemon juice over the cod fillets and cook for 1 minute.

Nutrition:

Calories: 246

Total Fat: 9g

Total Carbs: 1g

Sugar: 1g

Fiber: 1g

Protein: 39g

Sodium: 370mg

Halibut Curry

Preparation Time: 10 minutes

Cooking Time: 10 minutes

Servings: 4

Ingredients:

- 2 tbsp. Extra Virgin Olive Oil
- 2 tsp. Ground Turmeric
- 2 tsp. Curry Powder
- 1½ pound Halibut, skin, and bones removed, cut into 1 inch pieces
- 4 cups No-salt added chicken broth
- 1 (14 oz.) can Lite coconut milk
- ½ tsp. Sea Salt
- ¼ tsp. Freshly ground black pepper

Directions:

1. In a huge nonstick skillet at medium-high, heat the olive oil until it shimmers.
2. Add the turmeric and curry powder. Cook for 2 minutes, constantly stirring, to bloom the spices.
3. Add the halibut, chicken broth, coconut milk, salt, and pepper. Place to a simmer then lower the heat to medium. Simmer for 6 to 7 minutes, stirring occasionally, until the fish is opaque.

Nutrition:

Calories: 429

Total Fat: 47g

Total Carbs: 5g

Sugar: 1g

Fiber: 1g

Protein: 27g

Sodium: 507mg

Lemony Mussels

Preparation Time: 5 minutes

Cooking Time: 5 minutes

Servings: 4

Ingredients:

- 1 tbsp. extra virgin extra virgin olive oil
- 2 minced garlic cloves
- 2 lbs. scrubbed mussels
- Juice of one lemon

Directions:

1. Put some water in a pot, add mussels, bring with a boil over medium heat, cook for 5 minutes, discard unopened mussels and transfer them with a bowl.
2. In another bowl, mix the oil with garlic and freshly squeezed lemon juice, whisk well, and add over the mussels, toss and serve.
3. Enjoy!

Nutrition:

Calories: 140

Fat: 4 g

Carbs: 8 g

Protein: 8 g

Sugars: 4g

Sodium: 600 mg

Hot Tuna Steak

Preparation Time: 10 minutes

Cooking Time: 25 minutes

Servings: 6

Ingredients:

- 2 tbsps. Fresh lemon juice
- Pepper.
- Roasted orange garlic mayonnaise
- ¼ c. whole black peppercorns
- 6 sliced tuna steaks
- 2 tbsps. Extra-virgin olive oil
- Salt

Directions:

1. Bring the tuna in a bowl to fit. Put the oil, lemon juice, salt, and pepper. Turn the tuna to coat well in the marinade.
2. Rest for at least 15 to 20 minutes, turning once.
3. Put the peppercorns in a double thickness of plastic bags. Tap the peppercorns with a heavy saucepan or small mallet to crush them coarsely. Put on a large plate.
4. Once ready to cook the tuna, dip the edges into the crushed peppercorns. Heat a nonstick skillet over medium heat. Sear the tuna steaks, in batches if necessary, for 4 minutes per side for medium-rare fish, adding 2 to 3 tablespoons of the marinade to the skillet if necessary, to prevent sticking.
5. Serve dolloped with roasted orange garlic mayonnaise

Nutrition:

Calories: 124

Fat: 0.4 g

Carbs: 0.6 g

Protein: 28 g

Sugars: 0 g

Sodium: 77 mg

Marinated Fish Steaks

Preparation Time: 10 minutes

Cooking Time: 15 minutes

Servings: 4

Ingredients:

- 4 lime wedges
- 2 tbsps. Lime juice
- 2 minced garlic cloves
- 2 tsp. Olive oil
- 1 tbsp. snipped fresh oregano
- 1 lb. fresh swordfish
- 1 tsp. lemon-pepper seasoning

Directions:

1. Rinse fish steaks; pat dry using paper towels. Cut into four serving-size pieces, if necessary.
2. In a shallow dish, put and combine lime juice, oregano, oil, lemon-pepper seasoning, and garlic. Add fish; turn to coat with marinade.
3. Cover and marinate in the refrigerator for 30 minutes to 1-1/2 hours, turning steaks occasionally. Drain fish, reserving marinade.
4. Put the fish on the greased unheated rack of a broiler pan.
5. Broil 4 inches from the heat for at least 8 to 12 minutes or until fish starts to flake when tested with a fork, turning once and brushing with reserved marinade halfway through cooking.
6. Take off any remaining marinade.
7. Before serving, squeeze the lime juice on each steak.

Nutrition:

Calories: 240

Fat: 6 g

Carbs: 19 g

Protein: 12 g

Sugars: 3.27 g

Sodium: 325 mg

Baked Tomato Hake

Preparation Time: 10 minutes

Cooking Time: 20-25 minutes

Servings: 4

Ingredients:

- ½ c. tomato sauce

- 1 tbsp. olive oil
- Parsley
- 2 sliced tomatoes
- ½ c. grated cheese
- 4 lbs. de-boned and sliced hake fish
- Salt.

Directions:

1. Preheat the oven to 400 0F.
2. Season the fish with salt.
3. In a skillet or saucepan, stir-fry the fish in the olive oil until half-done.
4. Take four foil papers to cover the fish.
5. Shape the foil to resemble containers; add the tomato sauce into each foil container.
6. Add the fish, tomato slices, and top with grated cheese.
7. Bake until you get a golden crust, for approximately 20-25 minutes.
8. Open the packs and top with parsley.

Nutrition:

Calories: 265

Fat: 15 g

Carbs: 18 g

Protein: 22 g

Sugars: 0.5 g

Sodium: 94.6 mg

Cheesy Tuna Pasta

Preparation Time: 10 minutes

Cooking Time: 20 minutes

Servings: 2-4

Ingredients:

- 2 c. arugula
- ¼ c. chopped green onions
- 1 tbs. red vinegar
- 5 oz. drained canned tuna
- ¼ tsp. black pepper
- 2 oz. cooked whole-wheat pasta
- 1 tbsp. olive oil
- 1 tbsp. grated low-fat parmesan

Directions:

1. Cook the pasta in unsalted water until ready. Drain and set aside.
2. In a large-sized bowl, thoroughly mix the tuna, green onions, vinegar, oil, arugula, pasta, and black pepper.
3. Toss well and top with the cheese.
4. Serve and enjoy.

Nutrition:

Calories: 566.3

Fat: 42.4 g

Carbs: 18.6 g

Protein: 29.8 g

Sugars: 0.4 g

Sodium: 688.6 mg

Salmon and Roasted Peppers

Preparation Time: 5 minutes

Cooking Time: 25 minutes

Servings: 4

Ingredients:

- 1 cup red peppers, cut into strips
- 4 salmon fillets, boneless
- ¼ cup chicken stock
- 2 tablespoons olive oil
- 1 yellow onion, chopped
- 1 tablespoon cilantro, chopped
- Pinch of sea salt
- Pinch black pepper

Directions:

1. Warm a pan with the oil on medium-high heat; add the onion and sauté for 5 minutes.
2. Put the fish and cook for at least 5 minutes on each side.
3. Add the rest of the ingredients, introduce the pan in the oven, and cook at 390 degrees F for 10 minutes.
4. Divide the mix between plates and serve.

Nutrition:

Calories 265

Fat 7

Fiber 5

Carbs 15

Protein 16

Shrimp and Beets

Preparation Time: 10 minutes

Cooking Time: 10 minutes

Servings: 4

Ingredients:

- 1 pound shrimp, peeled and deveined
- 2 tablespoons avocado oil
- 2 spring onions, chopped
- 2 garlic cloves, minced
- 1 beet, peeled and cubed
- 1 tablespoon lemon juice
- Pinch of sea salt
- Pinch of black pepper
- 1 teaspoon coconut aminos

Directions:

1. Warm a pan with the oil on medium-high heat, add the spring onions and the garlic and sauté for 2 minutes.
2. Add the shrimp and the other ingredients, toss, cook the mix for 8 minutes, divide into bowls and serve.

Nutrition:

Calories 281

Fat 6

Fiber 7

Carbs 11

Protein 8

Shrimp and Corn

Preparation Time: 5 minutes

Cooking Time: 10 minutes

Servings: 4

Ingredients:

- 1 pound shrimp, peeled and deveined
- 2 garlic cloves, minced
- 1 cup corn
- ½ cup veggie stock
- 1 bunch parsley, chopped
- Juice of 1 lime
- 2 tablespoons olive oil
- Pinch of sea salt
- Pinch of black pepper

Directions:

1. Warm a pan with the oil on medium-high heat, then put the garlic and the corn and sauté for 2 minutes.
2. Add the shrimp and the other ingredients, toss, cook everything for 8 minutes more, divide between plates and serve.

Nutrition:

Calories: 343 kcal

Protein: 29.12 g

Fat: 10.97 g

Carbohydrates: 34.25 g

Chili Shrimp and Pineapple

Preparation Time: 10 minutes

Cooking Time: 10 minutes

Servings: 4

Ingredients:

- 1 pound shrimp, peeled and deveined
- 2 tablespoons chili paste
- Pinch of sea salt
- Pinch of black pepper
- 1 tablespoon olive oil
- 1 cup pineapple, peeled and cubed
- ½ teaspoon ginger, grated
- 2 teaspoons almonds, chopped
- 2 tablespoons cilantro, chopped

Directions:

1. Warm a pan with the oil on medium-high heat, add the ginger and the chili paste, stir and cook for 2 minutes.
2. Add the shrimp and the other ingredients, toss, cook the mix for 8 minutes more, divide into bowls, and serve.

Nutrition:

Calories 261

Fat 4

Fiber 7

Carbs 15

Protein 8

Curry Tilapia and Beans

Preparation Time: 5 minutes

Cooking Time: 20 minutes

Servings: 4

Ingredients:

- 1 tablespoon olive oil
- 2 tablespoons green curry paste
- 4 tilapia fillets, boneless
- Juice of ½ lime
- 1 cup canned red kidney beans, drained
- 1 tablespoon parsley, chopped

Directions:

1. Warm a pan with the oil on medium heat, put the fish, and cook for at least 5 minutes on each side.
2. Put the rest of the ingredients, toss gently, cook over medium heat for 10 minutes more, divide between plates and serve.

Nutrition:

Calories 271

Fat 4

Fiber 6

Carbs 14

Protein 7

Balsamic Scallops

Preparation Time: 5 minutes

Cooking Time: 10 minutes

Servings: 4

Ingredients:

- 1 pound sea scallops
- 4 scallions, chopped
- 2 tablespoons olive oil
- 1 tablespoon balsamic vinegar
- 1 tablespoon cilantro, chopped
- A pinch of salt and black pepper

Directions:

1. Warm a pan with the oil on medium-high heat, add the scallops, the scallions, and the other ingredients, toss, cook for 10 minutes, divide into bowls and serve.

Nutrition:

Calories 300

Fat 4

Fiber 4

Carbs 14

Protein 17

Whitefish Curry

Preparation Time: 10 minutes

Cooking Time: 15 minutes

Servings: 6

Ingredients:

- 1 chopped onion
- 1 lb. Firm white fish fillets
- ¼ c. chopped fresh cilantro
- 1 c. vegetable broth
- 2 minced garlic cloves
- 1 tbsp. Minced fresh ginger
- 1 tsp. Salt
- ¼ tsp. ground black pepper
- Lemon wedges
- 1 bruised lemongrass
- 2 c. cubed butternut squash
- 2 tsp. curry powder
- 2 tbsps. coconut oil
- 2 c. chopped broccoli
  - oz. coconut milk
- 1 thinly sliced scallion

Directions:

1. In a pot, add coconut oil and melt.
2. Add onion, curry powder, ginger, garlic, and seasonings then sauté for 5 minutes
3. Add broccoli, lemongrass and butternut squash and sauté for two more minutes
4. Stir in broth and coconut milk and bring to a boil. Lower the heat to simmer and add the fish.
5. Cover the pot, then simmer for 5 minutes, then discard the lemongrass.
6. Ladle the curry into a medium serving bowl.
7. Add scallion and cilantro to garnish before serving with lemon wedges.
8. Enjoy.

Nutrition:

Calories: 218 kcal

Protein: 18.1 g

Fat: 8.57 g

Carbohydrates: 18.2 g

Swordfish with Pineapple and Cilantro

Preparation Time: 10 minutes

Cooking Time: 20 minutes

Servings: 4

Ingredients:

- 1 c. fresh pineapple chunks
- 1 tbsp. coconut oil
- 2 lbs. sliced swordfish
- 2 tbsps. Chopped fresh parsley
- ¼ tsp. Ground black pepper.
- 2 minced garlic cloves
- ¼ c. chopped fresh cilantro
- 1 tbsp. coconut aminos
- 1 tsp. Salt.

Directions:

1. Preheat the oven to 4000F.
2. Grease a baking tray with coconut oil
3. Add cilantro, swordfish, coconut aminos, pepper, salt, garlic, parsley, and pineapple to the dish then mix well.
4. Put the dish in an already preheated oven and bake for 20 minutes.
5. Serve and enjoy.

Nutrition:

Calories: 444 kcal

Protein: 47.53 g

Fat: 20.32 g

Carbohydrates: 16.44 g

Sesame-Tuna Skewers

Preparation Time: 10 minutes

Cooking Time: 15 minutes

Servings: 6

Ingredients:

- 6 oz. cubed thick tuna steaks
- Cooking spray
- ¼ tsp. Ground black pepper.
- ¾ c. sesame seeds
- 1 tsp. Salt
- ½ tsp. Ground ginger.
- 2 tbsps. toasted sesame oil

Directions:

1. Preheat the oven to about 4000F.
2. Coat a rimmed baking tray with cooking spray.
3. Soak twelve wooden skewers in water
4. In a small mixing bowl, combine pepper, ground ginger, salt, and sesame seeds.
5. In another bowl, toss the tuna with sesame oil.
6. Press the oiled cubes into a sesame seed mixture and put the cubes on each skewer.
7. Put the skewers on a readily prepared baking tray and put the tray into the preheated oven.
8. Bake for 12 minutes and turn once.
9. Serve and enjoy.

Nutrition:

Calories: 196 kcal

Protein: 14.47 g

Fat: 15.01 g

Carbohydrates: 2.48 g

Trout with Chard

Preparation Time: 10 minutes

Cooking Time: 15 minutes

Servings: 4

Ingredients:

- ½ c. vegetable broth
- 2 bunches sliced chard
- 4 boneless trout fillets
- Salt
- 1 tbsp. extra-virgin olive oil
- 2 minced garlic cloves
- ¼ c. golden raisins
- Ground black pepper
- 1 chopped onion
- 1 tbsp. apple cider vinegar

Directions:

1. Preheat the oven to about 3750F.
2. Add seasonings to the trout
3. Add olive oil in a pan, then heat.
4. Add garlic and onion, then sauté for 3 minutes.
5. Add chard to sauté for 2 more minutes.
6. Add broth, raisins, and cedar vinegar to the pan.
7. Layer a topping of trout fillets
8. Cover the pan and put it in the preheated oven for 10 minutes.
9. Serve and enjoy.

Nutrition:

Calories: 284 kcal

Protein: 2.07 g

Fat: 30.32 g

Carbohydrates: 3.49 g

Sole with Vegetables

Preparation Time: 10 minutes

Cooking Time: 15 minutes

Servings: 4

Ingredients:

- 4 tsp. divided extra-virgin olive oil
- 1 thinly sliced and divided carrot

- Salt
- Lemon wedges
- ½ c. divided vegetable broth
- 5 oz. sole fillets
- 2 sliced and thinly divided shallots
- Ground black pepper
- 2 tbsps. divided snipped fresh chives
- 1 thinly sliced and divided zucchini

Directions:

1. Preheat the oven to about 4250F.
2. Separate the aluminum foil into medium-sized pieces
3. Put a fillet on one half of the aluminum foil piece and add seasonings
4. Add shallots, zucchini, and ¼ each of the carrot on top of the fillet. Sprinkle with 1 ½ teaspoon of chives
5. Drizzle 2 tablespoons of broth and a tablespoon of olive oil over the fish and vegetables
6. Seal to make a packet and put the packet on a large baking tray.
7. Repeat for the rest of the ingredients and make more packets
8. Put the sheet in a preheated oven and bake the packets for 15 minutes
9. Peel back the foil and put the contents with the liquid onto a serving plate.
10. Garnish with lemon wedges before serving.
11. Enjoy.

Nutrition:

Calories: 130 kcal

Protein: 9.94 g

Fat: 7.96 g

Carbohydrates: 4.92 g

Poached Halibut and Mushrooms

Preparation Time: 5 minutes

Cooking Time: 30 minutes

Servings: 8

Ingredients:

- 1/8 teaspoon sesame oil
- 2 pounds halibut, cut into bite-sized pieces
- 1 teaspoon fresh lemon juice
- ½ teaspoon soy sauce
- 4 cups mushrooms, sliced ¼ cup water
- Salt and pepper to taste ¾ cup green onions

Directions:

1. Place a heavy-bottomed pot on medium-high fire.
2. Add all ingredients and mix well.
3. Cover and bring to a boil. Once boiling, lower fire to a simmer. Cook for 25 minutes.
4. Adjust seasoning to taste.
5. Serve and enjoy.

Nutrition:

Calories: 217 Cal

Fat 15.8 g

Carbs: 1.1 g

Protein: 16.5 g

Fiber: 0.4 g

Halibut Stir Fry

Preparation Time: 5 minutes

Cooking Time: 20 minutes

Servings: 6

Ingredients:

- 2 pounds halibut fillets
- 2 tbsp. olive oil ½ cup fresh parsley
- 1 onion, sliced 2 stalks celery, chopped
- 2 tablespoons capers
- 4 cloves of garlic minced
- Salt and pepper to taste

Directions:

1. Place a heavy-bottomed pot on high fire and heat for 2 minutes. Add oil and heat for 2 more minutes.
2. Stir in garlic and onions. Sauté for 5 minutes. Add remaining ingredients except for the parsley and stir fry for 10 minutes or until fish is cooked.

3. Adjust seasoning to taste and serve with a sprinkle of parsley.

Nutrition:

Calories 331 Cal

Fat 26 g

Carbs 2 g

Protein 22 g

Fiber 0.5 g

Steamed Garlic-Dill Halibut

Preparation Time: 5 minutes

Cooking Time: 25 minutes

Servings: 4

Ingredients:

- 1-pound halibut fillet
- 1 lemon, freshly squeezed
- Salt and pepper to taste
- 1 teaspoon garlic powder
- 1 tablespoon dill weed, chopped

Directions:

1. Place a large pot on medium fire and fill up to 1.5-inches of water. Place a trivet inside the pot.
2. In a baking dish that fits inside your large pot, add all ingredients and mix well. Cover dish with foil. Place the dish on top of the trivet inside the pot.
3. Cover pot and steam fish for 15 minutes.
4. Let fish rest for at least 10 minutes before removing from pot.
5. Serve and enjoy.

Nutrition:

Calories: 270 Cal

Fat: 6.5 g

Carbs: 3.9 g

Protein: 47.8 g

Fiber: 2.1 g

Italian Halibut Chowder

Preparation Time: 5 minutes

Cooking Time: 20 minutes

Servings: 8

Ingredients:

- 2 tablespoons olive oil
- 1 onion, chopped
- 3 stalks of celery, chopped
- 3 cloves of garlic, minced
- 2 ½ pounds halibut steaks, cubed
- 1 red bell pepper, seeded and chopped
- 1 cup tomato juice
- ½ cup apple juice, organic and unsweetened
- ½ teaspoon dried basil
- 1/8 teaspoon dried thyme
- Salt and pepper to taste

Directions:

1. Place a heavy-bottomed pot on medium-high fire and heat pot for 2 minutes. Add oil and heat for a minute.
2. Sauté the onion, celery, and garlic until fragrant.
3. Stir in the halibut steaks and bell pepper. Sauté for 3 minutes.
4. Pour in the rest of the ingredients and mix well.
5. Cover and bring to a boil. Once boiling, lower fire to a simmer and simmer for 10 minutes.
6. Adjust seasoning to taste.
7. Serve and enjoy.

Nutrition:

Calories: 318 Cal

Fat: 23g

Carbs: 6g

Protein: 21g

Fiber: 1g

Dill Haddock

Preparation Time: 10 minutes

Cooking Time: 30 minutes

Servings: 4

Ingredients:

- 1-pound haddock fillets
- 3 teaspoons veggie stock
- 2 tablespoons lemon juice
- Salt and black pepper to the taste
- 2 tablespoons mayonnaise
- 2 teaspoons chopped dill
- A drizzle of olive oil

Directions:

1. Grease a baking dish with the oil, add the fish, and also add stock mixed with lemon juice, salt, pepper, mayo, and dill. Toss a bit and place in the oven at 350 degrees F to bake for 30 minutes. Divide between plates and serve.
2. Enjoy!

Nutrition:

Calories: 214

Fat: 12 Cal

Fiber: 4 g

Carbs: 7 g

Protein: 17 g

Chili Snapper

Preparation Time: 10 minutes

Cooking Time: 20 minutes

Servings: 2

Ingredients:

- 2 red snapper fillets, boneless and skinless
- 3 tablespoons chili paste
- A pinch of sea salt
- Black pepper
- 1 tablespoon coconut aminos
- 1 garlic clove, minced
- ½ teaspoon fresh grated ginger
- 2 teaspoons sesame seeds, toasted
- 2 tablespoons olive oil
- 1 green onion, chopped
- 2 tablespoons chicken stock

Directions:

1. Warm a pan with the oil on medium-high heat, add the ginger, onion, and the garlic, stir and cook for 2 minutes. Add chili paste, aminos, salt, pepper, and the stock stir and cook for 3 minutes more. Add the fish fillets, toss gently and cook for 5-6 minutes on each side.
2. Divide into plates, sprinkle sesame seeds on top, and serve.
3. Enjoy!

Nutrition:

Calories 261

Fat: 10 g

Fiber: 7 g

Carbs: 15 g

Protein: 16 g

Lemony Mackerel

Preparation Time: 10 minutes

Cooking Time: 15 minutes

Servings: 4

Ingredients:

- Juice of 1 lemon
- Zest of 1 lemon
- 4 mackerels
- 1 tablespoon minced chives
- Pinch of sea salt
- Pinch black pepper
- 2 tablespoons olive oil

Directions:

1. Warm a pan with the oil on medium-high heat, add the mackerel and cook for 6 minutes on each side. Add the lemon zest, lemon juice, chives, salt, and pepper then cook for 2 more minutes on each side. Divide everything between plates and serve.
2. Enjoy!

Nutrition:

Calories: 289 Cal

Fat: 20 g

Fiber: 0 g

Carbs: 1 g

Protein: 21 g

Honey Crusted Salmon with Pecans

Preparation Time: 20 minutes

Cooking Time: 20 minutes

Servings: 6

Ingredients:

- 3 tablespoons olive oil
- 3 tablespoons mustard
- 5 teaspoons raw honey
- ½ cup chopped pecans
- 6 salmon fillets, boneless
- 3 teaspoons chopped parsley
- Salt and black pepper to the taste

Directions:

1. In a bowl, whisk the mustard with honey and oil. In another bowl, mix the pecans with parsley and stir. Season salmon fillets with salt and pepper, place them on a baking sheet, brush with mustard mixture, top with the pecans mix, and place them in the oven at 400 degrees F to bake for 20 minutes. Divide into plates and serve with a side salad.
2. Enjoy!

Nutrition:

Calories 200

Fat 10

Fiber 5

Carbs 12

Protein 16

Salmon and Cauliflower

Preparation Time: 10 minutes

Cooking Time: 25 minutes

Servings: 4

Ingredients:

- 2 tablespoons coconut aminos
- 1 cauliflower head, florets separated and chopped
- 4 pieces salmon fillets, skinless
- 1 big red onion, cut into wedges
- 1 tablespoon olive oil
- Pinch of sea salt
- Pinch black pepper

Directions:

1. Put the salmon in a baking dish, put the oil all over, and season with salt and pepper. Place in preheated broiler over medium heat and cook for about 5 minutes. Add coconut aminos, cauliflower, and onion, then place in the oven and bake at 400 degrees F for 15 minutes more. Divide between plates and serve.
2. Enjoy!

Nutrition:

Calories 112

Fat 5

Fiber 3

Carbs 8

Protein 7

Ginger Salmon and Black Beans

Preparation Time: 10 minutes

Cooking Time: 30 minutes

Servings: 4

Ingredients:

- 1 cup canned black beans, drained
- 2 tablespoons coconut aminos
- ½ cup olive oil
- 1 ½ cup chicken stock
- 6 ounces salmon fillets, boneless

- 2 garlic cloves, minced
- 1 tablespoon fresh grated ginger
- 2 teaspoons white wine vinegar
- ¼ cup grated radishes
- ¼ cup grated carrots
- ¼ cup chopped scallions

Directions:

1. Meanwhile, in a bowl, mix the aminos with half of the oil and whisk. Cut halfway into each salmon fillet, place them in a baking dish and pour the aminos mixture all over. Toss and keep in the fridge for 10 minutes to marinate. Heat a pan with the rest of the oil over medium heat, add garlic, ginger, and black beans. Stir and cook for 3 minutes. Add vinegar and stock, stir, bring to a boil, cook for 10 minutes, and divide between plates. Broil fish for 4 minutes per side over medium-high heat then place a fillet next to the black beans and top with grated scallions, radishes, and carrots.
2. Enjoy!

Nutrition:

Calories 200

Fat 7

Fiber 2

Carbs 9

Protein 9

Clams with Olives Mix

Preparation Time: 10 minutes

Cooking Time: 10 minutes

Servings: 2

Ingredients:

- 3 tablespoons olive oil
- 2 pound little clams, scrubbed
- ½ teaspoon dried thyme
- 1 shallot, minced
- ½ cup veggie stock
- 2 garlic cloves, minced
- 1 apple, cored and chopped
- Juice of ½ lemon

Directions:

1. Warm a pan with the oil on medium-high heat, add shallot and garlic, stir and cook for 3-4 minutes. Add the stock, clams, thyme, apple, and lemon juice. Stir and cook for 6 minutes more, divide into bowls and serve.
2. Enjoy!

Nutrition:

Calories 180

Fat 9

Fiber 2

Carbs 8

Protein 10

Cod Curry

Preparation Time: 10 minutes

Cooking Time: 25 minutes

Servings: 4

Ingredients:

- 4 cod fillets, boneless
- ½ teaspoon mustard seeds
- Salt and black pepper to the taste
- 2 green chilies, chopped
- 1 teaspoon fresh grated ginger
- 1 teaspoon curry powder
- ¼ teaspoon ground cumin
- 4 tablespoons olive oil
- 1 small red onion, chopped
- 1 teaspoon ground turmeric
- ¼ cup chopped parsley
- 1½ cups coconut cream
- 3 garlic cloves, minced

Directions:

1. Heat a pot with half of the oil over medium heat. Add mustard seeds and cook for 2 minutes. Add ginger, onion, garlic,

turmeric, curry powder, chilies, and cumin, stir and cook for 10 minutes more. Add coconut milk, salt and pepper then stir. Bring to a boil, cook for 10 minutes and take off the heat. Warm another pan with the rest of the oil over medium heat, add fish, and then cook for 4 minutes. Transfer the fish on top of the curry mix, toss gently then cook for 6 more minutes. Divide between plates, sprinkle the parsley on top and serve.
2. Enjoy!

Nutrition:

Calories 210

Fat 14

Fiber 7

Carbs 6

Protein 16

Fast Fish Pie

Preparation Time: 15 minutes

Cooking Time: 45 minutes

Servings: 4

Ingredients:

- 2 slices prosciutto
- 1 cup frozen peas
- 2 sheets frozen puff pastry
- 600g firm white fish fillets
- 1/2 bunch dill
- 1 tbsp. corn flour
- 350g cauliflower
- 1 lemon
- 1 Coles Australian Free Range Egg
- 1 tbsp. sesame seeds

Directions:

1. Preheat broiler to 400°F. Spot the cauliflower, prosciutto, fish, peas, lemon pizzazz, dill & corn flour in an enormous bowl. Season. Delicately hurl until very much consolidated. Move the blend to a 6-cup round pie dish.
2. Cut 1 baked good sheet into 3 strips. Brush 2 contiguous edges of residual baked good sheet with egg. Spot 1 baked good strip, somewhat covering, over each edge, squeezing delicately to make an enormous square.
3. Brush sides of the pie dish with the use of egg. Spot pastry over fish blend, squeezing into the edge of the dish. Overlay overabundance baked good inwards. Brush the baked good with egg. Utilize a sharp blade to cut 3 cuts in the focal point of the baked good. Sprinkle with sesame seeds.
4. Bake the pie until the baked good is brilliant darker & puffed. Slice into wedges to serve.

Nutrition:

Calories: 364 kcal

Protein: 35.95 g

Fat: 20.51 g

Carbohydrates: 8.57 g

Quick Chermoula Fish Parcels

Preparation Time: 15 minutes

Cooking Time: 30 minutes

Servings: 4

Ingredients:

- 4 x 150g firm skinless white fish fillets
- 1/2 small red onion
- 400g can chickpeas
- Lemon wedges
- 100g roasted red capsicum
- Baby rocket
- Chermoula
- 1/4 cup olive oil
- 2 garlic cloves
- 1 long red chili
- 3/4 cup parsley leaves
- 3/4 cup coriander leaves
- 1 1/2 teaspoons ground cumin
- 2 tablespoons lemon juice

Directions:

1. Preheat a grill barbecue or hotplate on low warmth. Consolidate chickpeas, capsicum, & onion in a bowl.
2. Make Chermoula. Join all fixings in a bowl. Season with salt & pepper.
3. Cut four 30cm bits of foil. Top each with a 15cm bit of heating paper. Separation chickpea blend among bits of paper. Top with fish. Spoon 1/3 of chermoula over fish. Overlay up edges of paper & foil to encase fish, scrunching foil at the top to seal. Spot fish divides a foil heating plate. Spot plate on grill barbecue. Cook, with hood shut, until fish is cooked through.
4. Place fish divides serving plates. Cautiously open. Shower fish with remaining chermoula. Serve it.

Nutrition:

Calories: 316 kcal

Protein: 9.82 g

Fat: 18.27 g

Carbohydrates: 30.9 g

Healthy Fish Nacho Bowl

Preparation Time: 13 minutes

Cooking Time: 20 minutes

Servings: 4

Ingredients:

- 500g white fish fillets
- 400g red cabbage
- 3 green shallots
- 1 tablespoon yogurt
- 1 tablespoon olive oil
- 425g can black beans
- 50g gluten-free corn chips
- 200g cherry tomatoes
- 2-3 teaspoons gluten-free chipotle seasoning
- 1 small avocado
- 1/3 cup fresh coriander leaves
- 1 large lime, rind finely grated, juiced

Directions:

1. Combine the fish, stew powder/chipotle flavoring & 2 tsp oil in a bowl
2. Shred the cabbage in a nourishment processor fitted with the cutting connection. Move to a huge bowl with the tomato, lime skin, dark beans, yogurt, 2 tbs lime juice, 2 shallots, & the rest of the oil. Hurl well to consolidate.
3. Heat a huge non-stick skillet over high warmth. Cook the fish, turning until simply cooked through. Move to a plate.
4. Meanwhile, consolidate the avocado, coriander, remaining shallot & 1 tbs remaining lime squeeze in a little bowl.
5. Divide the cabbage blend, fish, guacamole & corn chips among serving bowls. Sprinkle with additional coriander & present with additional lime wedges.

Nutrition:

Calories: 388 kcal

Protein: 28.17 g

Fat: 16.64 g

Carbohydrates: 35.72 g

Fish & Chickpea Stew

Preparation Time: 5 minutes

Cooking Time: 10 minutes

Servings: 4

Ingredients:

- 2 cups fish stock
- 1 brown onion
- 400g can tomatoes
- 4 kale leaves
- 500g firm white fish fillets
- Sliced Coles Bakery Stone
- 2 garlic clove
- Finely grated parmesan
- 400g can chickpeas
- 1 carrot, peeled
- Salt & pepper to taste

Directions:

1. Spray a skillet with olive oil shower. Spot over medium-low warmth. Include the carrot & onion & cook, mixing, until delicate & brilliant. Include garlic & cook, blending, until sweet-smelling.
2. Add the chickpeas stock & tomato, & to the onion blend in the skillet. Bring to the bubble. Lessen warmth to medium-low & stew until the blend thickens somewhat.
3. Add the kale & fish to the dish & stew until the fish is simply cooked through. Season.
4. Divide the stew among serving bowls. Sprinkle with parmesan & present with the bread.

Nutrition:

Calories: 1447 kcal

Protein: 42.1 g

Fat: 127.85 g

Carbohydrates: 32.4 g

Easy Crunchy Fish Tray Bake

Preparation Time: 10 minutes

Cooking Time: 20 minutes

Servings: 4

Ingredients:

- 600g frozen crumbed whiting fish fillets
- 1/2 small red onion
- 2 x 250g punnets tomatoes
- 2 zucchini
- 180g baby stuffed peppers
- 1 tablespoon parmesan
- 2 teaspoons oregano leaves
- 1 lemon, cut into wedges

Directions:

1. Preheat the stove to 400F. Oil an enormous preparing plate. Spot the fish filets on the readied plate. Disperse the oregano & parmesan over the fish.
2. Add the zucchini, tomatoes & stuffed peppers to the plate. Disperse the onion rings over the top. Season well. Splash with olive oil. Heat until the fish is brilliant & cooked through.
3. Divide the fish & vegetables among plates & present with the rocket & lemon wedges.

Nutrition:

Calories: 346 kcal

Protein: 3.67 g

Fat: 2.8 g

Carbohydrates: 81.77 g

Ginger & Chili Sea Bass Fillets

Preparation Time: 5 minutes

Cooking Time: 10 minutes

Servings: 2

Ingredients:

- 2 Sea bass fillet
- 1 tsp. Black pepper
- 1 tbsp. Extra virgin olive oil
- 1 tsp Ginger, peeled and chopped
- 1 Garlic cloves, thinly slice
- 1 Red chili, deseeded and thinly sliced
- 2 Green onion stemmed, chopped

Directions:

1. Get a skillet and heat the oil on a medium to high heat.
2. Sprinkle black pepper over the Sea Bass and score the fish's skin a few times with a sharp knife.
3. Add the sea bass fillet to the very hot pan with the skin side down.
4. Cook for 5 minutes and turn over.
5. Cook for a further 2 minutes.
6. Remove seabass from the pan and rest.
7. Put the chili, garlic, and ginger and cook for approximately 2 minutes or until golden.
8. Remove from the heat and add the green onions.
9. Scatter the vegetables over your sea bass to serve.
10. Try with a steamed sweet potato or side salad.

Nutrition:

Calories: 306 kcal

Protein: 29.92 g

Fat: 8.94 g

Carbohydrates: 26.59 g

Nut-Crust Tilapia with Kale

Preparation Time: 5 minutes

Cooking Time: 15 minutes

Servings: 2

Ingredients:

- 2 tsp. Extra virgin olive oil
- 2 tbsp. Low-fat hard cheese, grated
- 1/2 cup Roasted and Ground Brazil Nuts/Hazelnuts/Any other hard nut
- 1/2 cup 100% Wholegrain breadcrumbs
- 2 Tilapia Fillet, skinless
- 2 tsp. Whole grain mustard
- 1 Head of kale, chopped
- 1 tbsp. Sesame seeds, lightly toasted
- 1 Garlic clove, minced

Directions:

1. Set the oven to 350°F.
2. Lightly oil a baking sheet with the use of 1 tsp. extra virgin olive oil.
3. Mix in the nuts, breadcrumbs, and cheese in a separate bowl.
4. Spread a thin layer of the mustard over the fish and then dip into the breadcrumb mixture.
5. Transfer to baking dish.
6. Bake for at least 12 minutes, till cooked through.
7. Meanwhile, warm 1 tsp. Oil in a skillet at medium heat temperature then sauté the garlic for 30 seconds, adding in the kale for a further 5 minutes.
8. Mix in the sesame seeds.
9. Serve the fish at once with the kale on the side.

Nutrition:

Calories: 475 kcal

Protein: 37.14 g

Fat: 33.44 g

Carbohydrates: 11.08 g

Wasabi Salmon Burgers

Preparation Time: 5 minutes

Cooking Time: 10 minutes

Servings: 1

Ingredients:

- 1/2 tsp. Honey
- 2 tbsp. Reduce-salt soy sauce
- 1 tsp. Wasabi powder
- 1 Beaten free-range egg
- 2 can Wild Salmon, drained
- 2 Scallion, chopped
- 2 tbsp. Coconut Oil
- 1 tbsp. Fresh ginger, minced

Directions:

1. Combine the salmon, egg, ginger, scallions, and 1 tbsp. oil in a bowl, mixing well with your hands to form 4 patties.
2. In a separate bowl, add the wasabi powder and soy sauce with the honey and whisk until blended.
3. Heat 1 tbsp. oil over medium heat in a skillet and cook the patties for 4 minutes each side until firm and browned.
4. Glaze the top of each patty with the wasabi mixture and cook for another 15 seconds before you serve.
5. Serve with your favorite side salad or vegetables for a healthy treat.

Nutrition:

Calories: 591 kcal

Protein: 63.52 g

Fat: 34.3 g

Carbohydrates: 3.83 g

Citrus & Herb Sardines

Preparation Time: 5 minutes

Cooking Time: 15 minutes

Servings: 2

Ingredients:

- 10 Sardines, scaled and clean
- 2 Whole Lemon zest
- Handful-Flat leafy parsley, chopped
- 2 Garlic cloves, finely chopped
- 1/2 cup Black Olives (pitted and halves)
- 3 tbsp. Olive oil
- 1 can Tomato, chopped, (optional)
- 1/2 can Chickpeas or Butterbeans, drained and rinsed
- 8 Cherry Tomatoes, halved (optional)
- Pinch of Black Pepper

Directions:

1. In a bowl, add the lemon zest to the chopped parsley (save a pinch for garnishing) and half of the chopped garlic, ready for later.
2. Put a very large skillet on the hob and heat on high.
3. Now add the oil and once very hot, lay the sardines flat on the pan.
4. Sauté for 3 minutes until golden underneath and turn over to fry for another 3 minutes. Place onto a plate to rest.
5. Sauté the remaining garlic (add another splash of oil if you need to) for 1 min until softened. Pour in the tin of chopped tomatoes, mix and let simmer for 4-5 minutes.
6. If you're avoiding tomatoes, just avoid this step and go straight to chickpeas.
7. Tip in the chickpeas or butter beans and fresh tomatoes and stir until heated through.
8. Here's when you add the sardines into the lemon and parsley dressing prepared earlier and add to the pan, cooking for a further 3-4 minutes.
9. Once heated through, serve with a pinch of parsley and remaining lemon zest to garnish.

Nutrition:

Calories: 493 kcal

Protein: 24.16 g

Fat: 35.67 g

Carbohydrates: 20.92 g

Daring Shark Steaks

Preparation Time: 35 minutes

Cooking Time: 40 minutes

Servings: 2

Ingredients:

- 2 Shark steak, skinless
- 2 tbsp. Onion powder
- 2 tsp. Chili powder
- 1 Garlic clove, minced
- ¼ cup Worcestershire sauce
- 1 tbsp. Ground black pepper
- 2 tbsp. Thyme, chopped

Directions:

1. In a bowl, put then mix all of the seasonings and spices to form a paste before setting aside.
2. Spread a thin layer of paste on all sides of the fish, cover, and chill for 30 minutes (If possible).
3. Preheat oven to 325°F/150°C/Gas Mark 3.
4. Bake the fish in parchment paper for 30-40 minutes, until well cooked.
5. Serve on a bed of quinoa or whole-grain couscous and your favorite salad.

Nutrition:

Calories: 112 kcal

Protein: 4.87 g

Fat: 3.65 g

Carbohydrates: 16.78 g

Spicy Kingfish

Preparation Time: 15 minutes

Cooking Time: 10 minutes

Servings: 2

Ingredients:

- 1 teaspoon dried unsweetened coconut
- 1 teaspoon cumin seeds
- 1 teaspoon fennel seeds
- 1 teaspoon peppercorns
- 10 curry leaves
- ½ teaspoon ground turmeric
- 1½ teaspoons fresh ginger, grated finely
- 1 garlic clove, minced
- Salt, to taste
- 1 tablespoon fresh lime juice
- 4 (4-ounce) kingfish steaks
- 1 tbsp. olive oil
- 1 lime wedge

Directions:

1. Heat a cast-iron skillet on low heat.
2. Add coconut, cumin seeds, fennel seeds, peppercorns, and curry leaves and cook, stirring continuously for about 1 minute.
3. Take off from the heat and cool completely.
4. In a spice grinder, add the spice mixture and turmeric and grind rill powdered finely.
5. Transfer the mixture into a large bowl with ginger, garlic, salt, and lime juice and mix well.
6. Add fish fillets and cat with the mixture evenly.
7. Refrigerate to marinate for about 3 hours.
8. In a huge nonstick skillet, warm oil on medium heat.
9. Put the fish fillets and cook for at least 3-5 minutes per side or till the desired doneness.
10. Transfer onto a paper towel-lined plate to drain.
11. Serve with lime wedges.

Nutrition:

Calories: 592 kcal

Protein: 67.03 g

Fat: 34.55 g

Carbohydrates: 4.91 g

Gingered Tilapia

Preparation Time: 15 minutes

Cooking Time: 6 minutes

Servings: 5

Ingredients:

- 2 tablespoons coconut oil
- 5 tilapia fillets
- 3 garlic cloves, minced
- 2 tablespoons unsweetened coconut, shredded
- 4-ounce freshly ground ginger
- 2 tablespoons coconut aminos
- 8 scallions, chopped

Directions:

1. In a huge skillet, melt coconut oil on medium heat.
2. Add tilapia fillets and cook for about 2 minutes.
3. Flip the side and add garlic, coconut, and ginger and cook for about 1 minute.
4. Add coconut aminos and cook for about 1 minute.
5. Add scallion and cook for about 1-2 minutes more.
6. Serve immediately.

Nutrition:

Calories: 135

Fat: 3g

Carbohydrates: 2g

Protein: 26g

Haddock with Swiss chard

Preparation Time: 15 minutes

Cooking Time: 10 minutes

Servings: 1

Ingredients:

- 2 tablespoons coconut oil, divided
- 2 minced garlic cloves
- 2 teaspoons fresh ginger, grated finely
- 1 haddock fillet
- Salt, to taste
- Freshly ground black pepper, to taste
- 2 cups Swiss chard, chopped roughly

- 1 teaspoon coconut aminos

Directions:

1. In a skillet, put 1 tablespoon of coconut oil then melt it on medium heat.
2. Add garlic and ginger and sauté for about 1 minute.
3. Add haddock fillet and sprinkle with salt and black pepper.
4. Cook for at least about 3-5 minutes per side or till the desired doneness.
5. Meanwhile, in another skillet, melt remaining coconut oil on medium heat.
6. Add Swiss chard and coconut aminos and cook for about 5-10 minutes.
7. Serve the salmon fillet over Swiss chard.

Nutrition:

Calories: 486 kcal

Protein: 39.68 g

Fat: 34.34 g

Carbohydrates: 5.57 g

Rockfish Curry

Preparation Time: 15 minutes

Cooking Time: 30 minutes

Servings: 8

Ingredients:

- 2 pound rockfish
- ¾ teaspoon ground turmeric, divided
- Salt, to taste
- 2 tablespoons coconut oil
- 12 pearl onions, halved
- 2 medium red onions, sliced thinly
- 2 Serrano peppers halved
- 40 small leaves, divided
- 1 (½-inch) piece fresh ginger, minced
- Freshly ground black pepper, to taste
- ¼ cup water
- 1½ (14-ounce) cans coconut milk, divided
- 1 teaspoon apple cider vinegar

Directions:

1. In a bowl, season the fish with ¼ teaspoon of the turmeric and salt and keep aside.
2. In a huge skillet, melt coconut oil on medium heat.
3. Add pearl onions, red onions, ginger, Serrano peppers, and 20 curry leaves and sauté for about 15 minutes.
4. Add ginger, remaining turmeric, salt, and black pepper and sauté for about 2 minutes.
5. Move half of the mixture into a bowl and keep aside.
6. Add remaining curry leaves, fish fillets, water, and 1 can of coconut milk and cook for about 2 minutes.
7. Now cook, covered for about 5 minutes.
8. Add apple cider vinegar and remaining half can of coconut milk and cook for about 3-5 minutes or till done completely.
9. Serve hot with the topping of reserved onion mixture.

Nutrition:

Calories: 331 kcal

Protein: 24.72 g

Fat: 18.38 g

Carbohydrates: 18.83 g

Coconut Rice with shrimps in Coconut curry

Preparation Time: 10 minutes

Cooking Time: 40 minutes

Servings: 2-3

Ingredients:

- 16 oz. Shrimp (deveined)
- 3 cloves Garlic (chopped)
- 2 Tsp. Curry powder
- ¼ cup Scallions (chopped)
- 15 oz. Coconut milk
- 1 ½ cup Water
- ⅛ cup Cilantro (chopped)
- 2 tbsp.
- Butter
- ½ Lime juice
- 2 tbsp. Ginger (shredded)

- 1 cup Jasmine rice
- Salt and red pepper flakes

Directions:
1. On medium heat, melt 1 tbsp. of butter, then add rice and stir to coat.
2. Pour 1 cup coconut milk and the water and cook for 30 minutes until rice is cooked.
3. Melt butter in a large pan on medium heat, add scallions, garlic, and ginger and leave to cook for 3 minutes.
4. In a separate bowl, mix coconut milk and curry powder
5. After the scallions are cooked, add the shrimps and cook till they are pink.
6. Add the coconut and curry mixture and cook then season accordingly.
7. Remove from heat and serve rice mixed with lime juice and cilantro alongside the shrimps.

Nutrition:

Calories: 400 kcal

Protein: 40.46 g

Fat: 18.01 g

Carbohydrates: 29.99 g

Grilled fish tacos
Preparation Time: 10 minutes

Cooking Time: 10 minutes

Servings: 8

Ingredients:
- 1 pound mahimahi fillets
- 2 tablespoons canola oil
- 2 tablespoons omega-3-rich margarine
- Juice of 1 lime
- 1 teaspoons salt, divided
- 1 teaspoon chili powder
- 1/2 teaspoon crushed red pepper
- 1/2 teaspoon garlic powder
- 1/2 teaspoon oregano
- 1/2 teaspoon ground cumin
- 2 mangoes
- 1/4 cup cilantro, chopped
- 8 wheat flour tortillas

Directions:
1. In a medium-size bowl, whisk together the canola oil, margarine, lime juice, one teaspoon of salt, and the residual dried spices. Pour mix over the fish. Cover and marinate for 45 minutes in the fridge.
2. In the meantime, peel mangoes and cut into cubes. Mix with cilantro and remaining salt.
3. Preheat grill to medium-high. Remove fish from the marinade, place on the grill, and cook 2 to 3 minutes on both sides. Place tortillas on the grill and heat 10 to 15 seconds on each side. Fill with fish fillets and mango topping.

Nutrition:

Calories: 231 kcal

Protein: 13.99 g

Fat: 17.04 g

Carbohydrates: 6.02 g

Curried Fish
Preparation Time: 10 minutes

Cooking Time: 35 minutes

Servings: 4

Ingredients:
- 1 1/2 cups basmati rice
- 2 tablespoons canola oil
- 1 yellow onion, finely chopped
- 1 tablespoon curry powder
- 1/2 teaspoon ground cumin
- 1/2 teaspoon ground coriander
- 1/4 teaspoon turmeric
- 1/2 teaspoon cayenne pepper, optional
- 1 bell pepper, cored and thinly chopped
- Four 5-ounce fish fillets
- 2 large tomatoes, diced
- 1/4 cup hot water

Directions:

1. Place the rice in a pan, add approximately 3 cups water, then leave to come to a boil; then reduce the heat and simmer for 20 minutes until all of the liquid is assimilated.
2. In a separate pan, heat canola oil over high heat. Add the onions and sauté for a couple of minutes. Add spices and bell pepper, and cook 1 to 2 minutes longer, stirring continually. Place fillets in the pan and spoon seasoning mixture over the top, then combine tomatoes and water to the dish. Once the liquid comes a to simmer, turn the heat down and cover. Cook 8 to 10 minutes longer.
3. Serve with rice.

Nutrition:

Calories: 362 kcal

Protein: 14.26 g

Fat: 24.98 g

Carbohydrates: 35.58 g

Herbed Rockfish

Preparation Time: 10 minutes

Cooking Time: 20 minutes

Servings: 8

Ingredients:

- 1 1/2 pounds rockfish fillets
- 2 egg whites
- 1 1/2 tablespoons nonfat milk
- 1/2 tablespoons canola oil
- 1 cup nonfat plain yogurt
- 1 tablespoon lemon juice
- 1 tablespoon oregano
- 1 tablespoon fresh parsley, chopped
- 1 tablespoon pimento, minced
- 1 teaspoon garlic, minced
- 1 teaspoon ground black pepper
- 6 slices wheat bread, toasted
- 1/4 cup flaxseed, ground fresh
- 1/4 cup extra virgin olive oil
- 1 pint cherry tomatoes, chopped
- 2 fresh lemons, wedges

Directions:

1. Clean rockfish fillets in cold water, remove the skin and remove any bones — Pat dry with paper towels. In a medium-size bowl, combine egg whites, nonfat milk, yogurt, canola oil, and lemon juice — place in a pie pan.
2. Put the next 8 ingredients (oregano-flaxseed) in a food processor until finely ground — place in a separate dish.
3. Heat the olive oil in a pan. First, soak the fillets in the spice mixture, succeeded by the yogurt blend, and then once again in the spice mixture, compressing the crumbs gently into the fish for the final layer.
4. Place the fillets in hot olive oil. When the underneath begins to brown, flip the fillets over, and reduce heat — Cook for a further 15 to 20 minutes.
5. Complete with tomatoes and lemon wedges.

Nutrition:

Calories: 178 kcal

Protein: 19.62 g

Fat: 8.96 g

Carbohydrates: 4.73 g

Salmon Sushi

Preparation Time: 30 minutes

Cooking Time: 20 minutes

Servings: 26

Ingredients:

- 1 1/2 cups water
- 1 cup of sushi rice
- 1/2 tablespoons rice vinegar
- 1/2 teaspoons sugar
- 1 teaspoon salt
- 4 ounces smoked salmon
- 4 nori seaweed sheets
- Optional: low-sodium soy sauce or wasabi paste.

Directions:

1. Using a pot with a lid, bring water to a boil. Combine rice, cover, and lessen the temperature.
2. Simmer 18 to 20 minutes, turn off the heat, and leave the rice to cool for 10 minutes. Place the rice in a bowl and dampen with vinegar, salt, and sugar. Blend with a wooden spoon, and allow the rice to stand. Chop smoked salmon into strips.
3. Make each sushi roll as follows:
4. Place 1 seaweed layer on a clean, dry surface.
5. Place 1/2 cup cooked rice over the seaweed, and delicately spread evenly over the sheet. Lay the strips of salmon in a perpendicular line in the center of the rice.
6. Delicately roll so as not to rip the seaweed, starting at the left edge, and ending just before the right edge — Tuck rice in at the sides of the roll.
7. Run a damp finger along the exhibited edge of the seaweed, and conclude rolling, pressing down to seal the border to the roll.
8. Slice into pieces using a cutting knife.

Nutrition:

Calories: 25 kcal

Protein: 1.78 g

Fat: 1.49 g

Carbohydrates: 2.33 g

Spicy herb catfish

Preparation Time: 10 minutes

Cooking Time: 25 minutes

Servings: 4

Ingredients:

- For the spice mixture:
- 1/4 cup coriander seeds
- 1/2 teaspoons cumin seeds
- 1/2 tablespoon ground red pepper
- 1/2 teaspoon crushed cardamom
- 1 tablespoon raw sugar
- 1 tablespoon kosher salt
- 1 teaspoon ground black pepper
- Four 6-ounce catfish fillets
- 1/2 cup flaxseed, freshly ground
- Canola oil spray
- For the garnish:
- Several sprigs of fresh cilantro 1 medium tomato and
- 1 lemon quartered

Directions:

1. Preheat oven to 350°F. Place the spice blend ingredients into a mixing bowl, and combine well. Place the mixture inside a pie pan.
2. Clean the catfish fillets and pat dry. Put ground flaxseed into an alternate pie pan. Dredge fillets in the spice mixture first, followed by flaxseed. Spray the baking sheet with canola oil and place fillets on a baking sheet and cook for 18 minutes. Boil the stock juices for an additional 6 minutes. Pour the juices over the fillets and serve decorated with cilantro, a portion of tomato, and a lemon quarter.

Nutrition:

Calories: 208 kcal

Protein: 13.5 g

Fat: 12.65 g

Carbohydrates: 13.66 g

Stuffed Trout

Preparation Time: 20 minutes

Cooking Time: 1 hour and 15 minutes

Servings: 4

Ingredients:

- 1 cup chicken broth
- 1/2 cup quinoa
- 2 tablespoons omega-3-rich margarine
- 1 yellow onion, finely dices
- 1 cup (100 g) mushrooms, sliced
- 2 teaspoons dehydrated tarragon
- Salt and pepper
- 1 cup cherry tomatoes, chopped
- 2 tablespoons lemon juice

- 2 tablespoons canola oil
- 2 whole lake trout
- 2 tablespoons flour

Directions:

1. In a pan, place the chicken broth on to simmer. Combine the quinoa, cover, and decrease the heat to low — Cook for 45 to 60 minutes.
2. Preheat oven to 400°F and proceed to line a baking tray with parchment paper.
3. To make the stuffing, melt margarine in a wide pan over medium heat. Sauté the onions and mushrooms till tender. Season by including tarragon, and salt and pepper. Combine cherry tomatoes and sauté 1 to 2 minutes further, mixing continually. Take off the heat and combine with cooked quinoa. Add in lemon juice and stir.
4. Spray the canola oil covering the trout. In a bowl, blend together flour, salt, and pepper. Glaze the interior and exterior of the trout with the flour batter. Stuff the trout with the stuffing blend.
5. Cook uncovered for 10 minutes per inch of trout.

Nutrition:

Calories: 342 kcal

Protein: 18.76 g

Fat: 19.1 g

Carbohydrates: 24.38 g

Thai Chowder

Preparation Time: 10 minutes

Cooking Time: 20 minutes

Servings: 6

Ingredients:

- 3 cups 98 % fat-free chicken broth
- 10 small red potatoes, diced
- 3 cobs fresh sweet corn
- 3/4 cup coconut milk
- 1/2 teaspoon fresh ginger, diced
- 1 teaspoon dried lemongrass
- 1 teaspoon green curry paste
- 1/2 cup cabbage, chopped
- Four 5-ounce tilapia fillets
- 2 tablespoons fish sauce
- 3/4 cup fresh shrimp, cleaned, with tails on
- 3/4 cup bay scallops
- 3/4 cup cilantro, chopped

Directions:

1. In a saucepan, boil chicken stock at high heat until it reaches a simmer. Decrease temperature and add the cabbage, ginger, coconut milk, lemongrass, sweet corn, and lemongrass, curry paste, and potatoes — cover and cook for 15 minutes.
2. Firstly, combine fish fillets and fish sauce, and cook for 6 minutes. Secondly, add the shrimp, and cook for a further 2 to 3 minutes. Finally, add the scallops and cook until scallops are opaque in color.
3. Serve with cilantro.

Nutrition:

Calories: 761 kcal

Protein: 33.25 g

Fat: 5.34 g

Carbohydrates: 150.45 g

Tuna-Stuffed Tomatoes

Preparation Time: 10 minutes

Cooking Time: 10 minutes

Servings: 2

Ingredients:

- 1 medium tomato
- 1 6oz. can tuna, drained and flaked
- 2 tbsp. mayonnaise
- 1 tbsp. celery, chopped
- ½ tsp. Dijon mustard
- ¼ tsp. seasoning salt
- Shredded mild cheddar cheese, to garnish

Directions:

1. Preheat oven to 375°. Wash tomato and cut in half from the stem. Using a tsp., scoop out tomato pulp and any seeds until you have two ½" shells remaining.
2. In a small mixing bowl, combine tuna, mayonnaise, celery, mustard, and seasoning salt. Stir until well blended.
3. Scoop an equal amount of tuna mixture into each ½ tomato shell. Place on a baking sheet and sprinkle shredded cheddar cheese over the top of each tuna-stuffed tomato shell. Bake for 7 to 8 minutes or until cheese is melted and golden-brown in color.
4. Serve immediately. Any remaining mixture can be safely stored, covered, in the fridge for up to 72 hours.

Nutrition:

Calories: 175 kcal

Protein: 21.24 g

Fat: 8.79 g

Carbohydrates: 3.04 g

Seared Ahi Tuna

Preparation Time: 10 minutes

Cooking Time: 15 minutes

Servings: 2

Ingredients:

- 2 (4-ounces each) ahi tuna steaks (3/4-inch thick)
- 2 tbsp. dark sesame oil
- 2 tbsp. soy sauce
- 1 tbsp. of grated fresh ginger
- 1 clove garlic, minced
- 1 green onion (scallion) thinly sliced, reserve a few slices for garnish
- 1 tsp. lime juice

Directions:

1. Begin by preparing the marinade. In a small bowl, put together the sesame oil, soy sauce, fresh ginger, minced garlic, green onion, and lime juice. Mix well.
2. Place tuna steaks into a sealable Ziploc freezer bag and pour marinade over the top of the tuna. Seal bag and shake or massage with hands to coat tuna steaks well with marinade. Bring the bag in a bowl, in case of breaks, and place tuna in the refrigerator to marinate for at least 10 minutes.
3. Place a large non-stick skillet over medium-high to high heat. Let the pan heat for 2 minutes, when hot, remove tuna steaks from the marinade and lay them in the pan to sear for 1-1½ minutes on each side.
4. Remove tuna steaks from pan and cut into ¼-inch thick slices. Garnish with a sprinkle of sliced green onion. Serve immediately.

Nutrition:

Calories: 213 kcal

Protein: 4.5 g

Fat: 19.55 g

Carbohydrates: 5.2 g

Bavette with Seafood

Preparation Time: 10 minutes

Cooking Time: 10 minutes

Servings: 4

Ingredients:

- Braised olive oil
- 200g clean medium shrimp
- 200g of clean octopus
- 200g mussel without shell
- 200g of clean squid cut into rings
- Salt to taste
- Black pepper to taste
- 1 clove minced garlic
- 400g peeled tomatoes
- 2 tablespoons coarse salt
- 350g of Bavette Barilla
- Chopped cilantro to taste
- ½ Lemon Juice

Directions:

1. In olive oil sauté the shrimp, the octopus, the mussel and the squid separately. Season with salt and black pepper.
2. In the same pan, sauté the garlic.
3. Add the peeled tomatoes, mix well — Cook for 2 minutes.
4. In a pan of boiling water, arrange 2 tablespoons of coarse salt and cook Bavette Barilla.
5. Remove Bavette Barilla 2 minutes before the time indicated on the package. Reserve the pasta cooking water if necessary.
6. Return the seafood to the sauce.
7. Arrange 1 scoop of the cooking water in the seafood sauce and add the drained pasta. Cook for another 2 minutes.
8. Finish with cilantro and lemon juice.
9. Serve immediately.

Nutrition:

Calories: 526 kcal

Protein: 40.59 g

Fat: 24 g

Carbohydrates: 38.02 g

Quick Shrimp Moqueca

Preparation Time: 10 minutes

Cooking Time: 10 minutes

Servings: 4

Ingredients:

- 600g Shrimp Peeled and Clean
- Salt to taste
- Juice of 2 lemons
- Braised olive oil
- 2 chopped purple onions
- 4 cloves garlic, minced
- 3 chopped tomatoes
- 1 chopped red pepper
- 1 chopped yellow pepper
- 1 cup tomato passata
- 200ml of coconut milk
- 2 finger peppers
- 2 tablespoons palm oil
- Chopped cilantro to taste

Directions:

1. In a container, arrange shrimp, season with salt and lemon juice and set aside.
2. In a hot pan, arrange olive oil and sauté onion and garlic.
3. Add the chopped tomatoes and sauté well.
4. Add the peppers and the tomato passata. Let it cook for a few minutes.
5. Add coconut milk, mix well.
6. Add the shrimp to the sauce.
7. Finally, add the finger pepper, palm oil, and chopped coriander.
8. Serve with rice and crumbs.

Nutrition:

Calories: 426 kcal

Protein: 46.15 g

Fat: 15.46 g

Carbohydrates: 26.26 g

Fried ball of cod

Preparation Time: 10 minutes

Cooking Time: 10 minutes

Servings: 4

Ingredients:

- Braised olive oil
- 1 red onion cut into strips
- 2 cloves garlic, minced
- 700g desalted and shredded cod
- ½ cup sliced black olive
- 3 minced boiled eggs
- Parsley to taste
- Salt to taste
- Black pepper

Directions:

1. In a hot skillet, arrange the olive oil and sauté the onion and then the garlic.
2. Add cod and sauté well.
3. Turn off the heat, then put the olives, the chopped eggs, and the parsley.
4. Correct salt if necessary, add pepper, and set aside to cool.

5. Stuff the pastry dough and close by brushing water and kneading with a fork.
6. Fry in hot oil by dipping until golden brown.
7. Drain on paper towels and serve.

Nutrition:

Calories: 253 kcal

Protein: 35.45 g

Fat: 9.61 g

Carbohydrates: 3.86 g

Seafood Paella

Preparation Time: 10 minutes

Cooking Time: 15 minutes

Servings: 2

Ingredients:

- Extra virgin olive oil
- 1 chopped onion
- 2 cloves minced garlic + 4 whole cloves garlic in shell
- ½ chopped green peppers
- ½ chopped yellow pepper
- ½ chopped red peppers
- 400g of the pump or parboiled rice
- 400g of sliced cooked octopus
- 400g squid in rings
- 2 packets of turmeric dissolved in 1.2 liters of fish stock
- Salt to taste
- Black pepper to taste
- 400g of pre-cooked shrimp
- 200g of frozen pea
- 500g mussel
- ½ packet of chopped parsley
- Chilies to decorate
- 4 units pre-cooked whole prawn
- Lemon juice

Directions:

1. In olive oil, sauté onion, garlic, peppers, and rice.
2. Add the octopus, the squid, and half the broth. Adjust salt and pepper.
3. As the liquid dries, add more broth taking care of the rice point.
4. When the stock is almost completely dry, add the shrimp and the pea.
5. Add the mussels and parsley.
6. Arrange peppers on top for garnish and prawns
7. Let it cook for 15 minutes with the pan covered.
8. Finish with lemon juice and olive oil.

Nutrition:

Calories: 1468 kcal

Protein: 177.19 g

Fat: 28.65 g

Carbohydrates: 115.89 g

Vietnamese Roll and Tarê

Preparation Time: 20 minutes

Cooking Time: 10 minutes

Servings: 4

Ingredients:

- 1 cup of soy sauce
- 1 cup of sake baby
- 1 cup of sugar
- 6 sheets of rice paper
- Warm water
- Mint leaves
- 250g sauteed medium prawns
- 1 cup carrot cut into sticks
- 1 cup chopped Japanese cucumber
- 6 shredded lettuce leaves
- 1 ½ cup rice noodles prepared per package instructions

Directions:

1. Bring the soy sauce, sake, and sugar to medium heat. Stir from time to time and cook the mixture until it reduces to ⅓ of the initial amount and obtain a soft syrup consistency. Set aside to cool.
2. Dip the rice leaf in warm water for about 30 seconds or until it softens.
3. Arrange on a flat surface and stuff the center of the rice paper with mint leaves,

prawns, carrot, cucumber, lettuce, and pasta.
4. Roll up, cut in half and half again. Repeat the process with the other sheets of rice paper.
5. Serve with taré sauce.

Nutrition:

Calories: 552 kcal

Protein: 10.54 g

Fat: 20.48 g

Carbohydrates: 82.12 g

Shrimp Pie

Preparation Time: 15 minutes

Cooking Time: 35 minutes

Servings: 4-8

Ingredients:

250g of flour

200g of unsalted cold butter

1 teaspoon salt

3 tbsp. water

2 tbsp. olive oil

2 cloves garlic, minced

400g peeled clean shrimp

1 tomato without skin and without chopped seed

2 tbsp. coconut milk

1 minced finger pepper

Salt

¼ cup sour cream

2 tbsp. chopped cilantro

1 gem

Directions:

Place the flour in a bowl then add the diced butter.

Knead with fingertips until crumbly.

Add salt and, gradually, water until it turns into dough. Cover with plastic and refrigerate for 1 hour.

Heat a frying pan, sprinkle with olive oil and brown the garlic and prawns.

Add the tomatoes, sauté for a couple of minutes, then add coconut milk and pepper and cook for another two minutes.

Season with salt, add the cream, turn off the heat and add the cilantro. Set aside to cool.

To open the dough in portions and cover the pancakes, stuff with the shrimp, and cover with a circle of dough.

Brush with the yolk and bake in the preheated oven at 180 degrees for about 30 minutes or until golden brown.

Nutrition:

Calories: 344 kcal

Protein: 15.6 g

Fat: 19.79 g

Carbohydrates: 25.33 g

Seafood Noodles

Preparation Time: 10 minutes

Cooking Time: 20 minutes

Servings: 2

Ingredients:

- Braised olive oil
- 4 cloves garlic, minced
- 300g of clean squid cut into rings
- 200g mussel without shell
- 200g shell-less volley
- 10 clean prawns
- 150g of dried tomatoes
- salt to taste
- black pepper to taste
- 500g of pre-cooked noodles
- ½ pack of watercress
- ½ Lemon Juice
- parsley to taste

Directions:

1. In olive oil, sauté the garlic and add the squid, the mussel, the shrimp, and the shrimp.
2. Put the dried tomatoes and season with salt and pepper.
3. Add the noodles, watercress, season with lemon juice, and parsley.

Nutrition:

Calories: 2049 kcal

Protein: 56.21 g

Fat: 143.36 g

Carbohydrates: 139.98 g

Potato Dumpling with Shrimp

Preparation Time: 15 minutes

Cooking Time: 50 minutes

Servings: 6-8

Ingredients:

- 500g of pink potatoes
- 1 egg
- salt to taste
- 1 tbsp. chopped parsley
- 2 tablespoons flour + flour for handling and breading
- 10 units of clean giant tailed shrimp
- black pepper to taste
- ½ packet of chopped cilantro
- 3 tablespoons palm oil
- 4 lemon juice
- frying oil

Directions:

1. Put the potato to cook for 40 minutes.
2. When very tender, remove from heat, let cool and mash potatoes already peeled.
3. Add the egg and mix well, season with salt and parsley and add the flour. Set aside in the fridge for 2 hours.
4. Make small transverse cuts on the belly of the shrimp, without cutting to the end. Season the shrimp with black pepper, salt, chopped coriander, palm oil, and lemon juice. Leave marinating for 15 minutes.
5. Take a portion of the potato flour dough in your hands and shape around a shrimp leaving the tail out.
6. Rinse flour again and fry in hot oil until golden.

Nutrition:

Calories: 159 kcal

Protein: 6.95 g

Fat: 8.42 g

Carbohydrates: 14.48 g

Shrimp Rissoles

Preparation Time: 10 minutes

Cooking Time: 30 minutes

Servings: 4

Ingredients:

- 1 tbsp. olive oil
- ½ diced onion
- 400g of shrimp
- 2 tbsp. tomato extract
- ½ packet of chopped parsley
- Salt to taste
- 250ml of water
- 250ml of milk
- 50g of butter
- 3 cups flour
- 100 g of curd
- 3 beaten eggs
- Breadcrumbs for breading

Directions:

1. Sauté with olive oil, onion, and shrimp.
2. Add tomato extract, parsley, and salt. Reserve.
3. In a pan, bring to medium heat water, milk and butter.
4. When the butter has melted, add 2 cups of wheat flour at a time and stir until the dough begins to unglue from the bottom of the pan. Set aside until warm.

5. When the dough is warm, knead, adding the remaining flour until it is smooth and elastic.
6. Roll the dough into a floured surface.
7. The format in circular portions.
8. Stuff with the shrimp and arrange a spoonful of curd. Close by tightening the ends.
9. Dip into beaten egg, breadcrumbs, and fry in hot oil until golden brown.

Nutrition:

Calories: 736 kcal

Protein: 42.45 g

Fat: 26.71 g

Carbohydrates: 78.58 g

Pumpkin Shrimp

Preparation Time: 20 minutes

Cooking Time: 1 hour and 10 minutes

Servings: 4-6

Ingredients:

- 1 average pumpkin
- 1kg medium shrimp
- 1 white onion
- 3 cloves of garlic
- 2 cans of peeled tomatoes
- 1 cup of white wine
- 1 box of sour cream
- 1 cup of curd
- salt
- Aluminum paper

Directions:

1. Cut the lid off the pumpkin, wrap in foil and bake at 180 degrees for 15 minutes.
2. Remove from oven, remove seeds and return to oven for another 40 minutes at 180 degrees.
3. In a pan, sauté the chopped onion. When golden, add the garlic and sauté until the aroma is released.
4. Add the peeled tomato cans and the white wine. Cook for 15 minutes over medium heat. Add water if it dries too fast.
5. When the tomato is already well crushed, add the cream and 1/2 cup of curd. Let reduce until thickened — season with salt.
6. In a skillet with olive oil, cook the prawns over high heat. When they are golden, add to the sauce. Remove the pumpkin from the oven, pass the remaining cream cheese on the inner walls, and place the shrimp sauce inside.

Nutrition:

Calories: 218 kcal

Protein: 29.55 g

Fat: 5.94 g

Carbohydrates: 10.65 g

Fish Sandwich

Preparation Time: 10 minutes

Cooking Time: 10 minutes

Servings: 4

Ingredients:

- 1 lb. quartered Salmon fillet
- 2 tsp. Cajun seasoning
- 1 pitted Avocado, peeled
- 2 tbsp. Mayonnaise
- 4 Wheat rolls
- 1 cup Arugula
- 2 Plum tomatoes, sliced thin
- .5 cup Red onion, sliced thin
- 2 tbsp. Coconut oil

Directions:

1. Coat the grill in coconut oil before ensuring it is heated to high heat.
2. Coat the fish using the seasoning before adding it to the grill and let it cook for approximately 3 minutes on each side.
3. Mash the avocado before blending it with the mayonnaise and spreading on the rolls before serving.
4. Season as required, serve hot and enjoy.

Nutrition:

Calories: 389 kcal

Protein: 26.88 g

Fat: 26.27 g

Carbohydrates: 12.21 g

Sardine Casserole

Preparation Time: 15 minutes

Cooking Time: 40 minutes

Servings: 4

Ingredients:

- 2 tbsp. Bread crumbs
- 1 tbsp. Basil
- 1 cloves Garlic, chopped
- .5 lbs. Cherry tomatoes, diced
- 17.5 oz. Sardines
- 3 tbsp. Coconut oil
- 1 lb. Russet potatoes

Direction:

1. Add the potatoes to a pot before covering them with salted water and letting the pot boil.
2. Once it boils, turn the heat to low/medium before placing a lid on it and letting the potatoes cook for 20 minutes.
3. Drain the potatoes and cover them in cold water to let them cool.
4. Slice and peel the potatoes.
5. Ensure your oven is heated to 350F.
6. Add the coconut oil to a casserole and coat well.
7. Alternate layers of potato and layers of sardine, adding the tomatoes to the sardine layers. Top with bread crumbs, basil, and garlic.
8. Let the casserole cook for 20 minutes, serve hot, and enjoy.

Nutrition:

Calories: 553 kcal

Protein: 37.22 g

Fat: 26.88 g

Carbohydrates: 40.95 g

Mexican Salad with Mahi-Mahi

Preparation Time: 20 minutes

Cooking Time: 75 minutes

Servings: 4

Ingredients:

- 1 lb. Ground beef
- Pepper (as desired)
- Salt (as desired)
- Hot pepper sauce (as desired)
- .5 tsp. Chili powder
- .5 tbsp. Cumin, ground
- .25 cup Cilantro, chopped
- 1 clove Garlic, crushed
- 2 tbsp. Agave sweetener
- 1 tbsp. Lemon juice
- 2 tbsp. Lime juice
- .5 cup Red wine vinegar
- .5 cup Coconut oil
- 1 Red onion, chopped
- 10 oz. Corn kernels, frozen
- 1 Red bell pepper, frozen
- 1 Green bell pepper, chopped
- 15 oz. Cannellini beans, rinsed and drained
- 15 oz. Kidney beans, rinsed and drained
- 15 oz. Black beans, rinsed and drained
- 32 oz. Mahi-mahi

Directions:

1. In a serving bowl, combine the red onion, frozen corn, bell peppers, and beans and mix well.
2. In a smaller separate bowl, combine the pepper, cumin, cilantro, hot pepper sauce, garlic, salt, sugar, lemon juice, lime juice, red wine vinegar, and coconut oil and whisk well.
3. Pour the dressing over the salad and toss well to coat, cover the salad with plastic wrap, and chill in the refrigerator and serve chilled.
4. Prior to serving Season the fish as desired.

5. Add the coconut oil to a pan before placing the pan on the stove over a medium heat burner.
6. Add in the fish and let it cook for approximately 5 minutes on each side.

Nutrition:

Calories: 709 kcal

Protein: 39.23 g

Fat: 47.12 g

Carbohydrates: 36.61 g

Fish Cakes

Preparation Time: 2 hours and 30 minutes

Cooking Time: 10 minutes

Servings: 4

Ingredients:

- 4 tbsp. Whole wheat flour
  - oz. Shrimp
- 9 oz. Tuna
- .5 cup Bread crumbs
- 1 tbsp. Italian seasoning
- 2 Chili pepper, seeded
- 6 Basil leaves
- 1 Egg
- 5 Sun-dried tomatoes, chopped
- 4 cloves Garlic
- .5 Onion
- 6 oz. Scallops
- 4 tbsp. Coconut oil

Directions:

1. Coat a pan in 1 T oil and place it on the stove above a burner that has been turned to a high/medium heat.
2. Add in the scallops and let them cook until they are completely white.
3. In a food processor, mix in 1 T coconut oil, the egg, tomatoes, garlic, and onion before adding in the seasoning, chilies, basil and parsley, and medium setting process.
4. Add in the shrimp, scallops, and tuna and process on a low setting.
5. Add in the breadcrumbs and keep processing until everything binds together.
6. Make the results into patties before adding them to a plate and placing the plate in the refrigerator for at least 2 hours.
7. Coat a pan in the remaining oil and place it on the stove above a burner that has been turned to medium heat.
8. Cook the patties in the pan until both sides have turned a golden brown.

Nutrition:

Calories: 396 kcal

Protein: 35.52 g

Fat: 19.68 g

Carbohydrates: 22.73 g

Crab Salad Cakes

Preparation Time: 10 minutes

Cooking Time: 5 minutes

Servings: 4

Ingredients:

- .5 tsp. Black pepper
- .5 tsp. Salt
- 1 tbsp. Extra virgin coconut oil
- .5 cup Swiss cheese, shredded
- 2 Hot sauce, dashes
- .25 tsp. Old Bay seasoning
- 1 tbsp. Mayonnaise
- 4 tsp. Lemon juice
- 1 Scallion, chopped
- .25 cup Red bell pepper, chopped
- .3 cup Celery, chopped
- 8 oz. Crabmeat
- 4 asparagus spears, sliced

Directions:

1. Pace the rack high in the oven and heat your broiler.
2. Microwave the asparagus in a covered bowl with 1 tsp. Water for 30 seconds.
3. Mix in the seasonings as desired and the mayonnaise, lemon juice, scallion, bell pepper, celery, and crab.

4. For the results into 4 patties and top with the cheese.
5. Broil the patties for 3 minutes.

Nutrition:

Calories: 310 kcal

Protein: 28.19 g

Fat: 12.45 g

Carbohydrates: 24.34 g

Simple Founder in Brown Butter Lemon Sauce

Preparation Time: 10 minutes

Cooking Time: 10 minutes

Servings: 4

Ingredients:

- For the Sauce:
- ½ cup unsalted grass-fed butter, cut into pieces
- Juice of 1 lemon
- Sea salt, for seasoning
- Freshly ground black pepper, for seasoning
- For the Fish:
- 4 (4-ounce) boneless flounder fillets
- Sea salt, for seasoning
- Freshly ground black pepper, for seasoning
- ¼ cup almond flour
- 2 tablespoons good-quality olive oil
- 1 tablespoon chopped fresh parsley

Directions:

1. To make the Sauce:
2. Brown the butter. In a medium saucepan at medium heat, cook the butter, stirring it once in a while, until it is golden brown, at least 4 minutes.
3. Finish the sauce. Remove the saucepan from the heat and stir in the lemon juice. Spice the sauce with salt and pepper and set it aside.
4. To make a Fish: Season the fish. Pat the fish fillets dry then spice them lightly with salt and pepper. Spoon the almond flour onto a plate, then roll the fish fillets through the flour until they are lightly coated. Cook the fish. In a large skillet at medium-high heat, warm the olive oil. Add the fish fillets and fry them until they are crispy and golden on both sides, 2 to 3 minutes per side.
Serve. Moved the fish to a serving plate and drizzle with the sauce. Top with the parsley and serve it hot.

Nutrition:

Calories: 389

Total fat: 33g

Total carbs: 1g

Fiber: 0g

Net carbs: 1g

Sodium: 256mg

Protein: 22g

Grilled Calamari

Preparation Time: 10 minutes

Cooking Time: 5 minutes

Servings: 4

Ingredients:

- 2 pounds calamari tubes and tentacles, cleaned
- ½ cup good-quality olive oil
- Zest and juice of 2 lemons
- 2 tablespoons chopped fresh oregano
- 1 tablespoon minced garlic
- ¼ teaspoon sea salt
- ⅛ teaspoon freshly ground black pepper

Directions:

1. Prepare the calamari. Score the top layer of the calamari tubes about 2 inches apart.
2. Marinate the calamari. In a large bowl, stir together the olive oil, lemon zest, lemon juice, oregano, garlic, salt, and pepper. Add the calamari and toss to coat it well, then

place it in the refrigerator to marinate for at least 30 minutes to 1 hour. Grill the calamari. Preheat a grill to high heat. Grill the calamari, turning once, for about 3 minute's total, until it's tender and lightly charred.
3. Serve. Divide the calamari between four plates and serve it hot.

Nutrition:

Calories: 455

Total fat: 30g

Total carbs: 8g

Fiber: 1g;

Net carbs: 7g

Sodium: 101mg

Protein: 35g

Souvlaki Spiced Salmon Bowls

Preparation Time: 10 minutes

Cooking Time: 20 minutes

Servings: 4

Ingredients:

- For the Salmon:
- ¼ cup good-quality olive oil
- Juice of 1 lemon
- 2 tablespoons chopped fresh oregano
- 1 tablespoon minced garlic
- 1 tablespoon balsamic vinegar
- 1 tablespoon smoked sweet paprika
- ½ teaspoon sea salt
- ¼ teaspoon freshly ground black pepper
- 4 (4-ounce) salmon fillets

Directions:

1. To make the Salmon:
2. Marinate the fish. In a medium bowl, put and mix the olive oil, lemon juice, oregano, garlic, vinegar, paprika, salt, and pepper. Put the salmon and turn to coat it well with the marinade. Cover the bowl and let the salmon sit marinating for 15 to 20 minutes.
3. Grill the fish. Preheat the grill to medium-high heat and grill the fish until just cooked through, 4 to 5 minutes per side. Set the fish aside on a plate.
4. For the Bowls:
5. 2 tablespoons good-quality olive oil
6. 1 red bell pepper, cut into strips
7. 1 yellow bell pepper, cut into strips
8. 1 zucchini, cut into ½-inch strips lengthwise
9. 1 cucumber, diced
10. 1 large tomato, chopped
11. ½ cup sliced Kalamata olives
12. 6 ounces feta cheese, crumbled
13. ½ cup sour cream

Directions:

1. To make the Bowls:
2. Grill the vegetables. In a medium bowl, put the oil, red and yellow bell peppers, and zucchini. Grill the vegetables, turning once, until they are lightly charred and soft, about 3 minutes per side.
3. Assemble and serve. Divide the grilled vegetables between four bowls. Top each bowl with cucumber, tomato, olives, feta cheese, and the sour cream. Put 1 salmon fillet on top of every bowl and serve immediately.

Nutrition:

Calories: 553

Total fat: 44g

Total carbs: 10g

Fiber: 3g;

Net carbs: 7g

Sodium: 531mg

Protein: 30g

Proscuitto-Wrapped Haddock

Preparation Time: 10 minutes

Cooking Time: 15 minutes

Servings: 4

Ingredients:

- 4 (4-ounce) haddock fillets, about 1 inch thick
- Sea salt, for seasoning
- Freshly ground black pepper, for seasoning
- 4 slices prosciutto (2 ounces)
- 3 tablespoons garlic-infused olive oil
- Juice and zest of 1 lemon

1. **Directions:**
   Preheat the oven. Set the oven temperature to 350°F. Line a baking sheet with parchment paper.
2. Prepare the fish. Pat the fish dry using paper towels then spice it lightly on both sides with salt and pepper. Wrap the prosciutto around the fish tightly but carefully so it doesn't rip.
3. Bake the fish. Bring the fish on the baking sheet and drizzle it with the olive oil. Bake for 15 to 17 minutes until the fish flakes easily with a fork.
4. Serve. Divide the fish between four plates and top with the lemon zest and a drizzle of lemon juice.

Nutrition:

Calories: 282

Total fat: 18g

Total carbs: 1g

Fiber: 0g;

Net carbs: 1g

Sodium: 76mg

Protein: 29g

Grilled Salmon with Caponata

Preparation Time: 15 minutes

Cooking Time: 20 minutes

Servings: 4

Ingredients:

- ¼ cup good-quality olive oil, divided
- 1 onion, chopped
- 2 celery stalks, chopped
- 1 tablespoon minced garlic
- 2 tomatoes, chopped
- ½ cup chopped marinated artichoke hearts
- ¼ cup pitted green olives, chopped
- ¼ cup cider vinegar
- 2 tablespoons white wine
- 2 tablespoons chopped pecans
- 4 (4-ounce) salmon fillets
- Freshly ground black pepper, for seasoning
- 2 tablespoons chopped fresh basil

Direction

1. Make the caponata. In a large skillet at medium heat, warm 3 tablespoons of the olive oil.

2. Add the onion, celery, garlic, and sauté until they have softened, about 4 minutes. Stir in the tomatoes, artichoke hearts, olives, vinegar, white wine, and pecans. Place the mixture to a boil, then reduce the heat to low and simmer until the liquid has reduced, 6 to 7 minutes. Take off the skillet from the heat and set it aside.

3. Grill the fish. Preheat a grill to medium-high heat. Pat the fish dry using paper towels then rub it with the remaining 1 tablespoon of olive oil and season lightly with black pepper. Grill the salmon, turning once, until it is just cooked through, about 8 minutes total.

4. Serve. Divide the salmon between four plates, top with a generous scoop of the caponata, and serve immediately with fresh basil.

Nutrition:

Calories: 348

Total fat: 25g

Total carbs: 7g

Fiber: 3g

Net carbs: 4g

Sodium: 128mg

Protein: 24g

Sweet Crab Cakes

Preparation Time: 15 minutes

Cooking Time: 10 minutes

Servings: 4

Ingredients:

- 1 pound cooked lump crabmeat, drained and picked over
- ¼ cup shredded unsweetened coconut
- 1 tablespoon Dijon mustard
- 1 scallion, finely chopped
- ¼ cup minced red bell pepper
- 1 egg, lightly beaten
- 1 teaspoon lemon zest
- Pinch cayenne pepper
- 3 tablespoons coconut flour
- 3 tablespoons coconut oil
- ¼ cup Classic Aioli

Directions:

1. Make the crab cakes. In a medium bowl, mix the crab, coconut, mustard, scallion, red bell pepper, egg, lemon zest, and cayenne until it holds together. Form the mixture into eight equal patties about ¾ inch thick.
2. Chill. Place the patties on a plate, cover the plate with plastic wrap, and chill them in the refrigerator for around 1 hour to 12 hours.
3. Coat the patties. Spread the coconut flour on a plate. Dip each patty in the flour until it is lightly coated.
4. Cook. In a large skillet at medium heat, warm the coconut oil. Fry the crab-cake patties, turning them once, until they are golden and cooked through, about 5 minutes per side.
5. Serve. Place two crab cakes on each of four plates and serve with the aioli.

Nutrition:

Calories: 370

Total fat: 24g

Total carbs: 12g

Fiber: 6g

Net carbs: 6g

Sodium: 652mg

Protein: 26g

Herbed Coconut Milk Steamed Mussels

Preparation Time: 10 minutes

Cooking Time: 15 minutes

Servings: 4

Ingredients:

- 2 tablespoons coconut oil
- ½ sweet onion, chopped
- 2 teaspoons minced garlic
- 1 teaspoon grated fresh ginger
- ½ teaspoon turmeric
- 1 cup coconut milk
- Juice of 1 lime
- 1½ pounds fresh mussels, scrubbed and debearded
- 1 scallion, finely chopped
- 2 tablespoons chopped fresh cilantro
- 1 tablespoon chopped fresh thyme

Directions:

1. Sauté the aromatics. In a huge skillet, warm the coconut oil. Add the onion, garlic, ginger, and turmeric and sauté until they have softened, about 3 minutes. Add the liquid. Mix in the coconut milk, lime juice then bring the mixture to a boil. Steam the mussels. Put the mussels to the skillet, cover, and steam until the shells are open, about 10 minutes. Take the skillet off the heat and throw out any unopened mussels.
Add the herbs. Stir in the scallion, cilantro, and thyme.
Serve. Divide the mussels and the sauce into 4 bowls and serve them immediately.

Nutrition:

Calories: 319

Total fat: 23g

Total carbs: 8g

Fiber: 2g;

Net carbs: 6g

Sodium: 395mg

Protein: 23g

Basil Halibut Red Pepper Packets

Preparation Time: 10 minutes

Cooking Time: 20 minutes

Servings: 4

Ingredients:

- 2 cups cauliflower florets
- 1 cup roasted red pepper strips
- ½ cup sliced sun-dried tomatoes
- 4 (4-ounce) halibut fillets
- ¼ cup chopped fresh basil
- Juice of 1 lemon
- ¼ cup good-quality olive oil
- Sea salt, for seasoning
- Freshly ground black pepper, for seasoning

Directions:

1. Preheat the oven. Set the oven temperature to 400°F. Cut into four (12-inch) square pieces of aluminum foil. Have a baking sheet ready. Make the packets. Divide the cauliflower, red pepper strips, and sun-dried tomato between the four pieces of foil, placing the vegetables in the middle of each piece. Top each pile with 1 halibut fillet, and top each fillet with equal amounts of the basil, lemon juice, and olive oil. Fold and crimp the foil to form sealed packets of fish and vegetables and place them on the baking sheet.
Bake. Bake the packets for about 20 minutes, until the fish flakes with a fork. Be careful of the steam when you open the packet!
Serve. Transfer the vegetables and halibut to four plates, season with salt and pepper, and serve immediately.

Nutrition:

Calories: 294

Total fat: 18g

Total carbs: 8g

Fiber: 3g

Net carbs: 5g

Sodium: 114mg

Protein: 25g

Sherry and Butter Prawns

Preparation Time: 5 minutes

Cooking Time: 5 minutes

Servings: 4

Ingredients:

- 1 ½ pounds king prawns, peeled and deveined
- 2 tablespoons dry sherry
- 1 teaspoon dried basil
- 1/2 teaspoon mustard seeds
- 1 ½ tablespoons fresh lemon juice
- 1 teaspoon cayenne pepper, crushed
- 1 tablespoon garlic paste
- 1/2 stick butter, at room temperature

Directions:

1. Whisk the dry sherry with cayenne pepper, garlic paste, basil, mustard seeds, lemon juice and prawns. Let it marinate for 1 hour in your refrigerator.
2. In a frying pan, melt the butter over medium-high flame, basting with the reserved marinade.
3. Sprinkle with salt and pepper to taste.

Nutrition:

294 Calories

14.3g Fat

3.6g Carbs

34.6g Protein

1.4g Fiber

Clams with Garlic-Tomato Sauce

Preparation Time: 5 minutes

Cooking Time: 20 minutes

Servings: 4

Ingredients:

- 40 littleneck clams
- For the Sauce:
- 2 tomatoes, pureed
- 2 tablespoons olive oil
- 1 shallot, chopped
- Sea salt, to taste
- Freshly ground black pepper, to taste
- 1/2 teaspoon paprika
- 1/3 cup port wine
- 2 garlic cloves, pressed
- 1/2 lemon, cut into wedges

Directions:

1. Grill the clams until they are open, for 5 to 6 minutes.
2. In a frying pan, heat the olive oil over moderate heat. Cook the shallot and garlic until tender and fragrant.
3. Stir in the pureed tomatoes, salt, black pepper and paprika and continue to cook an additional 10 to 12 minutes, up to well cook.
4. Heat off and add in the port wine; stir to combine. Garnish with fresh lemon wedges.

Nutrition:

134 Calories

7.8g Fat

5.9g Carbs

8.3g Protein

1g Fiber

Amberjack Fillets with Cheese Sauce

Preparation Time: 10 minutes

Cooking Time: 10 minutes

Servings: 4

Ingredients:

- 6 amberjack fillets
- 1/4 cup fresh tarragon chopped
- 2 tablespoons olive oil, at room temperature
- Sea salt, to taste
- Ground black pepper, to taste
- For the Sauce:
- 1/3 cup vegetable broth
- 3/4 cup double cream
- 1/3 cup Romano cheese, grated
- 3 teaspoons butter, at room temperature
- 2 garlic cloves, finely minced

Directions:

1. In a non-stick frying pan, warm the olive oil until sizzling.
2. Once hot, fry the amberjack for about 6 minutes per side or until the edges are turning opaque. Sprinkle them with salt, black pepper, and tarragon. Reserve.
3. To make the sauce, melt the butter in a saucepan over moderately high heat. Sauté the garlic until tender and fragrant or about 2 minutes.
4. Add in the vegetable broth and cream and continue to cook for 5 to 6 minutes more; heat off.
5. Stir in the Romano cheese and continue stirring in the residual heat for a couple of minutes more.

Nutrition:

285 Calories

20.4g Fat

1.2g Carbs

23.8g Protein

0.1g Fiber

Tilapia with Spicy Dijon Sauce

Preparation Time: 10 minutes

Cooking Time: 5 minutes

Servings: 4

Ingredients:

- 1 tablespoon butter, room temperature
- 2 chili peppers, deveined and minced
- 1 cup heavy cream
- 1 teaspoon Dijon mustard
- 1 pound tilapia fish, cubed
- Sea salt, to taste
- Ground black pepper, to taste
- 1 cup white onions, chopped
- 1 teaspoon garlic, pressed
- 1/2 cup dark rum

Directions:

1. Toss the tilapia with salt, pepper, onions, garlic, chili peppers and rum. Let it marinate for 2 hours in your refrigerator.
2. In a grill pan, melt the butter over a moderately high heat. Sear the fish in hot butter, basting with the reserved marinade.
3. Add in the mustard and cream and continue to cook until everything is thoroughly cooked, for 2 to 3 minutes.

Nutrition:

228 Calories

13g Fat

6.5g Carbs

13.7g Protein

1.1g Fiber

Garlic Butter Shrimps

Preparation Time: 13 minutes

Cooking Time: 16 minutes

Servings: 3

Ingredients:

- ½ pound shrimp, peeled and deveined
- 2 garlic cloves
- ½ white onion
- 3 tbsp. ghee butter
- 1 tsp black pepper
- 1 lemon (peeled)
- Himalayan rock salt to taste

Directions:

1. Preheat the oven to 425F
2. Mince the garlic and onion, cut the lemon in half
3. Season the shrimps with pink salt and pepper
4. Slice one-half of the lemon thinly, cut the other half into 2 pieces
5. Grease a baking dish with the butter; combine the shrimp with the garlic, onion and lemon slices, put in the baking dish
6. Bake the shrimps for 15 minutes, stirring halfway through
7. Remove the shrimps from the oven and squeeze the juice from 2 lemon pieces over the dish

Nutrition:

Carbs: 3, 9 g

Fat: 19, 8 g

Protein: 32 g

Calories: 338

Oven-Baked Sole Fillets

Preparation Time: 10 minutes

Cooking Time: 20 minutes

Servings: 4

Ingredients:

- 2 tablespoons olive oil
- 1/2 tablespoon Dijon mustard
- 1 teaspoon garlic paste
- 1/2 tablespoon fresh ginger, minced
- 1/2 teaspoon porcini powder
- Salt and ground black pepper, to taste
- 1/2 teaspoon paprika
- 4 sole fillets
- 1/4 cup fresh parsley, chopped

Directions:

1. Combine the oil, Dijon mustard, garlic paste, ginger, porcini powder, salt, black pepper, and paprika.
2. Rub this mixture all over sole fillets. Place the sole fillets in a lightly oiled baking pan.

3. Bake in the preheated oven at 400 degrees F for about 20 minutes.

Nutrition:

195 Calories

8.2g Fat

0.5g Carbs

28.7g Protein

0.6g Fiber

Keto Oodles with White Clam Sauce

Preparation Time: 10 minutes

Cooking Time: 10 minutes

Servings: 4

Ingredients:

- 2 pounds small clams
- 8 cups zucchini noodles
- 1/2 cup dry white wine
- 1/4 cup butter
- 1/4 cup fresh parsley (chopped)
- 2 tablespoons lemon juice
- 2 tablespoons olive oil
- 1 tablespoon garlic (minced)
- 1 teaspoon kosher salt
- 1 teaspoon lemon zest (grated)
- 1/4 teaspoon black pepper (ground)

Directions:

1. In a pan at medium heat, place the olive oil, butter, pepper, and salt. Stir to melt the butter.
2. Put in the garlic. Sautee the garlic until fragrant for at least 2 minutes
3. Set in the lemon juice and wine. Cook for at least 2 minutes, until the liquid is slightly reduced
4. Put in the clams. Cook the clams until they are all opened (about 3 minutes). Discard any clam that does not open after 3 minutes.
5. Remove the pan from the heat. Put in the zucchini noodles. Toss the mixture to combine well. Let the zoodles rest for a couple of minutes to soften them.
6. Put in the lemon zest and parsley. Stir. Serve.

Nutrition:

Calories: 311

Carbs: 9 g

Fats: 19 g

Proteins: 13 g

Fiber: 2 g

Fried Codfish with Almonds

Preparation Time: 8 minutes

Cooking Time: 18 minutes

Servings: 3

Ingredients:

- 16 oz. codfish fillet
- 3 oz. chopped almonds
- ½ tsp chili pepper
- 1 egg
- 1 tbsp. ghee butter
- 1 tsp psyllium
- 3 oz. cream
- 3 tbsp. keto mayo
- 1 tbsp. chopped fresh dill
- 1 tsp minced garlic
- ½ tsp onion powder
- Salt and pepper to taste

Directions:

1. In a small mixing bowl, combine the psyllium, onion powder, chili, and almonds
2. Beat the eggs in another bowl, mix well
3. Warm the butter in a skillet at medium heat.
4. Cut the fillet into 3 slices
5. Dip into the egg mixture, then into almonds and spices
6. Fry in the skillet for about 7 minutes each side
7. Meanwhile, in another bowl combine the cream, garlic, dill, and salt, stir well
8. Serve the fish with this sauce

Nutrition:

Carbs: 4, 9 g

Fats: 63 g

Protein: 33, 6 g

Calories: 709

Salmon Balls

Preparation Time: 5 minutes

Cooking Time: 13 minutes

Servings: 2

Ingredients:

- 1 can of tuna
- 2 tbsp. keto mayo
- 1 avocado
- 1 egg
- 1 garlic clove
- ½ cup heavy cream
- 3 tbsp. coconut oil
- ½ tsp ginger powder
- ½ tsp paprika
- ½ tsp dried cilantro
- 2 tbsp. lemon juice
- 2 tbsp. water
- Salt and ground black pepper to taste

Directions:

1. Drain the salmon, chop it
2. Mince the garlic clove, peel the avocado
3. In a bowl, combine the fish, mayo, egg, and garlic, season with salt, paprika, and ginger, mix well
4. Make 4 balls of it
5. Warm the oil in a skillet at medium heat
6. Put the balls and fry for 4-6 minutes each side
7. Meanwhile, put the heavy cream, avocado, cilantro, lemon juice, and 1 tablespoon of oil in a blender. Pulse well
8. Serve the balls with the sauce

Nutrition:

Carbs: 3, 9 g

Fats: 50 g

Protein: 20, 1 g

Calories: 555

Codfish Sticks

Preparation Time: 8 minutes

Cooking Time: 15 minutes

Servings: 2

Ingredients:

- 9 oz. codfish fillet
- 2 eggs
- 2 tbsp. ghee butter
- 2 tbsp. coconut flour
- ½ tsp paprika
- Salt and pepper to taste

Directions:

1. Slice the fish into sticks
2. In a bowl, put and mix the eggs, flour, paprika, pepper, and salt
3. Warm the butter in a skillet at medium heat.
4. Dip each fish slice into the spice mixture
5. Fry in the skillet over low heat for 4-5 minutes per side

Nutrition:

Carbs: 1, 5 g

Fat: 31 g

Protein: 22, 5 g

Calories: 329

Shrimp Risotto

Preparation Time: 10 minutes

Cooking Time: 15 minutes

Servings: 4

Ingredients:

- 14 oz. shrimps, peeled and deveined
- 12 oz. cauli rice
- 4 button mushrooms
- ½ lemon
- 4 stalks green onion

- 3 tbsp. ghee butter
- 2 tbsp. coconut oil
- Salt and black pepper to taste

Directions:

1. Preheat the oven to 400F
2. Put a layer of cauli rice on a sheet pan, season with salt and spices; sprinkle the coconut oil over it
3. Bake in the oven for 10-12 minutes
4. Cut the green onion, slice up the mushrooms and remove the rind from the lemon
5. Heat the ghee butter in a skillet over medium heat. Add the shrimps; season it and sauté for 5-6 minutes
6. Top the cauli rice with the shrimps, sprinkle the green onion over it

Nutrition:

Carbs: 9, 2 g

Fat: 26, 2 g

Protein: 25 g

Calories: 363

Lemony Trout

Preparation Time: 10 minutes

Cooking Time: 20 minutes

Servings: 2

Ingredients:

- 5 tbsp. ghee butter
- 5 oz. trout fillets
- 2 garlic cloves
- 1 tsp rosemary
- 1 lemon
- 2 tbsp. capers
- Salt and pepper to taste

Directions:

1. Preheat the oven to 400F
2. Peel the lemon, mince the garlic cloves and chop the capers
3. Season the trout fillets with salt, rosemary, and pepper
4. Grease a baking dish with the oil and place the fish onto it
5. Warm the butter in a skillet over medium heat
6. Add the garlic and cook for 4-5 minutes until golden
7. Remove from the heat, add the lemon zest and 2 tablespoons of lemon juice, stir well
8. Pour the lemon-butter sauce over the fish and top with the capers
9. Bake for 14-15 minutes. Serve hot

Nutrition:

Carbs: 3, 1 g

Fat: 25 g

Protein: 15, 8 g

Calories: 302

Quick Fish Bowl

Preparation Time: 11 minutes

Cooking Time: 15 minutes

Servings: 2

Ingredients:

- 2 tilapia fillets
- 1 tbsp. olive oil
- 1 avocado
- 1 tbsp. ghee butter
- 1 tbsp. cumin powder
- 1 tbsp. paprika
- 2 cups coleslaw cabbage, chopped
- 1 tbsp. salsa sauce
- Himalayan rock salt, to taste
- Black pepper to taste

Directions:

1. Preheat the oven to 425F. Line a baking sheet with the foil
2. Mash the avocado
3. Brush the tilapia fillets using olive oil, season with salt and spices
4. Place the fish onto the baking sheet, greased with the ghee butter
5. Bake for 15 minutes, then remove the fish from the heat and let it cool for 5 minutes

6. In a bowl, combine the coleslaw cabbage and the salsa sauce, toss gently
7. Add the mashed avocado, season with salt and pepper
8. Slice the fish and add to the bowl
9. Bake for 14-15 minutes. Serve hot

Nutrition:

Carbs: 5, 2 g

Fat: 24, 5 g

Protein: 16, 1 g

Calories: 321

Tender Creamy Scallops

Preparation Time: 15 minutes

Cooking Time: 21 minutes

Servings: 2

Ingredients:

- 8 fresh sea scallops
- 4 bacon slices
- ½ cup grated parmesan cheese
- 1 cup heavy cream
- 2 tbsp. ghee butter
- Salt and black pepper to taste

Directions:

1. Heat the butter in a skillet at medium-high heat
2. Add the bacon and cook for 4-5 minutes each side (till crispy)
3. Moved to a paper towel to remove the excess fat
4. Lower the heat to medium, sprinkle with more butter. Put the heavy cream and parmesan cheese, season with salt and pepper
5. Reduce the heat to low and cook for 8-10 minutes, constantly stirring, until the sauce thickens
6. In another skillet, heat the ghee butter over medium-high heat
7. Add the scallops to the skillet, season with salt and pepper. Cook for 2 minutes per side until golden
8. Transfer the scallops to a paper towel
9. Top with the sauce and crumbled bacon

Nutrition:

Carbs: 11 g

Fat: 72, 5 g

Protein: 24 g

Calories: 765

Salmon Cakes

Preparation Time: 10 minutes

Cooking Time: 10 minutes

Servings: 2

Ingredients:

- 6 oz. canned salmon
- 1 large egg
- 2 tbsp. pork rinds
- 3 tbsp. keto mayo
- 1 tbsp. ghee butter
- 1 tbsp. Dijon mustard
- Salt and ground black pepper to taste

Directions:

1. In a bowl, combine the salmon (drained), pork rinds, egg, and half of the mayo, season with salt and pepper. Mix well
2. With the salmon mixture, form the cakes
3. Heat the ghee butter in a skillet over medium-high heat
4. Place the salmon cakes in the skillet and cook for about 3 minutes per side. Moved to a paper towel to get rid of excess fat
5. In a small bowl, combine the remaining half of mayo and the Dijon mustard, mix well
6. Serve the salmon cakes with the mayo-mustard sauce

Nutrition:

Carbs: 1, 2 g

Fat: 31 g

Protein: 24, 2 g

Calories: 370

Salmon with Mustard Cream

Preparation Time: 10 minutes

Cooking Time: 12 minutes

Servings: 2

Ingredients:

- 2 salmon fillets
- ¼ cup keto mayo
- 1 tbsp. Dijon mustard
- 2 tbsp. fresh cilantro, minced
- 2 tbsp. ghee butter
- ½ tsp garlic powder
- Salt and pepper to taste

Directions:

1. Preheat the oven to 450F. Grease a baking dish with the ghee butter
2. Season the salmon with salt and pepper and put in the baking dish
3. In a mixing bowl, put and combine the Dijon mustard, mayo, parsley, and garlic powder. Stir well
4. Top the salmon fillets with the mustard sauce
5. Bake for 10 minutes

Nutrition:

Carbs: 2 g

Fat: 41, 5 g

Protein: 32, 9 g

Calories: 505

Shrimp and Black Beans Enchalada

Preparation Time: 5 minutes

Cooking Time: 15 minutes

Servings: 4

Ingredients:

- 2 cans (10 g) of red or green enchilada sauce
- 1 lb. shrimp
- 2 cans (15 oz.) black beans
- 2 cups grated Mexican cheese mixture
- 12 to 13 small flour tortillas

Directions:

1. Preheat the oven to 400° F. Put ¼ cup sauce (enchiladas) in a saucepan. Increase the heat and add the shrimp. Cook until the shrimp are clean and no longer transparent for about 5 minutes. Remove from the heated container.
2. Place the enchiladas in a 9 x 13-inch baking dish. Organize a pea breakfast, 3 or 4 shrimp, and a slice of cheese on an omelet. Fold the tortilla edges into the oven dish on the filling and with the seam facing down.
3. Repeat with the remaining tortillas. Pour out the rest of the enchilada sauce after preparing all the enchiladas.
4. Bake until all the cheese has melted for 15 minutes.

Nutrition:

Calories: 196

Fat: 12g

Net Carbs: 4g

Protein: 17g

Tuna Steaks with Shirataki Noodles

Preparation Time: 10 minutes

Cooking Time: 20 minutes

Servings: 4

Ingredients:

- 1 pack (7 oz.) miracle noodle angel hair
- 3 cups water
- 1 red bell pepper, seeded and halved
- 4 tuna steaks
- Salt and black pepper to taste
- Olive oil for brushing
- 2 tablespoons pickled ginger
- 2 tablespoons chopped cilantro

Directions:

1. Cook the shirataki rice based on the package instructions: In a colander, rinse the shirataki noodles with running cold water.

2. Place a pot of salted water to a boil; blanch the noodles for 2 minutes.
3. Drain and moved to a dry skillet over medium heat.
4. Dry roast for a few minutes until opaque.
5. Grease a grill's grate using a cooking spray and preheat on medium heat. Spice the red bell pepper and tuna with salt and black pepper, brush with olive oil, and grill covered.
6. Cook both for at least 3 minutes on each side. Moved to a plate to cool. Dice bell pepper with a knife.
7. Arrange the noodles, tuna, and bell pepper into the serving plate.
8. Top with pickled ginger and garnish with cilantro.
9. Serve with roasted sesame sauce.

Nutrition:

Calories: 310

Fat: 18.2g

Net Carbs: 2g

Protein: 22g

Tilapia with Parmesan Bark

Preparation Time: 4 minutes

Cooking Time: 12 minutes

Servings: 4

Ingredients:

- ¾ cup freshly grated Parmesan cheese
- 2 teaspoons pepper
- 1 tablespoon chopped parsley
- 4 tilapia fillets (4 us)
- Lemon cut into pieces

Directions:

1. Set the oven to 400° F. Mix cheese in a shallow dish with pepper and parsley and season with salt and pepper.
2. Mix the fish in the cheese with olive oil and flirt. Place on a baking sheet with foil and bake for 10 to 12 minutes until the fish in the thickest part is opaque.
3. Serve the lemon slices with the fish.

Nutrition:

Calories: 210

Fat: 9.3g

Net Carbs: 1.3g

Protein: 28.9g

Blackened Fish Tacos with Slaw:

Preparation Time: 14 minutes

Cooking Time: 6 minutes

Servings: 4

Ingredients:

- 1 tablespoon olive oil
- 1 teaspoon chili powder
- 2 tilapia fillets
- 1 teaspoon paprika
- 4 low carb tortillas

Slaw:

- ½ cup red cabbage, shredded
- 1 tablespoon lemon juice
- 1 teaspoon apple cider vinegar
- 1 tablespoon olive oil
- Salt and black pepper to taste

Directions:

1. Season the tilapia with chili powder and paprika. Heat the vegetable oil during a skillet over medium heat.
2. Add tilapia and cook until blackened, about 3 minutes per side. Cut into strips. Divide the tilapia between the tortillas. Blend all the slaw ingredients in a bowl and top the fish to serve.
3. **Nutrition:**

Calories: 268

Fat: 20g

Net Carbs: 3.5g

Protein: 13.8g

FRUIT AND DESERT RECIPES

Almond Butter Fudge

Preparation Time: 10 minutes

Cooking Time: 10 minutes

Servings: 18

Ingredients:

- 3/4 cup creamy almond butter
- 1 1/2 cups unsweetened chocolate chips

Directions:

1. Line 8*4-inch pan with parchment paper and set aside.

2. Add chocolate chips and almond butter into the double boiler and cook over medium heat until the chocolate-butter mixture is melted. Stir well.

3. Place mixture into the prepared pan and place in the freezer until set.

4. Slice and serve.

Nutrition:

Calories: 197

Fat: 16 g

Carbs: 7 g

Sugar: 1 g

Protein: 4 g

Cholesterol: 0 mg

Bounty Bars

Preparation Time: 20 minutes

Cooking Time: 0 minutes

Servings: 12

Ingredients:

- 1 cup coconut cream
- 3 cups shredded unsweetened coconut
- 1/4 cup extra virgin coconut oil
- 1/2 teaspoon vanilla powder
- 1/4 cup powdered erythritol
- 1 1/2 oz. cocoa butter
- 5 oz. dark chocolate

Directions:

1. Heat the oven at 350 °F and toast the coconut in it for 5-6 minutes. Remove from the oven once toasted and set aside to cool.

2. Take a bowl of medium size and add coconut oil, coconut cream, vanilla, erythritol, and toasted coconut. Mix the ingredients well to prepare a smooth mixture.

3. Make 12 bars of equal size with the help of your hands from the prepared mixture and adjust in the tray lined with parchment paper.

4. Place the tray in the fridge for around one hour and, in the meantime, put the cocoa butter and dark chocolate in a glass bowl.

5. Heat a cup of water in a saucepan over medium heat and place the bowl over it to melt the cocoa butter and the dark chocolate.

6. Remove from the heat once melted properly, mix well until blended and set aside to cool.

7. Take the coconut bars and coat them with dark chocolate mixture one by one using a wooden stick. Adjust on the tray lined with parchment paper and drizzle the remaining mixture over them.

8. Refrigerate for around one hour before you serve the delicious bounty bars.

Nutrition

Calories: 230

Fat: 25 g

Carbohydrates: 5 g

Protein: 32 g

Lean Granola

Preparation Time: 5 minutes

Cooking Time: 8 minutes

Servings: 3

Ingredients:

- 1 package Oatmeal
- 1 packet stevia
- 1 teaspoon vanilla extract
- 1/2 teaspoon apple spice or pumpkin pie spice

Directions:

1. Preheat the oven to 4000F. In a bowl, combine all ingredients and add enough water to get the granola to stick together.
2. Drop the granola onto a cookie sheet lined with parchment paper.
3. Bake for 8 minutes, but make sure to give the granola a fair shake for even browning halfway through the cooking time.

Nutrition

Calories 209

Fat: 3.2 g

Carbohydrates: 42 g

Protein: 5.8 g

Banana Bread

Preparation Time: 5 minutes

Cooking Time: 40 Minutes

Servings: 6

Ingredients:

- ¾ cup sugar
- 1/3 cup butter
- 1 tbsp. vanilla extract
- 1 egg
- 2 bananas
- 1 tbsp. baking powder
- 1 and ½ cups flour
- ½ tbsp. baking soda
- 1/3 cup milk
- 1 and ½ tbsp. cream of tartar
- Cooking spray

Directions:

1. Mix in milk with cream of tartar, vanilla, egg, sugar, bananas and butter in a bowl and turn whole.
2. Mix in flour with baking soda and baking powder.
3. Blend the 2 mixtures, turn properly, move into oiled pan with cooking spray, put into air fryer and cook at 320°F for 40 minutes.
4. Remove bread, allow to cool, slice.
5. Serve.

Nutrition:

Calories: 540

Fat: 16g

Carbs: 28g

Protein: 3g

Mini Lava Cakes

Preparation Time: 5 minutes

Cooking Time: 20 Minutes

Servings: 3

Ingredients:

- 1 egg
- 4 tbsp. sugar
- 2 tbsp. olive oil
- 4 tbsp. milk
- 4 tbsp. flour
- 1 tbsp. cocoa powder
- ½ tbsp. baking powder
- ½ tbsp. orange zest

Directions:

1. Mix in egg with sugar, flour, salt, oil, milk, orange zest, baking powder and cocoa powder, turn properly. Move it to oiled ramekins.

2. Put ramekins in air fryer and cook at 320°F for 20 minutes.

3. Serve warm.

Nutrition:

Calories: 329

Fat: 8.5g

Carbs: 12.4g

Crispy Apples

Preparation Time: 10 minutes

Cooking Time: 10 Minutes

Servings: 4

Ingredients:

- 2 tbsp. cinnamon powder
- 5 apples
- ½ tbsp. nutmeg powder
- 1 tbsp. maple syrup
- ½ cup water
- 4 tbsp. butter
- ¼ cup flour
- ¾ cup oats
- ¼ cup brown sugar

Directions:

1. Get the apples in a pan, put in nutmeg, maple syrup, cinnamon and water.

2. Mix in butter with flour, sugar, salt and oat, turn, put spoonful of blend over apples, get into air fryer and cook at 350°F for 10 minutes.

3. Serve while warm.

Nutrition:

Calories: 387

Fat: 5.6g

Carbs: 12.4g

Ginger Cheesecake

Preparation Time: 20 minutes

Cooking Time: 20 Minutes

Servings: 6

Ingredients:

- 2 tbsp. butter
- ½ cup ginger cookies
- 16 oz. cream cheese
- 2 eggs
- ½ cup sugar
- 1 tbsp. rum
- ½ tbsp. vanilla extract
- ½ tbsp. nutmeg

Directions:

1. Spread pan with the butter and sprinkle cookie crumbs on the bottom.

2. Whisk cream cheese with rum, vanilla, nutmeg and eggs, beat properly and sprinkle the cookie crumbs.

3. Put in air fryer and cook at 340° F for 20 minutes.

4. Allow cheese cake to cool in fridge for 2 hours before slicing.

5. Serve.

Nutrition:

Calories: 312

Fat: 9.8g

Carbs: 18g

461. Cocoa Cookies

Preparation Time: 10 minutes

Cooking Time: 14 Minutes

Servings: 12

Ingredients:

- 6 oz. coconut oil
- 6 eggs
- 3 oz. cocoa powder
- 2 tbsp. vanilla
- ½ tbsp. baking powder
- 4 oz. cream cheese
- 5 tbsp. sugar

Directions:

1. Mix in eggs with coconut oil, baking powder, cocoa powder, cream cheese, vanilla in a blender and sway and turn using a mixer.

2. Get it into a lined baking dish and into the fryer at 320°F and bake for 14 minutes.

3. Split cookie sheet into rectangles.

4. Serve.

Nutrition:

Calories: 149

Fat: 2.4g

Carbs: 27.2g

Special Brownies

Preparation Time: 10 minutes

Cooking Time: 22 Minutes

Servings: 4

Ingredients:

- 1 egg
- 1/3 cup cocoa powder
- 1/3 cup sugar
- 7 tbsp. butter
- ½ tbsp. vanilla extract
- ¼ cup white flour
- ¼ cup walnuts
- ½ tbsp. baking powder
- 1 tbsp. peanut butter

Directions:

1. Warm pan with 6 tablespoons butter and the sugar over medium heat, turn, cook for 5 minutes, move to a bowl, put salt, egg, cocoa powder, vanilla extract, walnuts, baking powder and flour, turn mix properly and into a pan.

2. Mix peanut butter with one tablespoon butter in a bowl, heat in microwave for some seconds, turn properly and sprinkle brownies blend over.

3. Put in air fryer and bake at 320° F and bake for 17 minutes.

4. Allow brownies to cool, cut.

5. Serve.

Nutrition:

Calories: 438

Fat: 18g

Carbs: 16.5g

Blueberry Scones

Preparation Time: 10 minutes

Cooking Time: 10 Minutes

Servings: 10

Ingredients:

- 1 cup white flour
- 1 cup blueberries
- 2 eggs
- ½ cup heavy cream
- ½ cup butter
- 5 tbsp. sugar
- 2 tbsp. vanilla extract
- 2 tbsp. baking powder

Directions:

1. Mix in flour, baking powder, salt and blueberries in a bowl and turn.

2. Mix heavy cream with vanilla extract, sugar, butter and eggs and turn properly.

3. Blend the 2 mixtures, squeeze till dough is ready, obtain 10 triangles from mix, put on baking sheet into air fryer and cook them at 320°F for 10 minutes.

4. Serve cold.

Nutrition:

Calories: 525

Fat: 21g carbs: 37g

Blueberries Stew

Preparation Time: 10 minutes

Cooking Time: 10 minutes

Servings: 4

Ingredients:

- 2 cups blueberries
- 3 tablespoons stevia
- 1 and ½ cups pure apple juice
- 1 teaspoon vanilla extract

Directions:

1. In a pan, combine the blueberries with stevia and the other ingredients, bring to a simmer and cook over medium-low heat for 10 minutes.

2. Divide into cups and serve cold.

Nutrition:

Calories 192

Fat 5.4

Fiber 3.4

Carbs 9.4

Protein 4.5

465. Mandarin Cream

Preparation Time: 20 minutes

Cooking Time: 0 minutes

Servings: 8

Ingredients:

- 2 mandarins, peeled and cut into segments
- Juice of 2 mandarins
- 2 tablespoons stevia
- 4 eggs, whisked
- ¾ cup stevia
- ¾ cup almonds, ground

Directions:

1. In a blender, combine the mandarins with the mandarin's juice and the other ingredients, whisk well, divide into cups and keep in the fridge for 20 minutes before serving.

Nutrition:

Calories 106

Fat 3.4

Fiber 0

Carbs 2.4

Protein 4

Creamy Mint Strawberry Mix

Preparation Time: 10 minutes

Cooking Time: 30 minutes

Servings: 6

Ingredients:

- Cooking spray
- ¼ cup stevia
- 1 and ½ cup almond flour
- 1 teaspoon baking powder
- 1 cup almond milk
- 1 egg, whisked
- 2 cups strawberries, sliced
- 1 tablespoon mint, chopped
- 1 teaspoon lime zest, grated

- ½ cup whipping cream

Directions:

2. In a bowl, combine the almond with the strawberries, mint and the other ingredients except the cooking spray and whisk well.

3. Grease 6 ramekins with the cooking spray, pour the strawberry mix inside, introduce in the oven and bake at 350 degrees F for 30 minutes.

4. Cool down and serve.

Nutrition:

Calories 200

Fat 6.3

Fiber 2

Carbs 6.5

Protein 8

Vanilla Cake

Preparation Time: 10 minutes

Cooking Time: 25 minutes

Servings: 10

Ingredients:

- 3 cups almond flour
- 3 teaspoons baking powder
- 1 cup olive oil
- 1 and ½ cup almond milk
- 1 and 2/3 cup stevia
- 2 cups water
- 1 tablespoon lime juice
- 2 teaspoons vanilla extract
- Cooking spray

Directions:

1. In a bowl, mix the almond flour with the baking powder, the oil and the rest of the ingredients except the cooking spray and whisk well.

2. Pour the mix into a cake pan greased with the cooking spray, introduce in the oven and bake at 370 degrees F for 25 minutes.

3. Leave the cake to cool down, cut and serve!

Nutrition:

Calories 200

Fat 7.6

Fiber 2.5

Carbs 5.5

Protein 4.5

Pumpkin Cream

Preparation Time: 5 minutes

Cooking Time: 5 minutes

Servings: 2

Ingredients:

- 2 cups canned pumpkin flesh
- 2 tablespoons stevia
- 1 teaspoon vanilla extract
- 2 tablespoons water
- A pinch of pumpkin spice

Directions:

1. In a pan, combine the pumpkin flesh with the other ingredients, simmer for 5 minutes, divide into cups and serve cold.

Nutrition

Calories 192

Fat 3.4

Fiber 4.5

Carbs 7.6

Protein 3.5

Chia and Berries Smoothie Bowl

Preparation Time: 5 minutes

Cooking Time: 0 minutes

Servings: 2

Ingredients:

- 1 and ½ cup almond milk
- 1 cup blackberries
- ¼ cup strawberries, chopped
- 1 and ½ tablespoons chia seeds
- 1 teaspoon cinnamon powder

Directions:

1. In a blender, combine the blackberries with the strawberries and the rest of the ingredients, pulse well, divide into small bowls and serve cold.

Nutrition

Calories 182

Fat 3.4g

Fiber 3.4 g

Carbs 8.4g

Protein 3g

Minty Coconut Cream

Preparation Time: 4 minutes

Cooking Time: 0 minutes

Servings: 2

Ingredients:

- 1 banana, peeled
- 2 cups coconut flesh, shredded
- 3 tablespoons mint, chopped
- 1 and ½ cups coconut water
- 2 tablespoons stevia
- ½ avocado, pitted and peeled

Directions:

1. In a blender, combine the coconut with the banana and the rest of the ingredients, pulse well, divide into cups and serve cold.

Nutrition:

Calories 193

Fat 5.4

Fiber 3.4

Carbs 7.6

Protein 3

Grapes Stew

Preparation Time: 10 minutes

Cooking Time: 10 minutes

Servings: 4

Ingredients:

- 2/3 cup stevia
- 1 tablespoon olive oil
- 1/3 cup coconut water
- 1 teaspoon vanilla extract
- 1 teaspoon lemon zest, grated
- 2 cup red grapes, halved

Directions:

1. Heat up a pan with the water over medium heat, add the oil, stevia and the rest of the ingredients, toss, simmer for 10 minutes, divide into cups and serve.

Nutrition:

Calories 122

Fat 3.7

Fiber 1.2

Carbs 2.3

Protein 0.4

Blueberry Matcha Smoothie

Preparation Time: 5 minutes

Cooking Time: 0 minutes

Servings: 2

Ingredients:

- 2 Cups Blueberries, Frozen
- 2 Cups Almond Milk
- 1 Banana
- 2 Tablespoons Protein Powder, Optional
- ¼ Teaspoon Ground Cinnamon
- 1 Tablespoon Chia Seeds
- 1 Tablespoon Matcha Powder
- ¼ Teaspoon Ground Ginger
- A Pinch Sea Salt

Directions:

1. Blend everything until smooth.

Nutrition:

Calories: 208

Protein: 8.7 Grams

Fat: 5.7 Grams

Carbs: 31 Grams

Pumpkin Pie Smoothie

Preparation Time: 5 minutes

Cooking Time: 0 minutes

Servings: 2

Ingredients:

- 1 Banana
- ½ Cup Pumpkin, Canned & Unsweetened
- 2-3 Ice Cubes
- 1 Cup Almond Milk
- 2 Tablespoons Almond Butter, Heaping
- 1 Teaspoon Ground Nutmeg
- 1 Teaspoon Ground Cinnamon
- 1 Teaspoon Vanilla Extract Pure
- 1 Teaspoon Maple Syrup, Pure

Directions:

1. Blend everything together until smooth.

Nutrition:

Calories: 235

Protein: 5.6 Grams

Fat: 11 Grams

Carbs: 27.8 Grams

Fig Smoothie

Preparation Time: 5 minutes

Cooking Time: 0 minutes

Servings: 2

Ingredients:

- 7 Figs, Halved (Fresh or Frozen)
- 1 Banana
- 1 Cup Whole Milk Yogurt, Plain
- 1 Cup Almond Milk
- 1 Teaspoon Flaxseed, Ground
- 1 Tablespoon Almond Butter
- 1 Teaspoon Honey, Raw
- 3-4 Ice Cubes

Directions:

1. Blend all together ingredients until smooth, and serve immediately.

Nutrition:

Calories: 362

Protein: 9 Grams

Fat: 12 Grams

Carbs: 60 Grams

Ginger, Carrot, and Turmeric Smoothie

Preparation Time: 5 minutes

Cooking Time: 0 minutes

Servings: 2

Ingredients:

- 1/8 tsp. Cayenne pepper
- 1 tsp. Turmeric, ground
- 1 tsp. Ginger, ground
- 1 tbsp. Hemp seeds, raw, shelled
- 1 cup Coconut water
- ½ cup Mango, fresh or frozen chunks
- 1 large Carrot, peeled and chopped

- 1 Orange, peeled and separated

Directions:

1. Puree all of the ingredients together with one-half cup of ice until smooth and drink immediately.

Nutrition:

Calories 250

35 grams sugar

4.5 grams fat

7 grams fiber

48 grams carbs

6 grams protein

Kiwi Strawberry Smoothie

Preparation Time: 10 minutes

Cooking Time: 0 minutes

Servings: 1

Ingredients:

- 1 Kiwi, peeled and chopped
- ½ cup Strawberries, fresh or frozen, chopped
- 1 cup Milk, almond or coconut
- 1 tsp. Basil, ground
- 1 tsp. Turmeric, ground
- 1 Banana, diced
- ¼ cup Chia seed powder

Directions:

1. Drink immediately after all the ingredients have been well mixed.

Nutrition:

Calories 250

9.9 grams sugar

1 gram fat

34 carbs grams

4.3 grams fiber

Blended Coconut Milk and Banana Breakfast Smoothie

Preparation Time: 10 minutes

Cooking Time: 0 minutes

Servings: 4

Ingredients:

- 4 ripe medium-sized bananas
- 4 tbsp. flax seeds
- 2 cups almond milk
- 2 cups coconut milk
- 4 tsp. cinnamon

Directions:

1. Peel the banana and slice it into ½-inch pieces. Put all the ingredients in the blender and blend into a smoothie. Add a dash of cinnamon at the top of the smoothie before serving.

Nutrition:

Calories: 332 kcal

Protein: 12.49 g

Fat: 14.42 g

Carbohydrates: 42.46 g

Kale Smoothie

Preparation Time: 10 minutes

Cooking Time: 0 minutes

Servings: 2

Ingredients:

- 10 kale leaves
- 5 bananas, peeled and cut into chunks
- 2 pears, chopped
- 5 tbsp. almond butter
- 5 cups almond milk

Directions:

1. In your blender, mix the kale with the bananas, pears, almond butter, and almond milk.

2. Pulse well, divide into glasses, and serve. Enjoy!

Nutrition:

Calories: 267

Fat: 11 g

Protein: 7 g

Carbs: 15 g

Fiber: 7 g

Raspberry Smoothie

Preparation Time: 10 minutes

Cooking Time: 0 minutes

Servings: 2

Ingredients:

- 1 avocado, pitted and peeled
- 3/4 cup raspberry juice
- 3/4 cup orange juice
- 1/2 cup raspberries

Directions:

1. In your blender, mix the avocado with the raspberry juice, orange juice, and raspberries.
2. Pulse well, divide into 2 glasses, and serve. Enjoy!

Nutrition:

Calories: 125

Fat: 11 g

Protein: 3 g

Carbs: 9 g

Fiber: 7 g

Pineapple Smoothie

Preparation Time: 10 minutes

Cooking Time: 0 minutes

Servings: 2

Ingredients:

- 1 cup coconut water
- 1 orange, peeled and cut into quarters
- 1 1/2 cups pineapple chunks
- 1 tbsp. fresh grated ginger
- 1 tsp. chia seeds
- 1 tsp. turmeric powder
- A pinch black pepper

Directions:

1. In your blender, mix the coconut water with the orange, pineapple, ginger, chia seeds, turmeric, and black pepper.
2. Pulse well, pour into a glass.
3. Serve for breakfast. Enjoy!

Nutrition:

Calories: 151

Fat: 2 g

Protein: 4 g

Carbs: 12 g

Fiber: 6 g

Beet Smoothie

Preparation Time: 10 minutes

Cooking Time: 0 minutes

Servings: 2

Ingredients:

- 10 oz. almond milk, unsweetened
- 2 beets, peeled and quartered
- 1/2 banana, peeled and frozen
- 1/2 cup cherries, pitted
- 1 tbsp. almond butter

Directions:

1. In your blender, mix the milk with the beets, banana, cherries, and butter.
2. Pulse well, pour into glasses, and serve. Enjoy!

Nutrition:

Calories: 165

Fat: 5 g

Protein: 5 g

Carbs: 22 g

Fiber: 6 g

Blueberry Smoothie

Preparation Time: 10 minutes

Cooking Time: 0 minutes

Servings: 1

Ingredients:

- 1 banana, peeled
- 2 handfuls baby spinach
- 1 tbsp. almond butter
- 1/2 cup blueberries
- 1/4 tsp. ground cinnamon
- 1 tsp. maca powder
- 1/2 cup water
- 1/2 cup almond milk, unsweetened

Directions:

1. In your blender, mix the spinach with the banana, blueberries, almond butter, cinnamon, maca powder, water, and milk.
2. Pulse well, pour into a glass, and serve. Enjoy!

Nutrition:

Calories: 341

Fat: 12 g

Protein: 10 g

Carbs: 54 g

Fiber: 12 g

Strawberry Oatmeal Smoothie

Preparation Time: 10 minutes

Cooking Time: 0 minutes

Servings: 1

Ingredients:

- 1 cup soy milk
- 1/2 cup rolled oats
- 1 banana, broken into chunks
- 14 frozen strawberries
- 1/2 tsp. vanilla extract
- 1 1/2 tsp. honey

Directions:

1. Add everything to a blender jug.
2. Cover the jug tightly.
3. Blend until smooth. Serve and enjoy!

Nutrition:

Calories: 172

Fat: 0.4 g

Protein: 5.6 g

Carbs: 8 g

Fiber: 2 g

Raspberry Banana Smoothie

Preparation Time: 10 minutes

Cooking Time: 0 minutes

Servings: 1

Ingredients:

- 1 banana
- 16 whole almonds
- 1/4 cup rolled oats
- 1 tbsp. flaxseed meal
- 1 cup frozen raspberries
- 1 cup raspberry yogurt
- 1/4 cup Concord grape juice
- 1 cup almond milk

Directions:

1. Add everything to a blender jug.
2. Cover the jug tightly.
3. Blend until smooth and then serve. Enjoy!

Nutrition:

Calories: 214

Fat: 0.4 g

Protein: 5.6 g

Carbs: 8 g

Fiber: 2.3 g

Almond Blueberry Smoothie

Preparation Time: 10 minutes

Cooking Time: 0 minutes

Servings: 1

Ingredients:

- 1 cup frozen blueberries
- 1 banana
- 1/2 cup almond milk
- 1 tbsp. almond butter
- Water, as needed

Directions:

1. Add everything to a blender jug.
2. Cover the jug tightly.
3. Blend until smooth. Serve and enjoy!

Nutrition:

Calories: 211

Fat: 0.2 g

Protein: 5.6 g

Carbs: 3.4 g

Fiber: 2.3 g

Green Vanilla Smoothie

Preparation Time: 10 minutes

Cooking Time: 0 minutes

Servings: 1

Ingredients:

- 1 banana, cut in chunks
- 1 cup grapes
- 1 tub (6 oz.) vanilla yogurt
- 1/2 apple, cored and chopped
- 1 1/2 cups fresh spinach leaves

Directions:

1. Add everything to a blender jug.
2. Cover the jug tightly.
3. Blend until smooth. Serve and enjoy!

Nutrition:

Calories: 131

Fat: 0.2 g

Protein: 2.6 g

Carbs: 9.1 g

Fiber: 1.3 g

Purple Fruit Smoothie

Preparation Time: 10 minutes

Cooking Time: 0 minutes

Servings: 1

Ingredients:

- 2 frozen bananas, cut in chunks
- 1/2 cup frozen blueberries
- 1 cup orange juice
- 1 tbsp. honey, optional
- 1 tsp. vanilla extract, optional

Directions:

1. Add everything to a blender jug.
2. Cover the jug tightly.
3. Blend until smooth. Serve and enjoy!

Nutrition:

Calories: 133

Fat: 1.1 g

Protein: 3.6 g

Carbs: 7.6 g

Fiber: 1.3 g

Vanilla Avocado Smoothie

Preparation Time: 10 minutes

Cooking Time: 0 minutes

Servings: 1

Ingredients:

- 1 ripe avocado, halved and pitted
- 1 cup almond milk
- 1/2 cup vanilla yogurt
- 3 tbsp. honey
- 8 ice cubes

Directions:

1. Add everything to a blender jug.
2. Cover the jug tightly.
3. Blend until smooth. Serve and enjoy!

Nutrition:

Calories: 143

Fat: 1.2 g

Protein: 4.6 g

Carbs: 21 g

Fiber: 2.3 g

Triple Fruit Smoothie

Preparation Time: 10 minutes

Cooking Time: 0 minutes

Servings: 1

Ingredients:

- 1 kiwi, sliced
- 1 banana, peeled and chopped
- 1/2 cup blueberries
- 1 cup strawberries
- 1 cup ice cubes
- 1/2 cup orange juice
- 1 container (8 oz.) peach yogurt

Directions:

1. Add everything to a blender jug.
2. Cover the jug tightly.
3. Blend until smooth. Serve and enjoy!

Nutrition:

Calories: 124

Fat: 0.4 g

Protein: 5.6 g

Carbs: 8 g

Fiber: 2.3 g

Peach Maple Smoothie

Preparation Time: 10 minutes

Cooking Time: 0 minutes

Servings: 1

Ingredients:

- 4 large peaches, peeled and chopped
- 2 tbsp. maple syrup
- 1 cup fat-free yogurt
- 1 cup ice

Directions:

1. Add everything to a blender jug.
2. Cover the jug tightly.
3. Blend until smooth. Serve and enjoy!

Nutrition:

Calories: 125

Fat: 0.4 g

Protein: 5.6 g

Carbs: 8 g

Fiber: 2.3 g

Pink California Smoothie

Preparation Time: 10 minutes

Cooking Time: 0 minutes

Servings: 1

Ingredients:

- 7 large strawberries
- 1 container (8 oz.) lemon yogurt
- 1/3 cup orange juice

Direction:

1. Add everything to a blender jug.
2. Cover the jug tightly.
3. Blend until smooth. Serve and enjoy!

Nutrition:

Calories: 144

Fat: 0.4 g

Protein: 5.6 g

Carbs: 8 g

Fiber: 2.3 g

Carrot and Orange Turmeric Drink

Preparation Time: 5 minutes

Cooking Time: 0 minutes

Servings: 2

Ingredients:

- 2 carrots, peeled, chopped
- 1 cup orange juice
- 1/2 inch ginger slice
- 2 tbsp. sugar
- 1 tbsp. lemon juice
- 1/4 tsp. turmeric powder

Direction:

1. In a blender, add orange juice, sugar, turmeric powder, carrots, and lemon juice. Blend well.
2. Pour into serving glasses. Serve and enjoy!

Nutrition:

Calories: 153 kcal

Protein: 4.47 g

Fat: 3.3 g

Carbohydrates: 27.02 g

Voluptuous Vanilla Hot Drink

Preparation Time: 10 minutes

Cooking Time: 0 minutes

Servings: 1

Ingredients:

- 3 cups unsweetened almond milk (or 1 1/2 cup full-fat coconut milk + 1 1/2 cups
- water)
- Stevia to taste
- 1 scoop of hemp protein
- 1/2 Tbsp. ground cinnamon (or more to taste)
- 1/2 Tbsp. vanilla extract

Directions:

1. Place the almond milk into a pitcher. Place ground cinnamon, hemp, vanilla extract in a small saucepan over medium-high heat. Heat until the pure liquid stevia is just melted and then pour the pure liquid stevia mixture into the pitcher.
2. Stir until the pure liquid stevia is well combined with the almond milk. Bring the pitcher in the fridge and allow to chill for at least two hours. Stir well before serving.

Nutrition:

Calories: 656 kcal

Protein: 42.12 g

Fat: 33.05 g

Carbohydrates: 44.45 g

Almond Butter Smoothies

Preparation Time: 5 minutes

Cooking Time: 0 minutes

Servings: 1

Ingredients:

- 1 scoop of hemp protein
- 1 Tablespoon natural almond butter
- 1 cup of hemp milk
- 1 banana, preferably frozen for a creamier shake
- few ice cubes

Directions:

1. Blend all ingredients together and enjoy!

Nutrition:

Calories: 533 kcal

Protein: 31.23 g

Fat: 26.31 g

Carbohydrates: 47.13 g

Baby Kale Pineapple Smoothie

Preparation Time: 5 minutes

Cooking Time: 0 minutes

Servings: 1

Ingredients:

- 1 cup almond milk

- 1/2 cup frozen pineapple
- 1 cup Kale
- 1 tablespoon hemp protein powder

Directions:

1. Place the almond milk, pineapple, and greens in the blender and blend until smooth.

Nutrition:

Calories: 389 kcal

Protein: 20.29 g

Fat: 16.2 g

Carbohydrates: 42.29 g

Vanilla Blueberry Smoothie

Preparation Time: 5 minutes

Cooking Time: 0 minutes

Servings: 1

Ingredients:

- 2 cups hemp milk
- 1 cup fresh blueberries
- Handful of ice/ 1 cup frozen blueberries
- 1 tbsp. flaxseed oil
- 2 tbsp. hemp protein powder

Directions:

1. Combine milk and fresh blueberries plus ice (or frozen blueberries) in a blender.
2. Blend for 1 minute, transfer to a glass, and stir in flaxseed oil.

Nutrition:

Calories: 1041 kcal

Protein: 35.21 g

Fat: 41.04 g

Carbohydrates: 140.4 g

Zesty Citrus Smoothie

Preparation Time: 5 minutes

Cooking Time: 0 minutes

Servings: 1

Ingredients:

- 1 cup almond milk
- half cup lemon juice
- 1 med orange peeled, cleaned, and sliced into sections
- Handful of ice
- 1 tbsp. flaxseed oil
- 2 tsp hemp protein powder

Directions:

1. Combine milk, lemon juice, orange, and ice in a blender.
2. Blend for 1 minute, transfer to a glass, and stir in flaxseed oil.

Nutrition:

Calories: 427 kcal

Protein: 17.5 g

Fat: 28.88 g

Carbohydrates: 24.96 g

Mango and Ginger Infused Water

Preparation Time: 5 minutes

Cooking Time: 5 minutes

Servings: 4

Ingredients:

- 1 cup fresh mango, chopped
- 2-inch piece ginger, peeled, cubed
- Water to cover ingredients

Directions:

1. Place ingredients in the mesh steamer basket.
2. Place basket in the instant pot.
3. Add water to cover contents.
4. Lock the lid. Cook on HIGH pressure 5 minutes.
5. Once done, release pressure quickly.
6. Remove steamer basket. Discard cooked produce.
7. Allow flavored water to cool. Chill completely. Serve.

Nutrition:

Calories: 209

Fat: 1g

Carbohydrates: 51g

Protein: 2g

White Hot Chocolate

Preparation Time: 5 minutes

Cooking Time: 6 minutes

Servings: 2

Ingredients:

- 3 cups coconut milk
- ¼ cup cocoa powder/butter
- 2 - 2½ Tbsp honey
- 2 tsp vanilla extract
- Pinch of sea salt

Directions:

1. Add milk, cocoa powder/butter, honey, vanilla extract, and salt to the instant pot.
2. Lock the lid. Cook on LOW pressure 6 minutes.
3. Release pressure quickly.
4. Using a hand blender, blend contents 25 seconds.
5. Serve hot.

Nutrition:

Calories: 331

Fat: 14g

Carbohydrates: 47g

Protein: 4g

Peach and Raspberry Lemonade

Preparation Time: 5 minutes

Cooking Time: 5 minutes

Servings: 4

Ingredients:

- 1 cup fresh peaches, chopped
- ½ cup fresh raspberries
- Zest and juice of 1 lemon
- Water to cover ingredients

Directions:

1. Place ingredients in mesh basket for instant pot. Place in pot.
2. Add water to barely cover the fruit.
3. Lock the lid. Cook on HIGH pressure 5 minutes.
4. Once done, release pressure quickly.
5. Remove steamer basket. Discard cooked produce.
6. Allow flavored water to cool. Chill completely before serving.

Nutrition:

Calories: 77

Fat: 0g

Carbohydrates: 19g

Protein: 0g

Hot Apple Cider

Preparation Time: 5 minutes

Cooking Time: 15 minutes

Servings: 4

Ingredients:

- 7 medium apples, cored, quarter
- 1 orange, peeled, cut into segments
- 1 lemon, peeled, cut into segments
- ½ cup fresh cranberries
- 2 cinnamon sticks
- ½ tsp whole cloves
- ½ star of anise
- ½ cup honey
- Water to cover ingredients

Directions:

1. Add apples, lemon, orange, and cranberries to the instant pot.
2. Add cinnamon stick, star anise, and cloves.
3. Pour in water to cover ingredients.
4. Lock the lid. Cook on HIGH pressure 15 minutes.
5. Release pressure naturally.
6. Mash fruit with a masher to release juices.

7. Strain the liquid. Chill completely before serving.

Nutrition:

Calories: 153

Fat: 9g

Carbohydrates: 14g

Protein: 4g

Blueberry Lime Juice

Preparation Time: 5 minutes

Cooking Time: 5 minutes

Servings: 4

Ingredients:

- 1 cup fresh blueberries
- Zest and juice of 1 lime
- Water to cover contents

Directions:

1. Place ingredients in a mesh steamer basket for instant pot. Place in pot.
2. Pour in water to cover contents.
3. Lock the lid. Cook on HIGH pressure 5 minutes.
4. Once done, release pressure quickly.
5. Remove steamer basket. Discard cooked produce.
6. Allow flavored water to cool. Chill completely before serving.

Nutrition:

Calories: 86

Fat: 0g

Carbohydrates: 22g

Protein: 0g

Sweet Cranberry Juice

Preparation Time: 5 minutes

Cooking Time: 8 minutes

Servings: 4

Ingredients:

- 4 cups fresh cranberries
- 1 cinnamon stick
- 1 gallon filtered water
- ½ cup honey
- Juice of 1 lemon

Directions:

1. Add cranberries, ½ of water, cinnamon stick to the instant pot.
2. Lock the lid. Cook on HIGH pressure 8 minutes.
3. Release pressure naturally.
4. Once cool, strain liquid. Add remaining water.
5. Stir in honey and lemon. Cool completely.
6. Chill before serving.

Nutrition:

Calories: 184

Fat: 0g

Carbohydrates: 49g

Protein: 1g

Hot Peppermint Vanilla Latte

Preparation Time: 5 minutes

Cooking Time: 5 minutes

Servings: 4

Ingredients:

- 4 cups almond milk
- 2 cups coffee
- 1 tsp vanilla
- ¼ cup honey
- 23 drops peppermint oil

Directions:

1. Add listed ingredients to the instant pot.
2. Lock the lid. Cook on HIGH pressure 5 minutes.
3. Once done, release pressure naturally.
4. Serve warm.

Nutrition:

Calories: 279

Fat: 3g

Carbohydrates: 61g

Protein: 3g

Berry Shrub

Preparation Time: 10 minutes

Cooking Time: 20 minutes

Servings: 4

Ingredients:

- 1 cup of dried elderberries
- 2 cups of apple cider vinegar
- 2 cups of water
- 2 cups of honey
- ½ a cup of chopped fresh oregano

Directions:

1. Add listed ingredients to the instant pot.
2. Lock the lid. Cook on HIGH pressure 20 minutes.
3. Once done, release pressure naturally.
4. Pour ingredients through a sieve into a jar.
5. Allow to cool down. Chill.

Nutrition:

Calories: 127

Fat: 0g

Carbohydrates: 6g

Protein: 0g

Cooked Iced Tea

Preparation Time: 2 minutes

Cooking Time: 4 minutes

Servings: 4

Ingredients:

- 4 regular tea bags
- 6 cups water
- 2 tbsp. honey

Directions:

1. Add ingredients to the instant pot.
2. Lock the lid. Cook on HIGH pressure 4 minutes.
3. Once done, release pressure naturally.
4. Allow to cool completely. Serve over ice.

Nutrition:

Calories: 22

Fat: 0g

Carbohydrates: 6g

Protein: 0g

Hibiscus Tea

Preparation Time: 5 minutes

Cooking Time: 10 minutes

Servings: 4

Ingredients:

- 2 cup dried hibiscus petals
- 10 cups water
- 1 tbsp. honey
- 1 tsp fresh ginger, grated
- Rind from 1 pineapple

Directions:

1. Rinse hibiscus leaves thoroughly with cold water.
2. Remove the dust.
3. Add water, honey, and ginger to the instant pot. Stir.
4. Stir in hibiscus petals and pineapple rind.
5. Lock the lid. Cook on HIGH pressure 10 minutes.
6. Once done, release pressure naturally.
7. Remove pineapple rind. Pass liquid through a fine-mesh strainer.
8. Cool completely. Chill before serving.

Nutrition:

Calories: 114

Fat: 0g

Carbohydrates: 28g

Protein: 0g

Apple Cinnamon Water

Preparation Time: 5 minutes

Cooking Time: 5 minutes

Servings: 4

Ingredients:

- 1 whole apple, diced
- 5 cinnamon sticks
- Water to cover contents

Directions:

1. Place ingredients in the steamer basket. Place in pot.
2. Add water cover contents.
3. Lock the lid. Cook on HIGH pressure 5 minutes.
4. Once done, release pressure quickly.
5. Remove steamer basket. Discard cooked produce.
6. Allow flavored water to cool. Chill completely before serving.

Nutrition:

Calories: 194

Fat: 0g

Carbohydrates: 12g

Protein: 0g

Wassail

Preparation Time: 5 minutes

Cooking Time: 10 minutes

Servings: 4

Ingredients:

- 8 cups apple cider
- 4 cups orange juice
- 5 cinnamon sticks
- 10 cloves
- ½ tsp nutmeg
- Zest and juice of 2 lemons
- 1 inch peeled ginger
- 2 vanilla beans, split or 2 Tbsp pure vanilla extract

Directions:

1. Pour cider and orange juice in the instant pot.
2. Place cinnamon sticks, nutmeg piece, cloves, lemon zest, vanilla beans in the steamer basket.
3. If you didn't use vanilla beans, pour in vanilla extract. Add lemon juice.
4. Lock the lid. Cook on HIGH pressure 10 minutes.
5. Once done, release pressure naturally.
6. Discard contents of the steamer basket.
7. Serve hot from the pot.

Nutrition:

Calories: 221

Fat: 0g

Carbohydrates: 42g

Protein: 0g

Instant Horchata

Preparation Time: 5 minutes

Cooking Time: 5 minutes

Servings: 4

Ingredients:

- 32 ounces rice milk
- 6 tbsp. honey
- 1 cinnamon stick, broken into small chunks

Directions:

1. Add listed ingredients to the instant pot.
2. Lock the lid. Cook on HIGH pressure 5 minutes.
3. Once done, release pressure naturally over 10 minutes.
4. Cool completely. Chill before serving.

Nutrition:

Calories: 226

Fat: 1g

Carbohydrates: 53g

Protein: 2g

Jamaican Hibiscus Tea

Preparation Time: 5 minutes

Cooking Time: 5 minutes

Servings: 4

Ingredients:

- 1 cup dried hibiscus flowers
- 8 cups water
- 1 tbsp. honey
- ½ tsp ginger, minced
- Juice of 1 lime
- Ice as needed

Directions:

1. Add hibiscus flowers, water, honey, and ginger to the instant pot.
2. Lock the lid. Cook on HIGH pressure 5 minutes.
3. Once done, release pressure naturally.
4. Cool completely. Transfer to glass decanter. Stir in lime Juice. Pour over ice.

Nutrition:

Calories: 197

Fat: 0g

Carbohydrates: 18g

Protein: 0g

Ginger Ale

Preparation Time: 5 minutes

Cooking Time: 30 minutes

Servings: 4

Ingredients:

- 1 pound fresh ginger, unpeeled, diced
- Juice and rind of 2 lemons
- 1 tbsp. honey
- 1 quart carbonated water
- Lime wedges
- Ice for serving

Directions:

1. Place ginger and lemon juice in a food processor. Pulse to smooth consistency.
2. Transfer puree to the instant pot. Stir in honey.
3. Add lemon peel to the instant pot.
4. Lock the lid. Cook on HIGH pressure 30 minutes.
5. Once done, release pressure naturally. Strain and chill.
6. Serve over ice.

Nutrition:

Calories: 108

Fat: 0g

Carbohydrates: 28g

Protein: 0g

Blackberry Italian Drink

Preparation Time: 5 minutes

Cooking Time: 15 minutes

Servings: 4

Ingredients:

- 1 cup blackberries
- 2 tbsp. honey
- 1 bottle sparkling water
- 1 lemon, sliced

Directions:

1. Add 1 cup (non-carbonated) water to the instant pot.
2. Add blackberries to the instant pot.
3. Lock the lid. Cook on HIGH pressure 10 minutes.
4. Once done, release pressure naturally.
5. Mash the berries in the instant pot. Transfer to dish. Allow to cool.
6. As blackberries cook, in a separate small saucepan with a heavy bottom. Add honey. Simmer 5 minutes. Cool down.
7. To make the drink. Spoon 1 teaspoon honey. Pour in fruit mixture. Add carbonated water. Stir.

Nutrition:

Calories: 249

Fat: 0.6g

Carbohydrates: 55g

Protein: 7.5g

Turmeric Hot Chocolate

Preparation Time: 5 minutes

Cooking Time: 10 minutes

Servings: 2

Ingredients:

- 2 cups milk
- 2 tsp. ground turmeric
- 1/8 tsp. pepper
- 4 tsp. honey
- 3 tbsp. cacao or cocoa powder
- 4 tsp. coconut oil
- 1/8 tsp. cayenne pepper, optional

Directions:

1. Add milk, turmeric, cocoa, and coconut oil into a saucepan. Place the saucepan over medium heat. Coconut oil and pepper are added because it helps to absorb the turmeric.
2. Whisk frequently until well incorporated.
3. When it begins to boil, take off from the heat. Add honey, cayenne pepper, and pepper and whisk well.
4. Divide into 2 cups and serve.

Nutrition:

Calories: 339 kcal

Protein: 12.76 g

Fat: 21.19 g

Carbohydrates: 30.35 g

Turmeric Tea

Preparation Time: 5 minutes

Cooking Time: 15 minutes

Servings: 2

Ingredients:

- 2 cups water
- ½ tsp ground cinnamon
- 2 lemon juices
- ½ teaspoon turmeric powder
- ½ teaspoon ground ginger
- 2 tablespoons honey

Directions:

1. Add water into a saucepan. Place the saucepan over medium heat.
2. When it begins to boil, add turmeric, cinnamon, and ginger and stir gently.
3. Turn off the heat. Cover and let the mixture steep for 12 – 15 minutes. Add honey and lemon juice.
4. Stir and pour into mugs.
5. Serve.

Nutrition:

Calories: 121 kcal

Protein: 3.57 g

Fat: 3.2 g

Carbohydrates: 21.97 g

Lemon Ginger Iced Tea

Preparation Time: 5 minutes

Cooking Time: 10 minutes

Servings: 2-3

Ingredients:

- 3-4 cups water
- ¼ teaspoon turmeric
- 1 tablespoon maple syrup
- 2 inches fresh ginger, peeled, thinly sliced or to taste
- 1 tablespoon fresh lemon juice or to taste (optional)
- A pinch ground cinnamon
- 2 – 3 lemon slices

Directions:

1. Pour water into a saucepan. Add ginger, turmeric, lemon slices, and cinnamon. Place the saucepan over medium heat.
2. Cover and simmer for 8 - 10 minutes.
3. Strain and pour into a jar. Put the maple syrup, and lemon juice, then stir. Chill for 8 – 10 hours.
4. Stir well. Pour into glasses and serve.

Nutrition:

Calories: 55 kcal

Protein: 2.32 g

Fat: 2.13 g

Carbohydrates: 7.47 g

Pineapple & Ginger Juice

Preparation Time: 5 minutes

Cooking Time: 0 minutes

Servings: 2

Ingredients:

- 8 celery stalks, chopped
- 2 cups chopped pineapple
- 2 cups spinach
- 2 inches ginger, peeled, sliced
- 2 cucumbers, chopped
- 2 apples, cored, chopped
- 2 lemons, peeled, halved

Directions:

1. Juice together all the ingredients in a juicer.
2. Pour into 2 glasses and serve.

Nutrition:

Calories: 339 kcal

Protein: 7.44 g

Fat: 4.23 g

Carbohydrates: 75.38 g

Parsley Ginger Green Juice

Preparation Time: 5 minutes

Cooking Time: 0 minutes

Servings: 2

Ingredients:

- 4 cups chopped parsley
- 2 green apples, cored
- 2 cucumbers, chopped
- 4 inches fresh ginger, peeled, sliced
- 4 cups chopped spinach
- 2 lemons, peeled, halved
- 6 stalks celery, chopped

Directions:

1. Juice together all the ingredients in a juicer.
2. Pour into 2 glasses and serve.

Nutrition:

Calories: 239 kcal

Protein: 10.74 g

Fat: 5.08 g

Carbohydrates: 44.86 g

Vanilla Turmeric Orange Juice

Preparation Time: 5 minutes

Cooking Time: 10 minutes

Servings: 2

Ingredients:

- 6 oranges, peeled, separated into segments, deseeded
- 2 teaspoons vanilla extract
- ½ teaspoon turmeric powder
- 2 cups unsweetened almond milk
- 1 teaspoon ground cinnamon
- Pepper to taste

Directions:

1. Juice the oranges. Add the rest of the ingredients.
2. Pour into 2 glasses and serve.

Nutrition:

Calories: 223 kcal

Protein: 11.47 g

Fat: 11.79 g

Carbohydrates: 15.9 g

Turmeric and Ginger Tonic

Preparation Time: 5 minutes

Cooking Time: 10 minutes

Servings: 4

Ingredients:

- 2 tablespoons grated, fresh ginger
- 2 tablespoons grated, fresh turmeric
- Juice of 2 lemons
- 6 cups water
- The rind of 2 lemons, peeled
- 1/8 teaspoon cayenne pepper
- Maple syrup or honey to taste

Directions:

1. Add water, ginger, turmeric, cayenne pepper, and lemon rind into a saucepan.
2. Place the saucepan over medium-high heat. (Don't boil)
3. When the mixture is hot, take off from the heat.
4. Strain into 4 mugs. Add honey and lemon juice and stir.
5. Serve warm.

Nutrition:

Calories: 48 kcal

Protein: 2.28 g

Fat: 1.81 g

Carbohydrates: 7.03 g

Flu Fighting Tonic

Preparation Time: 5 minutes

Cooking Time: 10 minutes

Servings: 2

Ingredients:

- Juice of 2 lemons
- ½ teaspoon turmeric powder
- 2 tablespoons clear honey preferably manuka
- Boiling water, as required
- Lemon slices to garnish

Directions:

1. Divide the lemon juice into 2 mugs. Add ¼ teaspoon turmeric powder into each mug.
2. Add a tablespoon of honey into each mug.
3. Pour boiling water to fill up the mugs. Stir.
4. Garnish with a slice of lemon and serve.

Nutrition:

Calories: 123 kcal

Protein: 3.59 g

Fat: 3.23 g

Carbohydrates: 22.78 g

Golden Chai Latte

Preparation Time: 5 minutes

Cooking Time: 10 minutes

Servings: 2

Ingredients:

- ½ cup water
- 1 ¼ cups cashew milk or any other non-dairy milk of your choice
- ½ tablespoon turmeric powder
- 1/8 teaspoon ground nutmeg
- 1 teaspoon loose leaf chai tea
- ½ cup water
- ¼ teaspoon ground cinnamon
- A pinch ground cardamom
- ½ tablespoon maple syrup

Directions:

1. Add water and 1-cup milk into a saucepan. Place the saucepan over medium heat.
2. Add chai leaves in a tea strainer (the type that that has a lid and you can close). Lower the strainer in the saucepan. Add spices.
3. When it just comes to a light boil, turn off the heat. Let it cool for 5 minutes. Take out the tea strainer and discard the leaves.
4. Add maple syrup and stir.
5. Pour into glasses. Drizzle remaining cashew milk on top. Garnish with cinnamon and nutmeg and serve.

Nutrition:

Calories: 142 kcal

Protein: 8.59 g

Fat: 6.26 g

Carbohydrates: 13.3 g

Chocolate Latte with Reishi

Preparation Time: 5 minutes

Cooking Time: 10 minutes

Servings: 2

Ingredients:

- 1 teaspoon Reishi powder
- A pinch sea salt
- 4 cups almond milk, unsweetened
- Sweetener of your choice
- 4 teaspoons raw cacao powder
- A pinch ground cinnamon
- 2 tablespoons coconut butter

Directions:

1. Add almond milk into a saucepan. Place the saucepan over low heat.
2. When the milk is warm and just begins to bubble, turn off the heat. Transfer into a blender.
3. Add the rest of the ingredients and blend for 30 – 40 seconds or until smooth.
4. Pour into mugs and serve.

Nutrition:

Calories: 461 kcal

Protein: 19.32 g

Fat: 30.57 g

Carbohydrates: 28.08 g

Mango Tomato Smoothie

Preparation Time: 5 minutes

Cooking Time: 0 minutes

Servings: 4

Ingredients:

- 2 mangoes, peeled, pitted
- 4 Campari tomatoes, chopped
- 2 cups chopped cilantro
- 1 cup almond milk
- 2 cups pineapple chunks
- 6 cups fresh baby spinach

Directions:

1. Put all together the ingredients into a blender and blend until smooth.
2. Pour into 4 tall glasses and serve.

Nutrition:

Calories: 395 kcal

Protein: 13.1 g

Fat: 8.19 g

Carbohydrates: 73.65 g

Spicy Tomato Smoothie

Preparation Time: 5 minutes

Cooking Time: 0 minutes

Servings: 2

Ingredients:

- 6 small vine tomatoes
- 1 small cucumber
- 1 small bunch cilantro, chopped
- ¼ cup chopped red onion
- 2 large carrots, chopped
- 2 cloves garlic, peeled
- Juice of 2 limes
- 1 jalapeño, sliced, deseed if desired

Directions:

1. Put all together the ingredients into a blender and blend until smooth.
2. Pour into 2 tall glasses and serve.

Nutrition:

Calories: 269 kcal

Protein: 24.87 g

Fat: 8.71 g

Carbohydrates: 26.89 g

Broccoli Smoothie

Preparation Time: 5 minutes

Cooking Time: 0 minutes

Servings: 4

Ingredients:

- 1 cup broccoli florets
- 2 cups frozen mango chunks
- 1 cup chopped spinach
- 1 ½ cups water
- 2 bananas, sliced, frozen
- 1 ½ cups strawberries
- 2 cups pineapple juice

Directions:

1. Put all together the ingredients into a blender and blend until smooth.
2. Pour into 4 tall glasses and serve.

Nutrition:

Calories: 222 kcal

Protein: 3.51 g

Fat: 1.98 g

Carbohydrates: 51.45 g

Cherry Smoothie

Preparation Time: 5 minutes

Cooking Time: 0 minutes

Servings: 4-6

Ingredients:

- 3 cups cherry juice
- 3 cups pitted, froze dark sweet cherries
- 2 bananas, sliced
- 1 ½ cups vanilla Greek yogurt
- To garnish: Optional
- Fresh cherries, pitted
- Mint sprigs

Directions:

1. Put all together the ingredients into a blender and blend until smooth.
2. Pour into 4 tall glasses.
3. Garnish with optional ingredients if using and serve.

Nutrition:

Calories: 114 kcal

Protein: 2.36 g

Fat: 1.88 g

Carbohydrates: 23.49 g

Chocolate Cherry Smoothie

Preparation Time: 5 minutes

Cooking Time: 0 minutes

Servings: 2

Ingredients:

- 4 cups pitted, frozen cherries
- 4 tablespoons cocoa or cacao powder
- 2 scoops protein powder or 4 tablespoons almond butter (optional)
- 2 cups almond milk, unsweetened
- 2 dates, pitted, chopped or 2 teaspoons pure maple syrup
- To serve: Optional
- Cacao nibs
- Granola
- Hemp hearts

Directions:

1. Put all together the ingredients into a blender and blend until smooth.
2. Pour into 2 tall glasses and serve topped with optional ingredients.

Nutrition:

Calories: 339 kcal

Protein: 16.37 g

Fat: 21.34 g

Carbohydrates: 27.99 g

Cucumber Kiwi Green Smoothie

Preparation Time: 5 minutes

Cooking Time: 0 minutes

Servings: 2

Ingredients:

- 2 ripe kiwi fruit
- 1 cup of seedless cucumber, chopped
- 1 cup of coconut water
- 6 to 8 ice cubes
- ice cubes

- ¼ cup of canned coconut milk
- 2 tbsps. of fresh chopped cilantro

Directions:
1. Combine the smoothie ingredients in your high-speed blender.
2. Pulse the ingredients a few times to chop them up.
3. Blend the mixture on the highest speed setting for 30 to 60 seconds.
4. Pour your finished smoothie into glasses and drink.

Nutrition:

Calories: 140 kcal

Protein: 5.1 g

Fat: 10.52 g

Carbohydrates: 7.4 g

Tropical Pineapple Kiwi Smoothie

Preparation Time: 5 minutes

Cooking Time: 0 minutes

Servings: 2

Ingredients:

- 1 ½ cup of frozen pineapple
- 1 ripe kiwi; peeled and chopped
- 1 cup of canned full-fat coconut milk
- 6 to 8 ice cubes
- 1 tsp of spiraling powder
- 3 tsp of lime juice

Directions:
1. Combine the smoothie ingredients in your high-speed blender.
2. Pulse the ingredients a few times to chop them up.
3. Blend the mixture on the highest speed setting.
4. Pour your finished smoothie into glasses and drink.

Nutrition:

Calories: 480 kcal

Protein: 7.38 g

Fat: 31.92 g

Carbohydrates: 48.35 g

Dreamy Yummy Orange Cream Smoothie

Preparation Time: 5 minutes

Cooking Time: 0 minutes

Servings: 2

Ingredients:

- 1 navel orange, peel removed
- 1 cup of almond milk
- 6 to 8 ice cubes
- ½ cup of canned full-fat coconut milk
- ¼ cup of fresh orange juice

Directions:
1. Combine the smoothie ingredients in your high-speed blender.
2. Pulse the ingredients a few times to chop them up.
3. Blend the mixture on the highest speed setting for 30 to 60 seconds.
4. Pour your finished smoothie into glasses and drink.

Nutrition:

Calories: 269 kcal

Protein: 8.63 g

Fat: 21.36 g

Carbohydrates: 12.75 g

Peachy Keen Smoothie

Preparation Time: 5 minutes

Cooking Time: 0 minutes

Servings: 2

Ingredients:

- 1 ½ cups of frozen peaches
- 1 small frozen banana
- 1 cup of almond milk
- 6 to 8 ice cubes
- 2 tbsp. of raw hemp seeds

- Pinch of ground ginger

Directions:

1. Combine the smoothie ingredients in your high-speed blender.
2. Pulse the ingredients a few times to chop them up.
3. Blend the mixture on the highest speed setting for 30 to 60 seconds.
4. Pour your finished smoothie into glasses and drink.

Nutrition:

Calories: 388 kcal

Protein: 10.59 g

Fat: 11.93 g

Carbohydrates: 64.08 g

Cucumber Melon Smoothie

Preparation Time: 5 minutes

Cooking Time: 0 minutes

Servings: 2

Ingredients:

- 1 ½ cups of chopped honeydew
- 1 cup of seedless cucumber, diced
- 1 cup of chilled coconut water
- 6 to 8 ice cubes
- 2 tbsp. of fresh mint

Directions:

1. Combine the smoothie ingredients in your high-speed blender.
2. Pulse the ingredients a few times to chop them up.
3. Blend the mixture on the highest speed setting for 30 to 60 seconds.
4. Pour your finished smoothie into glasses and drink.

Nutrition:

Calories: 300 kcal

Protein: 5.83 g

Fat: 8.55 g

Carbohydrates: 51.21 g

Tropical Mango Coconut Smoothie

Preparation Time: 5 minutes

Cooking Time: 0 minutes

Servings: 2

Ingredients:

- 1 ½ cups of frozen mango
- 1 medium frozen banana
- ½ cup of fresh orange juice
- ½ cup of canned coconut milk
- 1 tbsp. of fresh lemon juice
- 1 ½ tsp of honey

Directions:

1. Combine the smoothie ingredients in your high-speed blender.
2. Pulse the ingredients a few times to chop them up.
3. Blend the mixture on the highest speed setting for 30 to 60 seconds.
4. Pour your finished smoothie into glasses and drink.

Nutrition:

Calories: 354 kcal

Protein: 6.7 g

Fat: 18.09 g

Carbohydrates: 47.42 g

Blueberry Pomegranate Smoothie

Preparation Time: 5 minutes

Cooking Time: 0 minutes

Servings: 2

Ingredients:

- 2 cup of frozen blueberries
- 1 cup of pomegranate juice, unsweetened
- 6 to 8 ice cubes
- ¼ cup of canned coconut milk
- 1 tbsp. of hemp seeds

Directions:

1. Combine the smoothie ingredients in your high-speed blender.
2. Pulse the ingredients a few times to chop them up.
3. Blend the mixture on the highest speed setting for 30 to 60 seconds.
4. Pour your finished smoothie into glasses and drink.

Nutrition:

Calories: 282 kcal

Protein: 5.64 g

Fat: 13.8 g

Carbohydrates: 37.75 g

Pineapple and Greens Smoothie

Preparation Time: 5 minutes

Cooking Time: 0 minutes

Servings: 2

Ingredients:

- 1 cup of chopped spinach
- 1 cup of frozen pineapple
- 1 small frozen banana
- ¾ cup of almond milk
- 2 tbsp. Of chia seeds
- 1 tbsp. of honey

Directions:

1. Combine the smoothie ingredients in your high-speed blender.
2. Pulse the ingredients a few times to chop them up.
3. Blend the mixture on the highest speed setting for 30 to 60 seconds.
4. Pour your finished smoothie into glasses and drink.

Nutrition:

Calories: 272 kcal

Protein: 5.27 g

Fat: 4.5 g

Carbohydrates: 56.37 g

Blueberry and Spinach Shake

Preparation Time: 5 minutes

Cooking Time: 0 minutes

Servings: 2

Ingredients:

- 1 cup of low-fat Greek yogurt (optional)
- 1 cup of organic blueberries (or washed if non-organic)
- 1/2 cup of spinach
- ice cubes to the desired concentration

Directions:

1. Add ingredients together in a blender until smooth and then serve in a tall glass.
2. Sprinkle a few fresh berries on top if you wish!

Nutrition:

Calories: 233 kcal

Protein: 10.68 g

Fat: 5.38 g

Carbohydrates: 37.13 g

Wonderful Watermelon Drink

Preparation Time: 5 minutes

Cooking Time: 0 minutes

Servings: 2

Ingredients:

- 1 cup of watermelon chunks
- 2 cups of frozen mixed berries
- 1 cup of coconut water
- 2 tbsp. of chia seeds
- 1/2 cup of tart cherries

Directions:

1. Put all together the ingredients in a blender or juicer then blend until pureed.
2. Serve immediately and enjoy!

Nutrition:

Calories: 330 kcal

Protein: 10.22 g

Fat: 9.71 g

Carbohydrates: 53.3 g

Sweet & Savoury Smoothie

Preparation Time: 5 minutes

Cooking Time: 0 minutes

Servings: 2

Ingredients:

- 2 cups of carrots, peeled and sliced
- 2 cups of filtered water.
- 1 apple, peeled and sliced
- 1 banana, peeled and sliced
- 1 cup of fresh pineapple, peeled and sliced
- 1/2 tbsp. of ginger, grated
- 1/4 tsp of ground turmeric
- 1 tbsp. of lemon juice
- 1 cup of almond or soy milk

Directions:

1. Blend carrots and water to make a pureed carrot juice.
2. Pour into a Mason jar or sealable container, cover, and place in the fridge.
3. Once done, add the rest of the smoothie ingredients to a blender or juicer until smooth.
4. Add the carrot juice in at the end, blending thoroughly until smooth.
5. Serve with or without ice.

Nutrition:

Calories: 225 kcal

Protein: 6.03 g

Fat: 5.78 g

Carbohydrates: 39.93 g

Blackberry & Ginger Milkshake

Preparation Time: 5 minutes

Cooking Time: 0 minutes

Servings: 2

Ingredients:

- 1 thumb-sized piece of ginger, grated
- 2 cups of blackberries, washed
- 2 cups of chopped peaches
- 2 cups of almond milk

Directions:

1. Put all together the ingredients to a blender or juicer and blend until smooth.
2. Serve with a scattering of fresh blackberries and enjoy!

Nutrition:

Calories: 619 kcal

Protein: 15.42 g

Fat: 11.63 g

Carbohydrates: 123.04 g

Fresh Cranberry and Lime Juice

Preparation Time: 5 minutes

Cooking Time: 0 minutes

Servings: 2

Ingredients:

- 4 cups of cranberries
- 2 limes, juiced
- 1/2½ cups of spinach
- 1/2½ cups of mixed berries (frozen are fine)

Directions:

1. Mix all the ingredients with water in a juicer until pureed and served immediately over ice.

Nutrition:

Calories: 578 kcal

Protein: 6.83 g

Fat: 9.92 g

Carbohydrates: 119.35 g

Fresh Tropical Juice

Preparation Time: 5 minutes

Cooking Time: 0 minutes

Servings: 2

Ingredients:

- 1 whole pineapple, peeled and cut into chunks.
- 1/2 can of low-fat coconut milk
- 1 cup of water

Directions:

1. Add all ingredients to a juicer and blend until smooth.
2. Serve over ice.

Nutrition:

Calories: 116 kcal

Protein: 3.72 g

Fat: 3.13 g

Carbohydrates: 19.55 g

Mixed Fruit & Nut Milkshake

Preparation Time: 5 minutes

Cooking Time: 0 minutes

Servings: 2

Ingredients:

- 1/2½ grapefruit; peeled and chopped
- 2 tbsp. of chopped almonds
- 1/2½ inch piece of ginger, minced
- juice of 1 orange
- 1 tbsp. of honey
- 1/2 cup of almond milk
- 12 strawberries

Directions:

1. Put everything but the strawberries in a blender until smooth.
2. Add in the strawberries and blend until pureed, serving in a tall glass.

Nutrition:

Calories: 140 kcal

Protein: 5.89 g

Fat: 5.84 g

Carbohydrates: 17.36 g

Pineapple- Ginger Smoothie

Preparation Time: 5 minutes

Cooking Time: 0 minutes

Servings: 1

Ingredients:

- 1 cup pineapple slice
- ½ inch thick ginger, sliced
- 1 cup coconut milk

Directions:

1. Place all ingredients in a blender.
2. Pulse until smooth.
3. Chill before serving.

Nutrition:

Calories 299

Fats 8 g

Protein 9 g

Carbohydrates 51 g

Beet and Cherry Smoothie

Preparation Time: 5 minutes

Cooking Time: 0 minutes

Servings: 4

Ingredients:

- 10-ounce almond milk, unsweetened
- 2 small beets, peeled and cut into four
- ½ cup frozen cherries, pitted
- ½ teaspoon frozen banana
- 1 tablespoon almond butter

Directions:

1. Add all ingredients in a blender.
2. .Blend until smooth.

Nutrition:

Calories 470

Carbohydrates 24 g

Fats 38 g

Protein 16 g

Turmeric Delight

Preparation Time: 5 minutes

Cooking Time: 0 minutes

Servings: 2

Ingredients:

- 2 Cups Yogurt, Plain & Whole Milk
- 1 Tablespoon Lemon Juice, Fresh
- 1 Banana, Sliced
- 2 Teaspoons Honey, Raw
- 1 Teaspoon Turmeric
- ½ Teaspoon Cinnamon
- ¼ Teaspoon Ginger

Directions:

1. Put all together the ingredients into a blender then blend until smooth.

Nutrition:

Calories: 234

Protein: 9.3 Grams

Fat: 8.2 Grams

Carbs: 33.5 Grams

Hot Chocolate

Preparation Time: 5 Minutes

Cooking Time: 5 Minutes

Servings: 2

Ingredients:

- ½ tsp. Cinnamon
- 1 tbsp. Coconut Oil
- 2 cups Almond Milk
- 1 tbsp. Honey, raw
- 2 tbsp. Cocoa Powder, unsweetened
- ¼ tsp. Turmeric

Directions:

1. To begin with, bring the almond milk to a boil in a deep saucepan over medium heat.
2. Now, bring this mixture to a simmer and then stir in the cocoa powder to it.
3. After that, spoon in the turmeric powder and cinnamon to it. Mix well/
4. Then, add honey to it and once combined well, add the coconut oil
5. Give the drink a good mix until everything comes together.
6. Serve immediately.

Nutrition:

Calories: 150 Kcal

Proteins: 2.1g

Carbohydrates: 15.2g

Fat: 11.1gm

Tropical Popsicles

Preparation Time: 10 Minutes

Cooking Time: 10 Minutes

Servings: 6

Ingredients:

- 2 Kiwi, sliced
- 3 cups Pineapple, chopped
- 2 tbsp. Coconut Oil
- 2 tsp. Turmeric
- ½ tsp. Black Pepper

Directions:

1. First, place all the ingredients needed to make the popsicles excluding the kiwi in a high-speed blender for 2 minutes or until you get a smooth mixture.
2. Next, pour the smoothie into the Popsicle molds.
3. After that, insert the kiwi slices into the molds and then place the frames in the freezer until set.
4. Tip: If you want texture, you can blend it less.

Nutrition:

Calories: 101 Kcal

Proteins: 0.5g

Carbohydrates: 15g

Fat: 4g

Strawberry Ice Cream

Preparation Time: 5 Minutes

Cooking Time: 5 Minutes

Servings: 2-3

Ingredients:

- 1 Banana, frozen & sliced
- 1 cup Strawberries, frozen
- 1 tsp. Vanilla extract
- 2 tbsp. Coconut Milk

Directions:

1. Start by placing strawberries and banana in a high-speed blender and blend it for 2 to 3 minutes.
2. While blending, spoon in the coconut milk, and the vanilla extract.
3. Continue blending until the mixture is thick and smooth.
4. Serve the ice-cream immediately since it does not keep well in the freezer.

Nutrition:

Calories: 78 Kcal

Proteins: 1g

Carbohydrates: 13.6g

Fat: 2.7g

Blueberry Tarts

Preparation Time: 10 Minutes

Cooking Time: 30 Minutes

Servings: 5

Ingredients:

- To make the crust:
- 1 cup Dates
- 1 cup Cashews
- ½ cup Raisins
- ½ tsp. Himalayan Salt
- 1 cup Walnuts
- To make the filling:
- 1/8 tsp. Cinnamon
- 1 tbsp. Maple syrup
- 4 cups Blueberries

Directions:

1. To make this yummy dessert fare, keep all the nuts in a food processor and process the nuts until it becomes coarse flour.
2. Next, spoon in the dates, salt, and raisin to the nuts mixture and process them again.
3. Then, spread this mixture onto a greased parchment paper-lined baking sheet and place it in the refrigerator until set.
4. For the filling, mix all the ingredients needed in a medium-sized bowl and mix them well.
5. Finally, spoon in the filling on to the crust and spread across evenly on all sides.
6. Top with blueberries if desired.

Nutrition:

Calories: 544 Kcal

Proteins: 12.4g

Carbohydrates: 69.2g

Fat: 28.1g

Cookie Dough Bites

Preparation Time: 10 Minutes

Cooking Time: 5 Minutes

Servings: 2

Ingredients:

- ¼ cup Almond Flour
- 1 ½ cups Chickpeas, cooked
- ½ tsp. Salt
- ½ cup Almond Butter or any nut butter
- ¼ cup Chocolate Chips, dairy-free & sugar-free
- 1 tsp. Vanilla Extract
- 2 tbsp. Maple Syrup

Directions:

1. First, place all the ingredients excluding the chocolate chips in a high-speed blender for 3 minutes or until you get a thick, smooth mixture.
2. Next, transfer the mixture to a medium-sized bowl.
3. Then, fold in the chocolate chips into the batter.
4. Check for sweetness and add more maple syrup if needed.
5. Serve and enjoy.
6. Tip: Instead of maple syrup, you can also use Medjool dates.

Nutrition:

Calories: 373 Kcal

Proteins: 12.6g

Carbohydrates: 59.1g

Fat: 10g

Banana Cinnamon

Preparation Time: 2 minutes

Cooking Time: 8 minutes

Servings: 2-4

Ingredients:

- 1 large banana, chopped into ½ inch
- 2 tsp. honey
- 1 tsp. cinnamon

Directions:

1. In a small bowl, put the honey and cinnamon and combine well.
2. Heat the olive oil in a pan. Cook banana slices for 2 minutes or until browned all over.
3. Pour honey and cinnamon mixture over the bananas. Serve.

Nutrition:

Calories: 33 kcal

Protein: 1.64 g

Fat: 1.52 g

Carbohydrates: 3.43 g

Banana Cinnamon Cookies

Preparation Time: 5 minutes

Cooking Time: 10 minutes

Servings: 2

Ingredients:

- 2 ripe bananas, peeled
- 2/3 cup applesauce, unsweetened
- ¼ cup almond milk, unsweetened
- 4 pitted dates
- 1 tablespoon cinnamon
- 2/3 cup coconut flour
- 1 teaspoon vanilla
- 1 1/2 teaspoon lemon juice
- 3 tablespoons dried and chopped cranberries
- 1 teaspoon baking powder
- 2 tablespoons dried and chopped raisins

Directions:

1. Preheat the oven to 350 degrees F.
2. In a food processor, combine almond milk, applesauce, dates, and bananas. Blend until you achieve a smooth consistency.
3. Add in coconut flour, baking powder, cinnamon, vanilla, and lemon juice. Blend for 1 minute. Fold in cranberries and raisins.
4. Pour a baking sheet with the cookie dough. Place inside the oven for 20 minutes.
5. Allow to sit for 5 minutes and let it harden. Serve.

Nutrition:

Calories: 53 kcal

Protein: 9.28 g

Fat: 7.58 g

Carbohydrates: 65.87 g

Avocado Chia Parfait

Preparation Time: 5 minutes

Cooking Time: 20 minutes

Servings: 2

Ingredients:

- 1 tablespoon cashew nuts, chopped
- For the Avocado Jam
- 2 avocados, diced
- 2 tablespoons chia seeds
- ⅛ teaspoon nutmeg powder
- ¾ teaspoon cinnamon powder
- Pinch of sea salt
- For the Parfait Base
- 1¼ cups almond milk
- 1 banana, mashed
- ⅛ teaspoon nutmeg powder
- ½ teaspoon cinnamon powder
- 2 tablespoons pumpkin seeds

Directions:

1. In a bowl, combine almond milk, banana, nutmeg powder, cinnamon powder, and pumpkin seeds. Mix until well combined. Chill in the fridge.
2. Meanwhile, place the saucepan on medium heat. Combine avocados, nutmeg powder, cinnamon powder, and salt. Bring to a boil. Allow simmering for 20 minutes.
3. Turn off the heat. Mash half of the jam using a wooden spoon. Let cool. Set aside.
4. Spoon 2 tablespoons of parfait base and apple jam into parfait glasses. Garnish with cashew nuts. Serve.

Nutrition:

Calories: 671 kcal

Protein: 13.13 g

Fat: 54.86 g

Carbohydrates: 43.76 g

Choco Chia Cherry Cream

Preparation Time: 4 hours and 5 minutes

Cooking Time: 0 minutes

Servings: 4

Ingredients:

- 1½-cups almond milk
- ¼-cup chia seeds, powdered
- 3-Tbsps raw cacao, powdered
- 2-Tbsps pure maple syrup or honey
- ½-cup cherries, pitted and sliced + extra for plating
- Additional toppings: extra raw cacao nibs, cherries, and 70% or higher dark chocolate shavings

Directions:

1. Stir in all the ingredients, excluding the cherries in a mason jar. Mix well until thoroughly combined. Refrigerate overnight or for 4 hours.
2. When ready to serve, divide the pudding equally among four serving plates. Top each plate with the cherries. Garnish with the additional toppings.

Nutrition:

Calories: 502

Fat: 16.7g

Protein: 25.1g

Sodium: 68mg

Total Carbs: 86.3g

Dietary Fiber: 23.6g

Net Carbs: 62.7g

Avocado Choco Cake

Preparation Time: 10 minutes

Cooking Time: 25 minutes

Servings: 8

Ingredients:

- 1-pc large avocado
- 1-tsp vanilla extract
- ½-cup maple syrup
- ½-cup applesauce, unsweetened
- 3-pcs large eggs
- 1-tsp baking soda
- ½-cup cocoa powder, unsweetened and Dutch-processed
- ½-cup coconut flour
- ¼-tsp sea salt

Directions:

1. Preheat your oven to 350°F. Grease a baking pan with coconut oil.
2. Combine the avocado, vanilla, syrup, and applesauce in your food processor. Blend until thoroughly combined.
3. Transfer the mixture in a large mixing bowl. Whisk in the eggs. Add the baking soda, cocoa powder, coconut flour, and sea salt. Mix well until thoroughly combined.
4. Add the batter in the baking pan. Put the pan in the oven. Bake for 25 minutes.
5. Allow cooling for 20 minutes before cutting the cake into 16 squares.

Nutrition:

Calories: 253

Fat: 8.4g

Protein: 12.6g

Sodium: 245mg

Total Carbs: 43.9g

Dietary Fiber: 12.3g

Net Carbs: 31.6g

Date Dough & Walnut Wafer

Preparation Time: 15 minutes

Cooking Time: 18 minutes

Servings: 8

Ingredients:

- 1½-cup oats (divided)
- 6-pcs Medjool dates, pitted and sliced into quarters
- ½-cup coconut, unsweetened
- ½-tsp baking soda
- ¼-tsp sea salt
- ½-cup walnuts
- 2-Tbsps ground flaxseed
- 1-pc egg
- ¼-cup coconut oil
- For the Date Layer:
- 18-pcs Medjool dates, pitted
- 1-tsp lemon juice
- ½-tsp sea salt

Directions:

1. Preheat your oven to 325°F. Line a baking pan with parchment paper.
2. Pulse a cup of oats in your food processor until forming a flour consistency.
3. Add in the dates, coconut, baking soda, and sea salt. Pulse again until the dates entirely break up.
4. Add the remaining oats and walnuts, and pulse until the nuts break, but still a bit chunky. Add the flaxseed, egg, and oil. Pulse the mixture further until thoroughly combined.
5. Set aside ½-cup of the date mixture to use as a topping later. Press down the remaining mix to an even layer in the pan.
6. Rinse your food processor, and add all the date layer ingredients. Pulse the mixture until the dates entirely break up and take on a light caramel color.
7. With wet hands, press the mixture down, smoothing it on the date mixture. Crumble and sprinkle the reserved date mixture over the top.
8. Put the pan in the oven. Bake for 18 minutes. Allow the wafer to cool completely before slicing into 16 pieces.

Nutrition:

Calories: 203

Fat: 6.7g

Protein: 10.1g

Sodium: 76mg

Total Carbs: 28.3g

Dietary Fiber: 3g

Net Carbs: 25.3g

Pineapple Pie

Preparation Time: 15 minutes

Cooking Time: 50 minutes

Servings: 8

Ingredients:

- 5-Tbsps raw honey (divided)
- 15-pcs sweet cherries, fresh or frozen
- 2-pcs fresh pineapple, peeled, cored, and sliced into rings
- 3-Tbsps liquid coconut oil
- 2-pcs eggs
- 1-tsp pure vanilla extract
- 1-cup almond flour
- ½-tsp baking powder

Directions:

1. Preheat your oven to 350 °F.
2. Pour 1½-tablespoon of the honey in a round baking tin. Arrange the cherries and pineapple rings on the bed of honey in a decorative pattern. Place the pan in the oven, then bake for at least 15 minutes.
3. In the meantime, stir in all the remaining ingredients in a mixing bowl. Mix well until forming the mixture into dough. Set aside.
4. Take the pan out from the oven. Press down the batter over the pineapple rings, smoothing it at the top.
5. Return the pan in the oven, and bake further for 35 minutes.

Nutrition:

Calories: 213

Fat: 7.1g

Protein: 15.9g

Sodium: 39.2mg

Total Carbs: 23.7g

Dietary Fiber: 2.4g

Net Carbs: 21.3g

Citrus Cauliflower Cake

Preparation Time: 5 hours and 30 minutes

Cooking Time: 0 minutes

Servings: 10

Ingredients:

- For the Crust:
- 2½-cups pecan nuts
- 1-cup dates, pitted
- 2-Tbsps maple syrup or agave
- For the Filling:
- 3-pcs avocados, halved and pitted
- 3-cups cauliflower, riced
- 1½-cups pineapple, crushed
- ¾-cup maple syrup or agave
- 1-pc lemon, zest, and juice
- A pinch of cinnamon
- ½-tsp lemon extract
- ½-tsp pure vanilla extract
- For the Topping:
- 3-Tbsps maple syrup or agave
- 1-tsp pure vanilla extract
- 1½-cups plain coconut yogurt

Directions:

1. For the Crust:
2. Line a baking tray with parchment paper. Set the outer ring of a 9-inch spring form pan onto the baking tray.
3. Pulse the pecans in your food processor to a finely ground texture. Add the remaining crust ingredients, and pulse further until the mixture holds together.
4. Transfer and press the mixture to an even layer in the baking tray.
5. For the Filling:
6. Wipe the bowl of your food processor, and add in the avocado, cauliflower, pineapple, syrup, and lemon zest and juice. Process the mixture to a smooth consistency.
7. Add the cinnamon and the lemon and vanilla extracts. Pulse until thoroughly combined. Pour the mixture over the crust. Place the tray in your freezer overnight, or for 5 hours.
8. Take the cake out from your freezer, and let it sit at room temperature for 20 minutes. Remove the outer ring.
9. For the Topping:
10. Stir in all the topping ingredients in a mixing bowl. Pour the mixture over the cake and spread evenly.

Nutrition:

Calories: 667

Fat: 22.2g

Protein: 33.3g

Sodium: 237mg

Total Carbs: 88.1g

Dietary Fiber: 4.8g

Net Carbs: 83.3g

Creamy & Chilly Blueberry Bites

Preparation Time: 2 hours and 5 minutes

Cooking Time: 0 minutes

Servings: 2

Ingredients:

- 1-pint blueberries
- 2-tsp lemon juice
- 8-oz. vanilla yogurt

Directions:

1. Coat the blueberries with the lemon juice and yogurt in a mixing bowl. Toss carefully without squishing the berries.
2. Scoop out each of the coated berries and place them on a baking sheet lined with parchment paper. Put the sheet in your freezer for two hours before serving.

Nutrition:

Calories: 394

Fat: 13.1g

Protein: 19.7g

Sodium: 164mg

Total Carbs: 58.9g

Dietary Fiber: 9.7g

Net Carbs: 49.2g

Pistachioed Panna-Cotta Cocoa

Preparation Time: 18 minutes

Cooking Time: 2 minutes

Servings: 6

Ingredients:

- 12-oz. dark chocolate
- 1-Tbsp coconut oil
- 3-pcs large bananas, sliced into thirds
- Cocoa nibs, chopped
- Spiced or smoked almonds, chopped
- Salted pistachios, chopped

Directions:

1. Line a baking pan with parchment paper.
2. Melt the dark chocolate with oil in your microwave. Set aside.
3. Pierce a Popsicle stick halfway into one end of each banana.
4. Dip each banana into the melted chocolate. Place dipped bananas into the baking sheet. Sprinkle generously with the cocoa nibs, almonds, and pistachios. Place the sheet in your freezer to harden and set.

Nutrition:

Calories: 454

Fat: 15.1g

Protein: 22.7g

Sodium: 91mg

Total Carbs: 61.6g

Dietary Fiber: 4.9g

Net Carbs: 56.7g

Pure Avocado Pudding

Preparation Time: 3 hours

Cooking Time: 0 minutes

Servings: 4

Ingredients:

- 1 cup almond milk
- 2 avocados, peeled and pitted
- ¾ cup cocoa powder
- 1 teaspoon vanilla extract
- 2 tablespoons stevia
- ¼ teaspoon cinnamon
- Walnuts, chopped for serving

Directions:

1. Add avocados to a blender and pulse well

2. Add cocoa powder, almond milk, stevia, vanilla bean extract and pulse the mixture well
3. Place into serving bowls then top with walnuts
4. Chill for 2-3 hours and serve!

Nutrition:

Calories: 221

Fat: 8g

Carbohydrates: 7g

Protein: 3g

Sweet Almond and Coconut Fat Bombs

Preparation Time: 10 minutes + 20 minutes chill time

Cooking Time: 0 minutes

Servings: 4

Ingredients:

- ¼ cup melted coconut oil
- 9 and ½ tablespoons almond butter
- 90 drops liquid stevia
- 3 tablespoons cocoa
- 9 tablespoons melted almond butter, sunflower seeds

Directions:

1. Take a bowl and add all of the listed ingredients
2. Mix them well
3. Pour scant 2 tablespoons of the mixture into as many muffin molds as you like
4. Chill for 20 minutes and pop them out
5. Serve and enjoy!

Nutrition:

Total Carbs: 2g

Fiber: 0g

Protein: 2.53g

Fat: 14g

Spicy Popper Mug Cake

Preparation Time: 5 minutes

Cooking Time: 5 minutes

Servings: 2

Ingredients:

- 2 tablespoons almond flour
- 1 tablespoon flaxseed meal
- 1 tablespoon almond butter
- 1 tablespoon cashew cheese
- 1 large egg
- 1 bacon, cooked and sliced
- ½ a jalapeno pepper
- ½ teaspoon baking powder
- ¼ teaspoon sunflower seeds

Directions:

1. Take a frying pan then place it on medium heat
2. Put sliced bacon and cook until they have a crispy texture
3. Take a microwave proof container and mix all of the listed ingredients(including cooked bacon), clean the sides
4. Microwave for 75 seconds making to put your microwave to high power
5. Take out the cup and slam it against a surface to take the cake out
6. Garnish with a bit of jalapeno and serve!

Nutrition:

Calories: 429

Fat: 38g

Carbohydrates: 6g

Protein: 16g

The Most Elegant Parsley Soufflé Ever

Preparation Time: 5 minutes

Cooking Time: 6 minutes

Servings: 5

Ingredients:

- 2 whole eggs

- 1 fresh red chili pepper, chopped
- 2 tablespoons coconut cream
- 1 tablespoon fresh parsley, chopped
- Sunflower seeds to taste

Directions:

1. Preheat your oven to 390 degrees F
2. Almond butter 2 soufflé dishes
3. Put the ingredients to a blender and mix well
4. Divide batter into soufflé dishes and bake for 6 minutes
5. Serve and enjoy!

Nutrition:

Calories: 108

Fat: 9g

Carbohydrates: 9g

Protein: 6g

Fennel and Almond Bites

Preparation Time: 10 minutes + 3 hours freezing time

Cooking Time: 25 minutes

Servings: 10

Ingredients:

- 1 teaspoon vanilla extract
- ¼ cup almond milk
- ¼ cup of cocoa powder
- ½ cup almond oil
- A pinch of sunflower seeds
- 1 teaspoon fennel seeds

Directions:

1. Take a bowl and mix the almond oil and almond milk
2. Beat until smooth and glossy by using an electric beater
3. Mix in the rest of the ingredients
4. Take a piping bag and pour into a parchment paper-lined baking sheet
5. Freeze for 3 hours and stored in the fridge

Nutrition:

Total Carbs: 1g

Fiber: 1g

Protein: 1g

Fat: 20g

Coconut Butter Fudge

Preparation Time: 10 minutes

Cooking Time: 0 minutes

Servings: 6

Ingredients:

- 1 cup of coconut butter
- 2 tablespoons of raw honey
- ¼ teaspoon of salt
- 1 teaspoon of pure vanilla extract

Directions:

1. Begin by lining an 8 x 8 inch baking dish with parchment paper.
2. Melt the coconut butter, honey, and vanilla over low heat.
3. Put the mixture into the baking pan, and refrigerate for 2 hours before serving.

Nutrition:

Total Carbohydrates: 6g

Dietary Fiber: 0g

Net Carbs:

Protein: 0g

Total Fat: 36g

Calories: 334

Raspberry Gummies

Preparation Time: 5 minutes

Cooking Time: 15 minutes

Servings: 6

Ingredients:

- 1 cup of frozen raspberries
- 3 tablespoons of raw honey

- ¼ cup of grass-fed gelatin
- ¾ cup of cold water

Directions:
1. Place the water and frozen raspberries into a blender, and blend until smooth. Put into a large saucepan on medium heat.
2. Add the honey and gelatin and whisk together. Lower the heat, then whisk for another 5 minutes.
3. Pour into molds or a baking dish, and place in the refrigerator for at least 1 hour until firm. If you use a baking dish, cut the gelatin into squares; if not, just pop the gelatin out of the molds.

Nutrition:

Total Carbohydrates: 9g

Dietary Fiber: 1g

Net Carbs:

Protein: 0g

Total Fat: 0g

Calories: 37

Turmeric Milkshake

Preparation Time: 5 minutes

Cooking Time: 0 minutes

Servings: 2

Ingredients:
- 2 cups of unsweetened almond milk
- 3 tablespoons of raw honey
- 2 tablespoons of raw cocoa powder
- 1 tablespoon of ground flaxseeds
- 1 teaspoon of turmeric
- 2 frozen bananas

Directions:
1. Put all together the ingredients into a high-speed blender, and blend until smooth.
2. Divide between two serving glasses, and enjoy straight away.

Nutrition:

Total Carbohydrates: 74g

Dietary Fiber: 7g

Protein: 4g

Total Fat: 6g

Calories: 334

No-Bake Carrot Cake Bites

Preparation Time: 15 minutes

Cooking Time: 0 minutes

Servings: 6

Ingredients:
- 1 and a ½ cups of carrots
- 1 cup of pitted Medjool dates
- ½ teaspoon of ground ginger
- 1 tablespoon of pure maple syrup
- 1 teaspoon of cinnamon
- 1 cup of walnuts
- ¾ cup of shredded coconut

Directions:
1. Place all together the ingredients into a high-speed blender or food processor, and blend until the mixture comes together, adding a teaspoon of water at a time if needed.
2. Take the carrot mixture and press down into a cupcake tin, and refrigerate until firm.
3. Pop the carrot cakes out of the muffin tin, and enjoy!

Nutrition:

Total Carbohydrates: 32g

Dietary Fiber: 5g

Net Carbs:

Protein: 3g

Total Fat: 12g

Calories: 231

Chocolate Fudge Bites

Preparation Time: 10 minutes

Cooking Time: 3 minutes

Servings: 10

Ingredients:

- 1 and a ¼ cup of boiling water
- 3 tablespoons of grass-fed gelatin
- ½ cup of cold water
- ½ cup of raw cocoa powder
- ½ cup of coconut milk powder
- 1 cup of coconut oil
- 1/3 cup of pure maple syrup

Directions:

1. Mix one and a quarter cup of boiling water with the gelatin, and boil for 3 minutes. Then, place the gelatin mixture into a blender with the cold water and remaining ingredients. Blend for a couple of minutes to help the gelatin solidify.
2. Place the mixture into the bottom of a greased baking dish, then refrigerate until firm.
3. Cut into small serving squares.

Nutrition:

Total Carbohydrates: 30g

Dietary Fiber: 3g

Net Carbs:

Protein: 2g

Total Fat: 24g

Calories: 317

Blueberry Energy Bites

Preparation Time: 10 minutes

Cooking Time: 0 minutes

Servings: 6

Ingredients:

- ½ cup of gluten-free oat flour
- ¼ teaspoon of cinnamon
- 2 tablespoons of pure maple syrup
- 2 tablespoons of organic peanut butter
- ½ teaspoon of sea salt
- 2 tablespoons of dried blueberries
- ½ cup of unsweetened almond milk

Directions:

1. Place the dry ingredients into a mixing bowl, including the peanut butter, and stir until combined.
2. Put in the almond milk and maple syrup, and stir.
3. Form into 1 inch balls, and place in the refrigerator to firm up before serving.

Nutrition:

Total Carbohydrates: 13g

Dietary Fiber: 1g

Net Carbs:

Protein: 3g

Total Fat: 1g

Calories: 93

Beet Pancakes

Preparation Time: 10 minutes

Cooking Time: 12 minutes

Servings: 3

Ingredients:

- 4 Cups Roasted Beet, Puree
- 1 Cup Flour
- 3 Cup Whole Wheat Flour
- 6 Tsp. Brown Sugar
- 1 Tbsp. Baking Powder
- Salt
- 1/4 Tsp Baking Soda
- 1/2 Cup Heavy Milk
- 1/3 Cup Plain Greek Yoghurt
- 1 Large Egg
- 1/2 Cup Melted Butter
- 1 Tsp. Vanilla Extract

Directions:

1. .Mix the dry ingredients in a bowl.
2. In another bowl, mix the wet ingredients.
3. Combine both mixtures until smooth.
4. Fry the batter on a pan to make pancakes.

5. Serve with whip cream.

Nutrition:

Calories: 359 kcal

Carbs: 60 g

Fat: 3.0 g

Protein: 18.4 g.

Green Tea Pudding

Preparation Time: 20 minutes

Cooking Time: 10 minutes

Servings: 3

Ingredients:

- 1 Tsp. Matcha Green Tea Powder
- 3 Eggs
- 100g Butter
- 2 Cup Heavy Milk
- Salt
- 1/4 Cup Brown Sugar
- 1/4 Cup Corn Starch
- 1/8-Tbsp. Cinnamon Powder

Directions:

1. In a big pot, mix brown sugar, milk, cornstarch, and matcha powder.
2. In medium heat, keep whisking until mixed.
3. Mix the hot batter with whisked eggs slowly.
4. Cook for 3-5 minutes.
5. Strain the mixture and add butter.
6. Put the mixture in a container, refrigerate for a few hours and serve.

Nutrition:

Calories: 359 kcal

Carbs: 60 g

Fat: 3.0 g

Protein: 18.4 g

Banana Bars

Preparation Time: 10 minutes

Cooking Time: 60 minutes

Servings: 4

Ingredients:

- 5 Cup Ripe Mashed Banana
- 2 Eggs
- 2 Cup Brown Sugar
- 1/2 Cup Melted Butter
- 1/2 Cup Coconut Milk
- 1 Tsp. Pure Vanilla Extract
- 2 Cup Whole Wheat Flour
- 1 Tsp. Baking Soda
- 1/4 Tbsp. Cinnamon
- Salt
- 1 Cup Chocolate Chips

Direction:

1. Preheat oven to 170C.
2. Mix all together the ingredients to make the batter.
3. Place the batter in a wide tray and bake for 20 minutes at 170C.
4. Serve with liquid chocolate or fruits.

Nutrition:

Calories: 330 kcal

Carbs: 8.80 g

Fat: 13.0 g

Protein: 12.4 g.

Blueberry Sour Cream Cake

Preparation Time: 20 minutes

Cooking Time: 70 minutes

Servings: 4

Ingredients:

- 2 Cups Of Brown Sugar
- 2 Tbsp. All-Purpose Flour
- 1 Cup Of Melted Butter
- Salt
- 2 Large Eggs
- 1 Tsp Vanilla Extract

- 1 Tsp. Baking Powder
- 1 Cup Sour Cream
- 1 Tsp. Cinnamon Powder
- 1 Cup Blueberry

Direction:

1. Preheat oven on 175C.
2. Combine together the butter and sugar till light and fluffy.
3. Put sour cream, vanilla extract, and eggs into the mixture.
4. In another bowl, put all together the dry ingredients then mix.
5. Put the dry mixture into the butter mixture, adding blueberries, then combine well.
6. Place the batter into a greased pan then bake for 50-55 minutes at 170C.
7. Serve with sour cream and blueberries.

Nutrition:

Calories: 234 kcal

Carbs: 43 g

Fat: 21 g

Protein: 14.4 g.

Peanut Butter Balls

Preparation Time: 20 minutes

Cooking Time: 30 minutes

Servings: 5

Ingredients:

- 250g Creamy Peanut Butter
- 90g Melted Butter
- 200g Powdered Sugar
- 1 Tsp. Vanilla Extract
- 250g Chocolate
- 2 Tbsp. Peanut Oil.

Direction:

1. Mix everything except the oil and chocolates to form a batter
2. Refrigerate the batter for 45 minutes.
3. Make small balls with the batter using and place them on a parchment paper. Refrigerate for one more hour.
4. Melt some dark chocolate. Put the peanut balls into the chocolate and refrigerate for 20-25 minutes.
5. Serve with strawberry.

Nutrition:

Calories: 340 kcal

Carbs: 32 g

Fat: 21 g

Protein: 1.4 g.

Black Tea Cake

Preparation Time: 10 minutes

Cooking Time: 35 minutes

Servings: 10

Ingredients:

- 6 tablespoons black tea powder
- 2 cups coconut milk
- ½ cup coconut butter
- Chicory root powder to the taste
- 4 eggs
- 2 teaspoons vanilla extract
- ½ cup coconut oil
- 3 ½ cups almond flour
- 1 teaspoon baking soda
- 3 teaspoons baking powder

Directions:

1. Put the coconut milk in a pot and warm it up over medium heat. Add tea, stir well, take off the heat and cool down, in a bowl, mix the coconut butter with the chicory powder, eggs, vanilla, coconut oil, almond flour, baking soda, baking powder, and tea mix. Stir well, pour into a lined cake pan, and bake in the oven at 350 degrees F for 30 minutes. Slice, divide between plates, and serve.
2. Enjoy!

Nutrition:

Calories: 170

Fat: 4

Fiber: 5

Carbs: 6

Protein: 2

Matcha and Blueberries Pudding

Preparation Time: 3 hours

Cooking Time: 0 minutes

Servings: 2

Ingredients:

- 2 cups almond milk
- 1 cup matcha green tea powder
- 4 tablespoons chia seeds
- 1 cup blueberries
- 1 banana, sliced

Directions:

1. Put chia seeds, milk and matcha powder in a bowl. Stir, cover, and then place in the refrigerator for 3 hours. Divide into bowls, top with banana slices and blueberries and serve.
2. Enjoy!

Nutrition:

Calories: 324

Fat: 9

Fiber: 18

Carbs: 24

Protein: 8

Spiced Tea Pudding

Preparation Time: 10 minutes

Cooking Time: 10 minutes

Servings: 3

Ingredients:

- 1 can coconut milk
- ½ cup coconut flakes
- 1 cup almond milk
- 1 teaspoon nutmeg
- 1 tablespoon ground cinnamon
- ½ teaspoon cloves
- 1 teaspoon allspice
- 1 tablespoon raw honey
- 2 teaspoons ground ginger
- 1 teaspoon cardamom
- 2 tablespoons pumpkin seeds
- 1 ½ cups berries
- 1 tablespoon chia seeds
- 1 teaspoon green tea powder

Directions:

1. In your blender, puree tea powder with coconut milk, almond milk, cinnamon, coconut flakes, nutmeg, allspice, cloves, honey, cardamom, and ginger divide into bowls. Heat a pan over medium heat, add berries until bubbling, and then transfer to your blender and pulse well. Divide the berries into the bowls with the coconut milk mix, top with chia seeds and pumpkin seeds and serve.
2. Enjoy!
3. **Nutrition:**

Calories: 150

Fat: 6

Fiber: 5

Carbs: 14

Protein: 8

Lemonade Ice Pops

Preparation Time: 4 hours and 10 minutes

Cooking Time: 0 minutes

Servings: 4

Ingredients:

- 2 cups cold water
- 2 iced tea and lemonade tea bags
- 1 cup hot water

Directions:

1. Put hot water in a bowl, add tea bags, cover, and set aside for 10 minutes to steep. Squeeze the tea bags to take off all the water and then discard them. Add cold

water, divide into your ice pop maker, freeze for 6 hours, and serve.
2. Enjoy!

Nutrition:

Calories: 38

Fat: 0

Fiber: 0

Carbs: 0

Protein: 1

Café-Style Fudge

Preparation Time: 10 minutes + chilling time

Cooking Time: 0 minutes

Servings: 6

Ingredients:

- 1 tablespoon instant coffee granules
- 4 tablespoons confectioners' Swerve
- 4 tablespoons cocoa powder
- 1 stick butter
- 1/2 teaspoon vanilla extract

Directions:

1. Beat the butter and Swerve at low speed.
2. Add in the cocoa powder, instant coffee granules, and vanilla and continue to mix until well combined.
3. Spoon the batter into a foil-lined baking sheet. Refrigerate for 2 to 3 hours. Enjoy!

Nutrition:

144 Calories

15.5g Fat

2.1g Carbs

0.8g Protein

1.1g Fiber

Rum Butter Cookies

Preparation Time: 10 minutes + chilling time

Cooking Time: 5 minutes

Servings: 12

Ingredients:

- 1/2 cup coconut butter
- 1 teaspoon rum extract
- 4 cups almond meal
- 1 stick butter
- 1/2 cup confectioners' Swerve

Directions:

1. Melt the coconut butter and butter. Stir in the Swerve and rum extract.
2. Afterward, add in the almond meal and mix to combine.
3. Roll the balls and place them on a parchment-lined cookie sheet.
4. Keep in the refrigerator until ready to serve.

Nutrition:

400 Calories

40g Fat

4.9g Carbs

5.4g Protein

2.9g Fiber

Vanilla Cakes

Preparation Time: 10 minutes

Cooking Time: 15 minutes

Servings: 8

Ingredients:

- o tsp. Vanilla extract
- C.5 cup warmed coconut oil
- .5 tsp.
- Salt
- .5 tsp. Baking soda
- 2 tsp. Baking powder
- 1 cup Agave sweetener
- 2 cup Whole wheat flour
- 1 cup Almond milk
- 1 tbsp. Apple cider vinegar

Directions:

1. Ensure your oven is set to 350F.
2. Prepare two muffin pans (12 c) for use by greasing them.
3. Add the apple cider vinegar into a measuring c that is large enough to hold at least 2 c. Add in the almond milk for a total of 1.5 c. Allow the results to curdle approximately 5 minutes or until done.
4. Put together the salt, baking soda, baking powder, sugar, and flour together in a large bowl and whisk well.
5. Separately, combine the vanilla, coconut oil, and curdled almond in its bowl before combining the two bowls and blending well. Add the results to the muffin pans, dividing evenly.
6. Place the muffin pans in the oven and let them cook for about 15 minutes. You will know if it's all already cook when you can press down on the tops and spring back when pressed lightly.
7. All the cake pans to cool on a wire rack before removing the cakes for the best results.

Nutrition:

Calories: 336 kcal

Protein: 5.75 g

Fat: 16.25 g

Carbohydrates: 44.15 g

Strawberry Shortcake

Preparation Time: 15 minutes

Cooking Time: 0 minutes

Servings: 4

Ingredients:

- 1 tbsp. Low-calorie margarine
- .25 cup Semi-sweet chocolate chips
- 2.3-inch Shortcake, quartered
- 12 hulled Strawberries

Directions:

1. Using waxed paper, line a cookie sheet.
2. Thread 2 shortcake pieces and 3 strawberries on 4 skewers.
3. In a small saucepan, combine together the margarine and chocolate chips before placing the saucepan on the stove over a burner turned to low heat. Stir until the ingredients are well blended.
4. Drizzle the chocolate onto the kabobs and then place them in the refrigerator for 4 minutes to cool.

Nutrition:

Calories: 40 kcal

Protein: 1.85 g

Fat: 2.3 g

Carbohydrates: 3.32 g

Fried Pineapple Slice

Preparation Time: 10 minutes

Cooking Time: 8 minutes

Servings: 8

Ingredients:

- 1 fresh pineapple (peeled and cut into large slices)
- ¼ cup of coconut oil
- ¼ cup of coconut palm sugar
- ¼ teaspoon of ground cinnamon

Directions:

1. Warm a huge cast-iron skillet on medium heat.
2. Add oil and sugar and cook until the coconut oil has melted while stirring continuously.
3. Add the pineapple slices into two batches and cook for approximately 1-2 minutes.
4. Flip the medial side and cook for about a minute. Continue cooking for another minute.
5. Repeat the steps with the remaining slices.
6. Sprinkle with cinnamon and serve.

Nutrition:

Calories: 138,

Fats: 7g

Carbs: 20.9g

Sugar: 15.7g

Proteins: 0.6g

Sodium: 15mg

Grilled Peaches

Preparation Time: 10 minutes

Cooking Time: 10 minutes

Servings: 6

Ingredients:

- 3 medium peaches (halved and pitted)
- ½ cup of coconut cream
- 1 teaspoon of organic vanilla extract
- ¼ cup of walnuts, chopped
- Ground cinnamon

Directions:

1. Preheat the grill over medium-low heat. Grease the grill grate.
2. Arrange the peach slices on the grill with the cut-side down.
3. Grill each side for 3-5 minutes or until the desired doneness is attained.
4. .Meanwhile, mix coconut cream with vanilla extract in a bowl. Beat until smooth.
5. Spoon the whipped cream over each peach half.
6. Top with walnuts and sprinkle with cinnamon. Serve immediately.

Nutrition:

Calories: 110

Fats: 8g

Carbs: 8.8g

Sugar: 7.8g

Proteins: 2.4g

Sodium: 3mg

Pumpkin Ice Cream

Preparation Time: 15 minutes

Cooking Time: 0 minutes

Servings: 6

Ingredients:

- 1 (15-ounce) can of sugar-free pumpkin puree
- ½ cup of dates (pitted and chopped)
- 2 (14-ounce) cans of unsweetened coconut milk
- ½ teaspoon of vanilla flavor
- 1 ½ teaspoon of pumpkin pie spice
- ½ teaspoon of ground cinnamon
- Pinch of salt

Directions:

1. Put all together the ingredients in a high-speed blender and pulse.
2. Transfer the puree to an airtight container and freeze for approximately 1-120 minutes.
3. Transfer the frozen puree to an ice-cream maker and process following the manufacturers.
4. Return the ice-cream to the airtight container and freeze for about 1-120 minutes before serving.

Nutrition:

Calories: 373

Fats: 31.9g

Carbs: 24.7g

Sugar: 16.2g

Proteins: 4.2g

Sodium: 51mg

Lemon Sorbet

Preparation Time: 10 minutes

Cooking Time: 0 minutes

Servings: 2

Ingredients:

- 2 tablespoons of fresh lemon zest, grated
- ½ cup of raw honey
- 2 cups of filtered water
- ½ cups of fresh lemon juice

Directions:

1. Freeze the ice-cream maker tub for a day before making the sorbet.
2. Put all together the ingredients in a pan, excluding the freshly squeezed lemon juice and cook over medium heat.
3. Simmer for at least 1 minute, up to the sugar dissolves while stirring continuously.
4. Remove the mixture from the heat and add lemon juice.
5. Transfer the combination to an airtight container and refrigerate for around 2hours.
6. Put it into an ice-cream maker and process following the manufacturer's instructions.
7. Add one tablespoon of oil when the motor is running.
8. Return the ice-cream into the airtight container and freeze for approximately 2 hours.

Nutrition:

Calories: 305

Fats: 1.5g

Carbs: 74.9g

Sugar: 73.8g

Proteins: 1.9g

Sodium: 40mg

Banana & Avocado Mousse

Preparation Time: 10 minutes

Cooking Time: 0 minutes

Servings: 4

Ingredients:

- 2 cups of bananas (peeled and chopped)
- 2 ripe avocados (peeled, pitted, and chopped)
- 1 teaspoon of fresh lime zest, grated finely
- 1 teaspoon of fresh lemon zest, grated finely
- ½ cup of fresh lime juice
- ½ cup of fresh lemon juice
- 1/3 cup of raw honey

Directions:

1. Put all together the ingredients in a blender and pulse to puree.
2. Transfer the mousse to four serving glasses.
3. Refrigerate for around 3 hours before eating.

Nutrition:

Calories: 368

Fats: 20.1g

Carbs: 50.2g

Sugar: 33.6g

Proteins: 3.1g

Sodium: 14mg

Strawberry Soufflé

Preparation Time: 15 minutes

Cooking Time: 12 minutes

Servings: 6

Ingredients:

- 18 ounces of fresh strawberries, hulled
- 1/3 cup of raw honey, divided
- 5 organic egg whites, divided
- 4 teaspoons of fresh lemon juice

Directions:

1. Preheat the oven to 350F.
2. Put the strawberries in a blender then pulse until a puree form.
3. Strain the strawberry puree using a strainer while discarding the seeds.
4. Combine the strawberry puree to three tablespoons of honey, two egg whites, and fresh lemon juice. Pulse until a frothy and light-weight develops.
5. Beat the eggs in a separate bowl up to it becomes frothy.
6. Add the remaining honey and beat until a stiff peak forms.
7. Gently- fold the egg whites into the strawberry mixture.
8. Transfer the mixture into six large ramekins and arrange them on a baking sheet.

9. Bake for around 10-12 minutes.
10. Remove from the oven and serve immediately.

Nutrition:

Calories: 100

Fats: 0.3g

Carbs: 22.3g

Sugar: 19.9g

Proteins: 3.7g

Sodium: 30mg

Tropical Fruit Crisp

Preparation Time: 10 minutes

Cooking Time: 15 minutes

Servings: 6

Ingredients:

For the Filling:

- 2 tablespoons of coconut oil
- 2 tablespoons of coconut sugar
- 1 large mango (cut into chunks)
- 1 large pineapple (cut into chunks)
- 1/8 teaspoon of ground cinnamon
- 1/8 teaspoon of ground ginger

For the Topping:

- ¾ cup of almonds
- 1/3 cup of unsweetened coconut, shredded
- ½ teaspoon of ground allspice
- ½ teaspoon of ground cinnamon
- ½ teaspoon of ground ginger

Directions:

1. Preheat the oven to 375 degrees F.
2. For the filling: melt the coconut oil in a pan on medium-low heat and cook the coconut sugar for 1-2 minutes while stirring.
3. Add the remaining ingredients then cook for at least 5 minutes. Stir.
4. Remove the contents from heat and transfer it to a baking dish.
5. For the topping: Put all together the ingredients in a mixer and pulse until a coarse meal forms.
6. Place the topping over the filling.
7. Bake for at least 15 minutes or until the top becomes golden brown.

Nutrition:

Calories: 265

Fats: 12.4g

Carbs: 38g

Sugar: 23.3g

Proteins: 4.3g

Sodium: 17mg

No-Bake Cheesecake

Preparation Time: 20 minutes

Cooking Time: 0 minutes

Servings: 12

Ingredients:

For Crust:

- 1 cup of dates (pitted and chopped)
- 1 cup of raw almonds
- 2-3 tablespoons of unsweetened coconut, shredded

For Filling:

- 3½ cups of cashews, soaked overnight
- ½ cup of coconut oil, melted
- 2 tablespoons of fresh lemon rind, grated finely
- ¾ cup of fresh lemon juice
- ¾ cup of raw honey
- 10 drops of liquid stevia
- 1 teaspoon of organic vanilla extract
- Salt
- A thinly sliced lemon

Directions:

1. Put together the dates, almonds, and coconut in a blender and pulse.

2. Transfer the puree a greased spring form pan.
3. Smooth the outer lining of the crust using a spatula.
4. Put cashews and oil in a food processor and pulse.
5. Add the remaining ingredients except for lemon slices and pulse until it turns creamy and smooth.
6. Place the combination over the crust evenly.
7. Smooth the counter of filling using the corner of a spatula.
8. Refrigerate for one hour.
9. Take it off from the refrigerator and garnish with lemon slices.
10. Cut it into desired sized slices and serve.

Nutrition:

Calories: 468

Fats: 32g

Carbs: 6.6g

Sugar: 44.1g

Proteins: 8.4g

Sodium: 23mg

Citrus Strawberry Granita

Preparation Time: 15 minutes

Cooking Time: 0 minutes

Servings: 4

Ingredients:

- 12 ounces of fresh strawberries, hulled
- 1 grapefruit (peeled, seeded, and sectioned)
- 2 oranges (peeled, seeded and sectioned)
- ¼ lemon
- ¼ cup of raw honey

Directions:

1. Put strawberries, grapefruit, oranges, and lemon in a juicer and extract juice following the manufacturer's instructions.
2. Put 1½ cups of the veggie juice and honey to a pan and cook over medium heat for 5 minutes while stirring continuously.
3. Remove it from heat and add it to the remaining juice.
4. Set aside for approximately 30 minutes.
5. Transfer the juice mixture into an 8x8-inch glass baking dish.
6. Freeze for 4 hours while scraping after every 30 minutes.

Nutrition:

Calories: 145

Fats: 0.4g

Carbs: 37.5g

Sugar: 32.4g

Proteins: 1.7g

Sodium: 2mg

Glazed Banana

Preparation Time: 10 minutes

Cooking Time: 5 minutes

Servings: 2

Ingredients:

- 1 tbsp. of olive oil
- 1 peeled and sliced under-ripened banana
- 1 tbsp. of filtered water
- 1 tbsp. of raw honey
- 1/8 tsp. of ground cinnamon

Directions:

1. In a nonstick skillet, warm oil on medium heat.
2. Add banana slices and cook for about 1-2 minutes per side.
3. Meanwhile, in a small bowl, add water and honey and beat well.
4. Transfer the banana slices on a serving plate.
5. Immediately, pour honey mixture over banana slices.
6. Keep aside to cool completely. Serve with the sprinkling of cinnamon.

Nutrition:

Calories: 145

Fat: 7.2g

Carbs: 22.2g

Protein: 0.7g

Fiber: 1.6g

Refreshing Raspberry Jelly

Preparation Time: 10 minutes + 1 hour freezing

Cooking Time: 30 minutes

Servings: 4

Ingredients:

- 2 pound of fresh raspberries
- ¼ cup of water
- 1 tbsp. of fresh lemon juice

Directions:

1. In a medium pan, add raspberries and water on low heat and cook for about 8-10 minutes until done completely.
2. Add lemon juice and cook for about 30 minutes, stirring occasionally.
3. Remove from heat and place the mixture into a sieve.
4. Arrange a strainer over a bowl.
5. Through strainer, strain the mixture by pressing with the back of a spoon.
6. Put the mixture into a blender then pulse till a jelly-like texture is formed.
7. Transfer into serving glass bowls and refrigerate for at least for about 1 hour.

Nutrition:

Calories: 119

Fat: 1.5g

Carbs: 27.2g

Protein: 2.8g

Fiber: 14.8g

Comforting Baked Rice Pudding

Preparation Time: 10 minutes

Cooking Time: 20 minutes

Servings: 8

Ingredients:

- 2 cups of cooked brown rice
- 2 cups of unsweetened almond milk
- 2 large organic eggs
- ¼ cup of raw honey
- 1 tsp. fresh lemon zest, finely grated
- 1 tsp. of ground cinnamon
- ½ tsp. of ground ginger
- ½ tsp. of ground cardamom
- 1 peeled and sliced banana
- ¼ cup of almond flakes

Directions:

1. Set the oven to 390 F, then grease a baking dish.
2. Spread cooked rice at the bottom of the prepared baking dish evenly.
3. In a large bowl, put together the coconut milk, eggs, honey, lemon zest, spices, and beat until well combined.
4. Place the egg mixture over the rice evenly.
5. Arrange banana slices over egg mixture evenly and sprinkle with almonds.
6. Bake for about 20 minutes.
7. Serve warm.

Nutrition:

Calories: 264

Fat: 4.9g

Carbs: 50g

Protein: 6.2g

Fiber: 2.9g

Fall-Time Custard

Preparation Time: 15 minutes

Cooking Time: 60 minutes

Servings: 6

Ingredients:

- 1 cup of canned pumpkin
- 1 tsp. of ground cinnamon
- ¼ tsp. of ground ginger
- 2 pinches of freshly grated nutmeg
- Pinch of salt

- 2 organic eggs
- 1 cup of coconut milk
- 8-10 drops of liquid stevia
- 1 tsp. of organic vanilla extract

Directions:

1. Preheat the oven to 350 degrees F.
2. In a large bowl, put together pumpkin and spices then mix.
3. In another bowl, add the eggs and beat well.
4. Add the remaining ingredients then whisk till well combined.
5. Add egg mixture into pumpkin mixture and mix till well combined.
6. Transfer the mixture into 6 ramekins.
7. Arrange the ramekins in a baking dish,
8. Add enough water in the baking dish about 2-inch high around the ramekins.
9. Bake for about 1 hour or till a toothpick inserted in the center comes out clean.

Nutrition:

Calories: 131

Fat: 11.1g

Carbs: 6.1g

Protein: 3.3g

Fiber: 2.3g

Creamy Frozen Yogurt

Preparation Time: 10 minutes + 2-3 hours freezing

Cooking Time:

Servings: 3

Ingredients:

- 2 peeled, pitted and chopped medium avocados
- ½ cup of unsweetened almond milk
- ½ cup of coconut yogurt
- 1 tbsp. of raw honey
- 2 tbsp. of fresh lemon juice
- 1 tsp. of organic vanilla extract
- 1 tsp. of fresh mint leaves

Directions:

1. In a blender, put all together the ingredients except mint leaves and pulse till creamy and smooth.
2. Place into an airtight container then freeze for at least 2-3 hours.
3. Take off from the freezer and keep aside for 10-15 minutes.
4. With a spoon stir well.
5. Top with fresh mint leaves and serve.

Nutrition:

Calories: 105

Fat: 1.3g

Carbs: 20.3g

Protein: 2.8g

Fiber: 1.4g

Yummy Fruity Ice-Cream

Preparation Time: 20 minutes + 3-4 hours freezing

Cooking Time: 0 minutes

Servings: 4

Ingredients:

- 1 cup fresh strawberries, hulled and sliced
- ½ peeled and sliced small banana
- 2 tbsp. of shredded coconut
- ½ cup of coconut cream

Directions:

1. In a powerful blender, put all together the ingredients and pulse till smooth.
2. Place it into an ice cream maker, then process according to the manufacturer's directions.
3. Now, transfer into an airtight container. Freeze to set for at least 3-4 hours, stirring after every 30 minutes.

Nutrition:

Calories: 103

Fat: 8.2g

Carbs: 8.2g

Protein: 1.2g

Fiber: 2g

Glorious Blueberry Crumble

Preparation Time: 10 minutes

Cooking Time: 30 minutes

Servings: 6

Ingredients:

- For Crust:
- 1 cup of almond meal
- 1 cup of toasted and finely crushed almonds
- 2 tbsp. of coconut sugar
- ½ tsp. of ground cinnamon
- ½ cup of softened coconut oil
- 4 cups of fresh blueberries

Directions:

1. Set the oven to 350F then lightly, grease a pie dish.
2. In a huge bowl, mix together all ingredients except blueberries.
3. Divide half of the almond mixture at the bottom of the prepared pie dish.
4. Place blueberries over almond mixture evenly.
5. Top with the remaining almond mixture evenly.
6. Bake for at least 30 minutes or till the top becomes golden brown.
7. Serve warm.

Nutrition:

Calories: 411

Fat: 34.3g

Carbs: 24.9g

Protein: 7.4g

Fiber: 6.4g

30 Days Meal Plan

DAYS	BREAKFAST	LUNCH	DINNER
1	TURKEY CRUST MEATZ	BASILCHICKEN SAUTE	RED PEPPER AND MOZARELLA STUFFED CHICKEN
2	BLUE CHEESE BUFFALO CHICKEN BALLS	WINTER CHICKEN WITH VEGETABLES	PEANUT CRUSTED CHICKEN
3	CHCKEN & CHEESE FILLED AVOCADOS	SLOW COOKER JERK CHICKEN	BASIL CHICKEN SAUTE
4	TOMATO &CHEESE CHICKEN CHILI	FETA & BACON CHICKEN	FLYING JACOB CASSEROLE
5	TARRAGON CHICKEN WITH ROASTED BALSAMIC TURNIPS	CHICKEN PIE WITH BACON	CASHEW CHICKEN CURRY
6	VODKA DUCK FILLETS	CHICKEN QUICHEN	CURRY CHICKEN LETTUCE WRAPS
7	BUFFOLA BALLS	BBQ CHICKEN LIVER AND HEARTS	BEEF WITH CARROT & BROCCOLI
8	TURKEY CHILI	BEEF WITH ZUCCHINI NOODLES	CITRUS BEEF WITH BOK CHOY
9	PORK WITH CHILI ZUCCHINIS AND TOMATOES	PORK WITH MUSHROOMS AND CUCUMBERS	OREGANO PORK
10	GROUND PORK PAN	CRANBERRY PORK	CREAMY PORK
11	PORK AND LEEKS	SPICY BEEF	BEEF STUFFED CABBAGE
12	SPICY BEEF	CHICKEN ENCHALADAS	GREEK CHICKEN STIFADO
13	MIDDLE EASTERN SHISH KEBAB	CHEESY MEXICAN STYLE CHICKEN	TANGY CHICKEN WITH SCALLONS
14	ASAIN SAUCY CHICKEN	BLUEBEERY MATCHA SMOOTHIE	PUMPKIN PIE
15	FIG SMOOTHIE	PORK AND LEEKS	HOT CHICKEN MEATBALLS
16	GOLDEN CHAI LATTE	FLU FIGHTING TONIC	CHOCOLATE LATTE WITH REISHI
17	PINEAPPLE PIE	TROPICAL POPSICLES	MANGO TOMATOES SMOOTHIE
18	CHOCOLATE CHEER SMOOTHIE	BLUEBERRY TARTS	COOKIE DOUGH BITES
19	SPICY POPPER MUG CAKE	AVOCADE CHAI PAARFAIT	HOT CHOCOLATE

20	COOCNUT BUTTER FUDGE	NO BAKE CARROT CAKE BITES	BEET PANCAKE
21	GREEN TEA	BANANA BARS	BLUEBERRY SOUR CREAM CAKE
22	PEANUT BUTTER BALLS	TURMERIC MILKSHAKE	RASPBERRY GUMMIES
23	NO BAKE CHEESECAKE	GLAZED BANANA	GRILLED PEACHES
24	VANILLA CAKES	LEMONADE ICE POPS	BLACK TEA CAKE
25	BRAISED KALE	STIR FRIED GINGERY VEGGIES	CELERY ROOT HASH BROWNS
26	CURRIED OKRA	VEGETABLE POTPIE	EGGPLANTS GRATIN
27	CASHEW PESTO & PARSLEY	TOASTED CUMIN CRUCH	KOREAN BARBECUE TOFU
28	VEGETABLE PIE	TURMERIC NACHOS	TASTY SPRING SALAD
29	PURE DELISH SPINACH SALAD	CITRUS CAULIFLOWER CAKE	DATE DOUGH & WALNUT
30	BERRY SHRUB	COOKED ICES TEA	INSTANT HORCHATA

CONCLUSION

Thank you for making it to the end. An Inflammation-Free Diet will help to rebalance the pro- & anti-inflammatory channels in your body & lessen excessive inflammation. If you currently have symptoms related to an inflammation, such as hay fever, joint pain, asthma, or skin allergies, you will most likely notice a substantial improvement in these symptoms within a few weeks. An Inflammation-Free Diet will also help rejuvenate your skin, smoothing fine lines & wrinkles & improving your skin's texture and clarity. In addition to these immediate benefits, is not it wonderful to know that by reducing inflammation, you are also lowering your chances of serious disease in the future like heart diseases, Alzheimer and cancer, among others.

What if achieving a long-sought after weight loss and/or improving health is easier than you think? The Anti-Inflammatory Diet Cookbook is the perfect answer to your prayers. This free and easy to use cookbook offers yummy recipes that are low in sodium, fat, sugars, and gluten. Plus, it provides valuable information on anti-inflammatory foods that can help with reducing chronic inflammation.

The Anti-Inflammatory Diet Cookbook offers many of the same tasty recipes you know and love with a few new twists. If you need some healthy recipes that are both delicious and nutritious, then this is the perfect cookbook for you to try first.

Some of the recipes included in this cookbook are our favorite anti-inflammatory dishes as well as limited edition recipes that are not featured on our other websites. This cookbook is a great way to try some of our favorite and newest anti-inflammatory recipes.

The best diet Cookbook is a must have for anyone looking to improve their health and lifestyle. The Anti-Inflammatory Diet Cookbook covers all aspects of this amazing program. It will help you use the right foods in your diet and cook delicious dishes that can show you how easy it is to maintain a healthy weight, reduce inflammation, and even improve your mood. In addition, it provides an easier way for those who are just starting out on this journey to make sure they are eating the right things.

The diet plan outlined in this book will not only make you feel better, but it can eliminate numerous health problems. The more comfortable you are while eating the right foods, the less likely it is that cancer, heart disease and other diseases will develop. In addition, even though you won't be able to completely eliminate all weight gain, your body will be able to burn fat instead of storing it. This is a huge benefit for those who have tried other diets before and had no success.

This diet Cookbook covers every aspect of the plan so you can start to feel better in a healthier body. There are recipes for breakfast, lunch, dinner and even snacks. You will be able to follow this diet plan right away and it is easy to understand. The recipes are easy to follow and don't require any exotic ingredients. The result is more energy, less inflammation, a leaner figure and even more confidence in yourself.

The Anti-Inflammatory Diet Cookbook is easier than most other diet plans out there. While some dieters may have to change the type of food they eat, this one does not. The diet plan is made up of foods that are easy for you to recognize. They have been around for years and you will be able to use them right away without any trouble. All you need to do is add the proper amount of these foods into your daily routine and you can begin to feel better in a healthier body.

The recipes are easy to follow, making it easier than most other diet plans out there. There are numerous different recipes that you can use if you don't have time to cook everything right away. You do not need to use exotic ingredients for some of the recipes since many of them can be made with common items found in your pantry.

This book is a must have for everyone looking to improve their health and lifestyle. It will teach you how to start eating the right foods that you can use to improve your health. It not only helps eliminate inflammation, but it can also prevent other diseases from developing. In addition, this book is a great for those who are just starting out on their journey so they can make sure that they are eating the right type of foods.

In conclusion, this diet Cookbook has shown you how to change your lifestyle and which foods to eat in order to get rid of many of today's most common health problems. It is a great choice for anyone who is looking to improve their health and lifestyle.

I hope you enjoyed and have learned something new1

Manufactured by Amazon.ca
Bolton, ON

30095072R00131